A-Z of EVERGREEN TREES & SHRUBS

Consultant editor: Lizzie Boyd

Typeset in Century Schoolbook

PRINTED IN SPAIN

ISBN 0 276 42096 9

Opposite: Low-growing heathers form a happy association with dwarf
conifers and thrive in the same conditions as rhododendrons.

Overleaf: In early summer, the Cambridge-blue *Ceanothus thyrsiflorus
repens* takes pride of place, yielding later to the silver-blue spruce *Picea
pungens* 'Koster' and the prostrate bright green *Juniperus conferta*.

Pages 6-7: The constant green of an imposing conifer adds life to a winter
landscape rimmed by frost.

PUBLISHED BY THE READER'S DIGEST ASSOCIATION LIMITED
LONDON NEW YORK MONTREAL SYDNEY CAPE TOWN

Originally published in partwork form
by Eaglemoss Publications Limited

SUCCESSFUL GARDENING

A-Z of EVERGREEN TREES & SHRUBS

CONTENTS

Evergreen trees and shrubs

The enduring colours in the garden come from evergreens – broad-leaved and coniferous trees and shrubs. Handsome at all times, they are especially valued during the dark winter months when all other plant life has died down. Evergreens bring a sense of comfort and security: they surround our homes with protective barriers, they carpet the ground and clothe the walls. The more unassuming species form backgrounds for flowering plants, while others eclipse everything else with their magnificent blooms. Some rise like sentinels above other plants and yet others snuggle into tiny pockets in the rock garden.

Above all, evergreens add an unending source of greenery to the garden. They can be so dark and glossy as to appear black or so luminous and pale that they seem almost white, with leaves varying from the minute, scale-like foliage of heathers and the needles of conifers to the massive leaves of magnolias and some rhododendrons.

Conifer plantation A silver-blue spruce dominates a grouping of prostrate, pyramid and bun-shaped conifers.

A-Z of evergreen trees

Most evergreen trees are conifers, native to the Northern Hemisphere. Although the massive forest conifers, grown for their timber, are unsuitable for gardens, hundreds of man-made cultivars have been bred from them and do not reach the overwhelming proportions of their ancestors. Even so, conifers can still outgrow the average garden, and while there is always the option of felling a tree, it is preferable to consider the eventual height and spread before making a choice. The magnificent Atlas cedar, for example, should be planted only in very large gardens and park landscapes, but its relation, the Himalayan cedar, better known as the deodar, is a splendid specimen tree for average gardens.

The spruces, pines and cypresses all have spectacular varieties whose foliage differs in colour and texture, from bunches of stiff needles to soft and feathery leaf sprays. Their habits are equally diverse, ranging from tiers of symmetrical branches to perfect cones and pyramids, slender columns and broad, wide-spreading heads. Junipers are among the most accommodating conifers, suitable for small gardens and growing as slender pillars or narrow pyramids, with green, grey, blue or golden foliage and small berry-like fruits instead of the cones produced by other conifers.

There are few broad-leaved evergreen trees, but they include the impressive holm oaks of English landscape scenes, the ultra-hardy, bright-berried hollies and the graceful and aromatic eucalyptus from Australia. Gum trees require a little tender care, but their elegant blue-grey foliage and their beautiful trunks with peeling bark are well worth the extra cosseting.

Grow evergreen trees as specimen plants, in small groups where space allows or in spectacular isolation so that their outline and foliage can be admired and enjoyed throughout the year.

CHOOSING CONIFERS

Conifers – hardy, easy to grow and colourful all year round – are among the most versatile garden plants.

Conifers are essentially trees of cool northern climates. They range from tall forest trees to dense hummocks and types that creep over bare mountain faces. Their common characteristics are the needle-like foliage and their ability to bear seed-holding woody cones.

Between the extremes is an astonishing range of shapes, sizes, colours and growth rates. When choosing conifers for the garden it is a good idea to double check their suitability for the purpose you have in mind. Majestic conifers, such as the blue spruce, the weeping deodar or the Weymouth pine, are suitable only for large gardens and park landscapes. Fast-growing conifers, like the Leyland and the Lawson cypresses, are unsurpassed for hedg-ing and screening but hardly qualify as ornamental specimen trees. Most conifers are evergreens, the exceptions being the deciduous larch, swamp cypress and dawn redwood, all of which are too large for general garden planting.

Evergreen conifers are hardy and long-lived; they require little care once established and add a feeling of maturity to even a new garden. They contrast well with flowering plants and deciduous and broad-leaved evergreen trees and shrubs, and provide the bulk of winter colour in the garden.

Garden conifers

For the average-sized garden it is sensible to choose conifers of slow growth and restricted spread – columnar and pyramid-shaped types should be chosen in preference to tall and wide-spreading conifers. Numerous cultivars have been bred from the species, and there are conifers to suit gardens of every size and situation. A few conifers are genuinely dwarf, never exceeding 60cm (2ft) in height and spread, but the majority eventually grow to medium-sized trees and shrubs though they take decades to do so.

Compact dwarf conifers are especially useful for small gardens, as a whole range of colours, foliage and forms can be fitted into

▼ **Conifer planting** The diversity of form, foliage, texture, colour and scale is given full expression in a group planting of mature conifers.

▲ **Conifer hedges** The Western red cedar (*Thuja plicata*) is splendid for hedging. The bright glossy green foliage is pleasantly aromatic and responds well to clipping. It thrives in sun or shade and on chalky soils.

▼ **Weymouth pine** Named after Lord Weymouth rather than the seaside resort, *Pinus strobus* is a round-headed tree. The variety 'Pendula', however, is a picturesque dwarf form with gnarled drooping branches.

a limited space. There are miniature conifers, suitable for windowboxes or troughs; low-growing, wide-spreading types ideal for ground cover; and dwarf conifers of all descriptions which fit perfectly into a rock, scree or heather garden.

Garden centres and large DIY centres sell conifers, often in a separate section, though the choice can be limited. There are many specialist nurseries with hundreds of species and varieties to choose from.

Soil and site

Most conifers prefer a sunny open position, though yews (*Taxus*) will grow in shade and some yellow-foliaged conifers need light shade to prevent sun scorch. They all need good drainage. Neutral soil is ideal, but certain junipers (*Juniperus*), pines (*Pinus*), thujas and yews tolerate alkaline soil, and some pines and firs (*Abies*) prefer acid soil. The richer the soil, the faster the growth rate, and poorish soil can be an advantage. Avoid frost pockets as spring frosts can kill young growth. While some junipers, chamaecyparis, yews and thujas are extensively used as windbreaks, other conifers need shelter from drying winds.

Using conifers

Conifers, particularly dwarf forms, have strong characters and should be chosen and sited with care. Before choosing, consider what you want from each plant, and where it will perform best in the garden.

Year-round interest Conifers provide a valuable array of year-round colour in the garden. Foliage ranges from pale to rich yellow, through pale, bright and deep green to grey, silver-blue and bronze.

Some conifers create extra interest by having variegated foliage or contrasting leaf undersides, or different juvenile and adult foliage. A few change colour dramatically in winter.

Cones also vary considerably. Some are borne upright on the branches, others droop from the undersides; some cones are squat or barrel-shaped, others long and narrow, while yet others, such as those of junipers, are fleshy berries rather than woody cones.

Beds and borders Dwarf conifers are traditionally associated with heaths and heathers. They also mix well with low-

▲ **Blue spruce** The Glauca (blue) varieties of the Colorado spruce (*Picea pungens*) are admirable trees for creating focal points. They are slow-growing, taking many years to reach maturity as medium-sized trees, with horizontal branches densely clothed with blue-green foliage. The colour appears even more intense against a background of dark green trees.

▲ ▶ **Golden juniper** Superb as ground cover, *Juniperus communis* 'Depressa Aurea' grows only 30cm (12in) high but spreads its slender branches to 1.2m (4ft). The branches are packed with sprays of foliage that turn from butter yellow in spring to golden in summer and bronze in winter. It glows most brightly in full sun.

▶ **Lawson cypress** A tub-grown *Chamaecyparis lawsoniana* exerts a calming influence on the riotous colours of summer bedding plants. Conical in shape, with broad fan-like leaf sprays, it is slow-growing for several years and later transplants easily to the open garden.

growing hebes, Japanese maples, cotoneasters and brooms, and make delightful neighbours for spring bulbs and summer-flowering, low-growing plants, such as sun roses, shrubby cinquefoil and pinks. Slow-growing, narrowly columnar conifers are excellent in large mixed borders, adding height and contrast to deciduous shrubs and herbaceous perennials.
Conifers as focal points Upright conifers, such as *Juniperus scopulorum* 'Skyrocket', make outstanding focal points above low-growing plants. The same is true for conifers shaped like cones, pyramids, globes, ovals and buns. Weeping standards and irregular, picturesque forms have more impact as isolated specimen plants.

The perfect symmetry of upright, shrubby or pyramidal conifers is ideal for adding formality to a garden. A pair of identical conifers flanking a front door or garden gate has the same formal effect as standard clipped bay trees – for a fraction of the price.
Conifer hedges Tall and fast-growing conifers, such as x *Cupressocyparis leylandii* and *Chamaecyparis lawsoniana* are used extensively for screening and shelterbelts. They are too vigorous for informal hedging, but several dwarf conifers can be used for edging: a row of the bun-shaped, dwarf pine, *Pinus leucodermis* 'Schmidtii', for example, or the conical golden false cypress, *Chamaecyparis lawsoniana* 'Minima Aurea', make a delightful boundary line between different garden compartments.

Large conifer hedges and windbreaks cast shade and rain shadow as well as shelter, and their roots compete with nearby ornamental plants for food and nutrients from the soil. Dwarf conifer hedges cause no such problems, but they are comparatively expensive; the cost of dwarf conifers is high, and they must be planted close together for a solid effect.
Alpine and rock gardens For landscapes in miniature, dwarf conifers provide excellent scaled-down versions of windswept mountain trees. Weeping varieties can cascade over rocks, and prostrate varieties can hug the ground in the company of sedums, sempervivums and saxifrages. Slender columns of *Juniperus communis* 'Compressa' or feathery globes of dwarf Japanese cedar (*Cryptomeria japonica*) add proportionate height.

▲ **Flowering yew** The common yew (*Taxus baccata*) is a frequently used hedging plant. Here it plays host to the bright red flowers of a climbing nasturtium; it will continue to flourish long after this annual has withered and gone.

◄ **Japanese spirals** Junipers respond well to close clipping and artistic topiary. Years of training and pruning have created an arresting focal point from the erect-growing, bright green *Juniperus chinensis* 'Kaizuka'.

Conifers as ground cover Provided you are prepared to weed by hand for the first two or three years, prostrate conifers make excellent ground cover, smothering weeds and hiding all traces of soil. They are a sensible alternative to lawns on sloping ground, as well as on steep or uneven banks where mowing is difficult and where soil erosion might occur.

Prostrate junipers, with their tidy, dense growth, are especially useful, and *Juniperus* x *media* and *J. sabina* varieties tolerate light shade. The taller-growing golden yew (*Taxus baccata* 'Dovastonii Aurea') makes good, large-scale ground cover, adding impressive splashes of yellow to the landscape.
Window boxes and troughs True miniature conifers are ideal for container gardening. Upright forms that barely reach a height of 30cm (1ft), such as the tiny *Juniperus communis* 'Compressa', or slow-growing hummock forms such as the aptly named *Cedrus deodara* 'Pygmy', which grows 15mm (½in) in a year, make excellent companions for polyanthus and trailing ivy in a window box, or choice alpines in a sink garden.

13

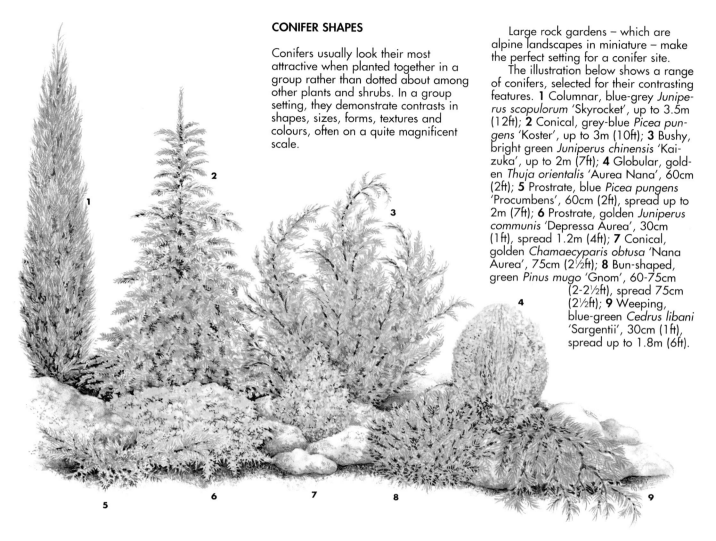

CONIFER SHAPES

Conifers usually look their most attractive when planted together in a group rather than dotted about among other plants and shrubs. In a group setting, they demonstrate contrasts in shapes, sizes, forms, textures and colours, often on a quite magnificent scale.

Large rock gardens – which are alpine landscapes in miniature – make the perfect setting for a conifer site.

The illustration below shows a range of conifers, selected for their contrasting features. **1** Columnar, blue-grey *Juniperus scopulorum* 'Skyrocket', up to 3.5m (12ft); **2** Conical, grey-blue *Picea pungens* 'Koster', up to 3m (10ft); **3** Bushy, bright green *Juniperus chinensis* 'Kaizuka', up to 2m (7ft); **4** Globular, golden *Thuja orientalis* 'Aurea Nana', 60cm (2ft); **5** Prostrate, blue *Picea pungens* 'Procumbens', 60cm (2ft), spread up to 2m (7ft); **6** Prostrate, golden *Juniperus communis* 'Depressa Aurea', 30cm (1ft), spread 1.2m (4ft); **7** Conical, golden *Chamaecyparis obtusa* 'Nana Aurea', 75cm (2½ft); **8** Bun-shaped, green *Pinus mugo* 'Gnom', 60-75cm (2-2½ft), spread 75cm (2½ft); **9** Weeping, blue-green *Cedrus libani* 'Sargentii', 30cm (1ft), spread up to 1.8m (6ft).

► **Dwarf blue spruce** Sharp blue-green needles are crowded along the branches of the dwarf *Picea pungens* 'Procumbens'. Rarely more than 60cm (2ft) high but eventually spreading to 2m (7ft), it forms the centrepiece in a group of shrubby conifers, its silver-blue hues accentuated by violet-purple iris.

▼ **A clutch of conifer**s Cones and pyramids, buns and wide-spreading hummocks are just a few of the outlines presented by conifers. They thrive in each other's company and associate well with low-growing heathers.

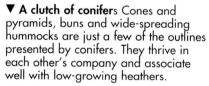

▲ **Autumn colours** Golden conifers add shafts of light to an autumn garden. They retain their brightness long after the deciduous shrubs have shed their vivid foliage.

▶ **Cedar of Lebanon** Slow-growing, the graceful *Cedrus libani* 'Nana' droops its feathery foliage over a heather footing. It rarely exceeds 90cm (3ft) in height, but becomes flat-topped with age.

▼ **Sculptural juniper** Prostrate *Juniperus sabina* 'Tamariscifolia' drapes its horizontal green-blue branches over low walls and sunny banks, spreading almost indefinitely.

THE ART OF TOPIARY

Topiary has classical origins and evergreen hedges and shrubs can be sculptured into formal geometric designs or whimsical shapes.

Topiary has a chameleon-like quality, changing its appearance to suit its surroundings. Roman noblemen, Italian Renaissance princes and great English landowners of the 16th and 17th centuries filled their gardens with topiary, but it can be equally at home in modern-day settings.

Depending on its size, shape and symbolism, topiary can add dignity and style to a garden, or display a sense of humour, and it often reveals a great deal about the owner's personality.

A sculptural obelisk or ball seen against classical architecture, for example, reinforces its formal backdrop. In a country cottage garden, that same topiary serves as a pleasant contrast to the informality of most cottage-garden plants.

A tall, crenellated topiary hedge extending as far as the eye can see indicates wealth, in terms of maintenance costs as well as land ownership. In a suburban garden, a scaled-down crenellated boundary hedge indicates tidiness, skill, patience and a pride in gardening.

Choosing the plants

Topiary plants need a rigid, woody framework, since training and pruning is pointless if the branches hang limply or die back to ground level every autumn. Topiary plants should have a dense, or potentially dense, growth habit, so that the form created is easy to identify; and they should respond well to regular pruning.

They should have small leaves, since close clipping of large leaves, such as those of laurel, is time-consuming to do attractively, and looks sloppy if done hurriedly. The texture of large leaves, even from a distance, makes 'reading' a geometric shape difficult, unless the topiary is very large.

Topiary plants are usually evergreen or semi-evergreen, so that they retain their shape and beauty throughout the year. Lime, hornbeam, thorn and willow can also be pruned into ornamental shapes, such as pleached lime walks, or allées. Such deciduous trees grow naturally thick and dense so that even when leafless they appear solid.

Suitable plants should grow reasonably quickly but not so fast that they expend themselves in a few years.

In spite of such precise requirements, there are many topiary plants from which to choose. Box (*Buxus sempervirens*) and dwarf edging box (*Buxus sempervirens* 'Suffruticosa') are especially popular; other suitable broad-leaved evergreens include bay, firethorn and holly. Yew is the best conifer for topiary, especially for hedging; juniper and cypress are good alternatives. Popular semi-evergreen shrubs include privet and evergreen honeysuckle.

Gold- or silver-leaved varieties make stunning topiary, especially when seen against a dark background. They are, however, often slower-growing than their all-green counterparts, and very strong variegation can distract from the overall clarity of form.

Ready-made topiary

Topiary adds interest and individuality to a garden, and creates a link, however light-hearted, with the past. A piece of topiary, even if bought fully trained, takes some of the rawness away from a new garden, in the same way as planting a large, semi-mature tree.

Topiary's main drawback is that it requires ongoing commitment: it takes at least five years to train a small specimen, and ready

◄ **Bird sculptures** Close-leaved yew responds well to clipping, but topiary work like these bird figures demands skill, patience and artistic ability. It takes about five years to create such impressive examples, but thereafter maintenance is simple.

trained specimens need regular maintenance. If you are enthusiastic about topiary, but not sure about their long-term future, grow topiary plants in containers so that they can be transported to a new home or discarded.

Imported, ready-grown topiary comes in various sizes, often in geometric shapes or as standard-trained box or bay trees. Because they are commercially grown they are very expensive, and perfect in shape, but their cost gives them a rarity value – topiary in every garden would be as boring as an endless row of classical statues. Another reason, apart from cost, for not buying ready-made topiary is the personal satisfaction from topiary of your own making, like bringing on shrubs and trees from tiny cuttings.

◄ **Architectural designs** Deceptively simple, large-scale topiary in the shape of an archway, a horseshoe and a Doric column creates a formal elegance and a sense of tranquillity.

▼ **Cottage garden charm** A topiary cottage, fashioned from a yew boundary hedge, will be at least ten years in the making. Pruned around a large wire frame, it demands annual trimming.

▲ **Oriental topiary** Low-growing box has been meticulously pruned into a decorative feature of Chinese characters. An annual trim preserves their shape.

▼ **Visual art** A bold example of topiary in yew, complete with facial expression, demonstrates a move away from formal geometric shapes.

▲ **Animal shapes** Popular for topiary designs, trained and pruned over wire frames, favourite topics include goats, hounds, pigs and elephants.

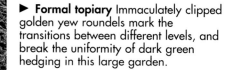

► **Formal topiary** Immaculately clipped golden yew roundels mark the transitions between different levels, and break the uniformity of dark green hedging in this large garden.

▼ **Humorous sculptures** A hunt in full cry across a vast lawn displays artistic skills, infinite patience and a delightful sense of humour.

Types of topiary
Topiary work can be divided into two main types: architectural and sculptural.

Architectural topiary is generally linear, often in the form of hedges or edging, and ranges in size from 30cm (1ft) to well above head height. It is used to mark boundaries, extend the lines of the house into the garden, make internal garden 'walls' which subdivide a large plot into separate compartments, or neatly define beds, borders and paths.

Large-scale architectural topiary can lead the eye to a beautiful view, or frame a small landscape scene. It can hide eyesores or mundane views of neighbours' gardens. Architectural topiary can also create three-dimensional garden buildings: cottage-, castle- or beehive-shaped hideaways or follies of greenery.

Large-scale architectural topiary can take the form of mazes – intricate geometric hedging patterns in a plan which offers a puzzling challenge to all who enter. Intricate geometric patterns of small-scale clipped hedges are the basis of parterre gardening. (Topiary and parterres are different aspects of the same approach: using plants as raw materials for art, rather than allowing the plants to develop their natural and more usual form.)

Sculptural topiary is used in the same way as garden sculptures made of stone: as free-standing, three-dimensional ornamental garden features and focal points. Sculptural topiary can enhance the main entrance to a garden or house, marking it out from minor gates or doors. Pairs of container-grown topiary plants can decorate a flight of steps, for a sense of grandeur. Like architectural topiary, sculptural topiary ranges in size from little round box bushes 20cm (8in) across to huge pieces 3m (10ft) or more high.

Architectural and sculptural topiary may also be combined. A crenellated topiary hedge can be topped at regular intervals by topiary sculptures such as balls, animals or cubes. Half-way between architectural and sculptural topiary are huge hedges, often of yew, clipped into fluid abstract bulges and curves, like an extended modern sculpture.

Formal topiary
In a sense, all topiary is formal, since plants are trained and pruned to form shapes they would not develop naturally. Geometric topiary, however, tends to have more formal overtones than topiary in the shape of animals – for example, leafy ducks, dogs and cats have homely, friendly connotations and character.

▲ **Evergreen colonnade** Topiary can richly enhance planting schemes. This carefully trained and trimmed row of *Chamaecyparis leylandii* provides an elegant see-through division between shrub and herbaceous borders.

Again, much depends on symbolism and scale. A row of elegant topiary peacocks marching across a grand lawn, or a full-sized topiary hunt, complete with horses, riders and hounds, appear impressively formal because of their size and the scale of the work carried out.

Ideas for topiary
Simple geometric shapes, such as cubes, balls, cones and pyramids, are easier than complex ones needing special wire frames. You can prune geometric shapes starting at ground (or pot) level, or lollipop fashion on standard or half-standard stems.

A more challenging approach is to stack two or more geometric shapes over each other on a straight trunk – like stringing beads on a vertical necklace. A topiary cone, spiral or pyramid can be topped with a topiary ball or cube. You can also trim a large topiary cone or pyramid to form two or three separate tiers, with gaps between, revealing the bare central trunk.

◀ **Cottage topiary** A far cry from the formality of large-scale topiary in stately landscapes, a tiny front garden becomes a show-place for the topiarist's skills and sense of fun. Here, a horse and rider, a lion and baby elephant adorn the tall plinth of close-clipped hedge.

▼ **Privet wizardry** Simple forms of topiary can be as arresting as complicated designs. Here, the ordinary privet (*Ligustrum ovalifolium*) and its golden cultivar 'Aureum' have been intertwined and clipped into roundels to create a fascinating focal point by the waterside.

A topiary cube, ball or cone can be topped by a topiary bird, or you can create pedestals – basically elongated cubes – of topiary, and place a geometric shape or animal on top.

Tapering topiary obelisks can alternate with fruit trees or ornamental trees, or simply line both sides of a driveway. Where people constantly take short cuts across a lawn, a small topiary hedge is as effective in stopping this as a trip rail, and more ornamental.

You can spell out the name of your house, its street number, or even your own name in dwarf box topiary. Mounding the ground up slightly to form an angled plane makes it easier to 'read'.

In classical times, high topiary hedges were clipped into a series of niches in which sculptures were displayed. Instead of sculptures, consider placing standard roses, fuchsias or colourful annuals in the niches. Topiary alcoves holding a seat or bench also have classical origins, but are just as attractive today. Topiary walls over a metre high create a windbreak and introduce a sense of privacy and containment. A topiary alcove large enough to hold a table and chairs would be equally enchanting.

On a more modest scale, topiary in a large pot can conceal a manhole cover, or the foundation of a collapsible clothes line.

Cheating at topiary
You can achieve the effect of topiary with no extra work by choosing cultivars of dwarf conifers

with pronounced geometric shapes: usually balls, columns or cones. They are slow-growing and ideal for small gardens and provide an immediate head start on pruning. For an instant ball shape, try *Cryptomeria japonica* 'Compressa', a perfectly round miniature Japanese cedar; or *Picea abies* 'Gregoryana', a bun-shaped miniature spruce, or the even slower-growing variety 'Echiniformis'.

For columns, consider *Juniperus communis* 'Compressa', a

dwarf slender juniper; or the narrowest of all conifers, blue-grey *J. scopulorum* 'Skyrocket'. Conical conifer shapes include the dwarf golden false cypress (*Chamaecyparis lawsoniana* 'Aurea Densa'), and the golden and bronze Chinese dwarf arbor vitae (*Thuja orientalis* 'Aurea Rogersii').

These dwarf conifers are particularly effective in multiples, and container-grown. Maintain their shape by trimming any sprigs or shoots that break the shape in spring and early summer.

Abies
silver fir, true fir

Abies pinsapo

Abies pinsapo, foliage

- Height at 25 years 4.5-11m (15-36ft)
- Mature height 10-30m (33-100ft)
- Spread 1.8-6m (6-20ft)
- Moist, acid soil
- Hardy conifer
- Features – needle-like foliage, oval cones

The majestic silver fir is a handsome tree, suitable for background planting, screening, or as a specimen tree. The tiered branches of this aromatic conifer usually form a conical shape with needle-like dark to grey-green leaves, which are often white underneath. The narrow, oval, erect cones, usually 5-10cm (2-4in) long, are borne on the upper branches of mature trees.

Popular species
Abies bracteata (Santa Lucia fir) is a fast-growing species up to 9m (30ft) high and 4.5m (15ft) across. It forms a rough pyramid shape with drooping lower branches and hard, spine-tipped needles which are dark green above and banded with silver underneath. The cones are bristly.

Abies concolor (Colorado white fir), up to 10m (33ft) high and 4.5m (15ft) across, has smooth grey bark, grey-green leaves and green and purple cones. Varieties include 'Candicans' (silver-white) and 'Violacea' (grey-blue).

Abies delavayi forrestii, syn. *A. forrestii*, grows up to 9m (30ft) high and 3.5m (12ft) across. The dense, dark green leaves are silver underneath and the cones are a rich purple-blue.

Abies fargesii is up to 9m (30ft) high and 4.5m (15ft) across, and eventually 24m (80ft) or more tall. It has dark green leaves and purple-brown cones.

Abies koreana (Korean fir) is a neat, slow-growing tree up to 4.5m (15ft) high and 1.8m (6ft) across. Grown for its upright rows of pink, crimson or green flowers in late spring, it has rather sparse, dark green leaves which are glistening white underneath. Blue-green cones are borne on even young trees. 'Compact Dwarf' is a neat and spreading variety; it does not produce cones.

Abies lasiocarpa var. *arizonica* (cork fir), up to 10m (33ft) high and 3.5m (12ft) across, has grey, corky bark and silvery blue leaves; it bears small brown cones.

Abies nordmanniana (Caucasian fir) grows 15m (50ft) high and 4.5m (15ft) wide. Glossy bright green needles, silvery on the undersides, crowd the downward-sweeping branches. The dark brown cones are 15cm (6in) long.

Abies pinsapo (Spanish or hedgehog fir) is up to 6m (20ft) high and 2.4m (8ft) across and eventually 24m (80ft) or more high. Stiff, dark green leaves grow densely all round the twigs; the cones are purple-brown. It tolerates chalky soils. 'Glauca' has blue-grey leaves.

Abies veitchii is a fast-growing tree up to 10m (33ft) high and 4.5m (15ft) across. It has a broad conical shape with dense bright green leaves which are white underneath; mature trees bear numerous small, bluish-purple cones.

Cultivation
Plant young silver firs before they exceed 30cm (1ft) in height, ideally in a site protected from spring frosts. They do best in deep, well-drained but moisture-retentive and slightly acid soils. However, *A. pinsapo* tolerates dry and alkaline soil. Plant in late autumn on light soil or mid spring on heavy soils.

Abies nordmanniana 'Golden Spreader'

Abies koreana, cones

Abies koreana

Maintain a weed-free root run about 90cm (3ft) across for several years. Thereafter, mulch and top dress with a general fertilizer annually in late spring.

Pruning No pruning is necessary, except to maintain a single leader. If the leading shoot forks, remove the shoot furthest from the main axis, cutting flush with the main stem.

Pests and diseases Adelgids suck sap and produce tufts of white waxy wool. Rust shows as small white blisters on the leaves and may cause witches' brooms.

Abies concolor

Abies lasiocarpa var. *arizonica*

Acacia
mimosa, silver wattle

Acacia dealbata

☐ Height at 25 years 6m (20ft)
☐ Mature height 9m (30ft)
☐ Spread 1.5m (5ft)
☐ Well-drained soil
☐ Half-hardy broadleaf
☐ Features – foliage, flowers

Wattle trees are native to Australia and generally thrive outdoors only in Mediterranean climates. However, one species, *Acacia dealbata*, will survive most winters in southern Britain if grown in the shelter of a warm sunny wall.

This is the florist's mimosa, a fast-growing tree or tall, multi-stemmed shrub under suitable conditions, whose branches bear silver-grey, fern-like leaves. In spring it is draped with drooping clusters of sweetly fragrant, bright yellow flower balls.

Cultivation
In frost-free regions, plant young pot-grown specimens in early autumn. Acacias need sun and shelter from winds and will grow in any well-drained soil; they are extremely drought-tolerant.
Pruning None is necessary, but the branches are brittle and easily broken off by strong winds; cut them back flush with the main stem if damage occurs.
Pests and diseases Trouble free.

Araucaria
monkey puzzle

Araucaria araucana

☐ Height at 25 years 9m (30ft)
☐ Mature height 20m (65ft) or more
☐ Spread 3m (10ft)
☐ Rich, moist soil
☐ Hardy conifer
☐ Features – foliage

A striking specimen tree from Chile and Argentina, monkey puzzle (*Araucaria araucana*, syn. *A. imbricata*) has stiff, rope-like branches. A young tree, which may take ten years to reach a height of 1.2m (4ft), is a broad columnar shape, becoming domed with age.

Suitable only for large gardens, the monkey puzzle was popular with Victorian gardeners. It is notable for its symmetrical tiers of branches that sometimes sweep upwards and sometimes downwards. The dark green leathery, needle-like leaves, rigid and spine-tipped, are set closely along the branches; they point upwards, and it is said that a monkey can easily climb up, but not down – hence the common name.

Monkey puzzle trees are either male or female; male trees bear clusters of banana-shaped catkins which shed pollen in early summer before turning brown. Mature female trees bear globular cones, 15cm (6in) or more long, on the upper branches; they are covered with golden spines and take three

Araucaria araucana

years to mature before breaking up and expelling large seeds.

Cultivation
The monkey puzzle thrives in moist but well-drained, loamy soil. It is highly wind-resistant. Plant young container-grown specimen trees in mid autumn, and in early spring in northern gardens.
Pruning None required.
Pests and diseases Honey fungus may kill trees.

ARBOR VITAE – see *Thuja*

Arbutus

strawberry tree

Arbutus unedo, flowers

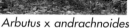
Arbutus x *andrachnoides*

Arbutus unedo, fruits

☐ Height at 25 years 3.5-7.5m (12-25ft)
☐ Mature height 9m (30ft) or more
☐ Spread 2-6m (7-20ft)
☐ Well-drained acid soil
☐ Hardy broadleaf
☐ Features – flowers, fruits, bark

The strawberry tree is one of the loveliest evergreen trees for the garden. Its dark green, oval leaves are decorated in spring or autumn with sprays of white or pink urn-shaped flowers. The red or orange, strawberry-like fruits are edible, though rather tasteless. The bark is attractive too, the smooth top layer often peeling to reveal the new bark beneath.

See also page 62.

Popular species

Arbutus andrachne, from south-east Europe, is up to 6m (20ft) high and 4.5m (15ft) across. It has smooth, peeling, cinnamon-red bark and leathery, dark green leaves which are sometimes shallowly toothed. Sprays of white flowers appear in early to mid spring, later followed by orange-red fruits. This species is tender when young but will mature into a hardy tree if given a sheltered position.

Arbutus x *andrachnoides*, syn. *A.* x *hybrida*, up to 3.5m (12ft) high and 2m (7ft) across, has cinnamon-red bark and dark green, shallowly toothed leaves. Nodding sprays of 7.5cm (3in) long ivory-white flowers appear in late autumn or early to mid spring. Red fruits sometimes appear. This species is hardy in all but the coldest areas and tolerates some lime in the soil.

Arbutus menziesii (madrona), from western North America, is up to 7.5m (25ft) high and 6m (20ft) across, or more in sheltered areas. The smooth terracotta-coloured bark peels away to reveal the young green bark beneath. The glossy dark green leaves are sometimes shallowly toothed. Upright sprays of white flowers appear in late spring and are fol-lowed by round, orange-yellow fruits.

Arbutus unedo (Killarney straw-berry tree), from the Mediter-ranean and south-west Ireland, grows into a gnarled tree up to 4.5m (15ft) high and 3m (10ft) across. It has deep brown, rough and shredding bark which is red underneath, and shiny toothed leaves. The drooping white or pink flower clusters appear in autumn, often at the same time as the orange-red fruits.

Cultivation

Plant in mid autumn or spring in well-drained lime-free loam, although *A.* x *andrachnoides* and *A. unedo* tolerate lime. All do best in full sun and a sheltered site. In winter, protect young plants with bracken or straw. Protect *A. men-ziesii* and *A. andrachne* from cold north and east winds.

Pruning Cut back straggly shoots in mid spring.

Pests and diseases Leaf spot shows as small brown spots.

Cedrus
cedar

Cedrus atlantica 'Pendula'

Cedrus deodara, cones

Cedrus deodara (young tree)

□ Height at 25 years 3-12m (10-40ft)
□ Mature height 24-30m (80-100ft)
□ Spread 1.8-12m (6-40ft)
□ Any well-drained soil
□ Hardy conifer
□ Features – beautiful specimen tree; handsome foliage

The hardy, long-lived cedar is a magnificent aromatic specimen tree for a large lawn. The young tree is usually conical, but may lose its lower branches later, revealing a massive, smooth, dark grey trunk, and becoming broad and flat-topped. The species are generally too large for most gardens, but several compact, slow-growing or dwarf varieties are available, including weeping trees, for smaller gardens.

The slender needle-like leaves, in shades of green, grey-green or golden-yellow, are 2.5-5cm (1-2in) long and carried in tufts arranged spirally along the branches. Male and female flowers are borne on the same tree, but only the male flowers are noticeable, studding the branches with bright yellow in autumn and shedding clouds of golden pollen. Mature trees carry upright, barrel-shaped cones, up to 12.5cm (5in) long, on the upper branches.

Popular species
Cedrus atlantica (Atlas cedar) is a fast-growing species from the Atlas Mountains of Algeria and Morocco. It grows 12m (40ft) or more high and wide, with dark green foliage and horizontal branches which may ascend slightly when young. The cones are up to 10cm (4in) long. Varieties include: 'Aurea' (golden-yellow); 'Fastigiata' (grey-blue, narrow, upright); 'Glauca' (blue cedar, spectacular and popular variety with silver-blue foliage); 'Glauca Pendula' (a weeping form of 'Glauca'); and 'Pendula' (slow-growing when young, green to grey-green leaves on weeping branches).
Cedrus deodara (deodar, Himalayan cedar) from the western Himalayas, is up to 9m (30ft) high and 6m (20ft) across. It has gracefully drooping branches and blue-grey young leaves maturing to dark green. Varieties include: 'Albospica' (cream-white tips to young shoots); 'Aurea' (to 3m/10ft high, 1.8m/6ft across, slow-growing, golden young foliage in spring maturing to greenish-yellow); 'Aurea Pendula' (weeping form of 'Aurea'); 'Golden Horizon' (semi-prostrate, graceful form, up to

75cm (2½ft) high and 1.2m (4ft) across, with spreading, drooping branches and golden-yellow foliage); 'Pendula' (top-grafted tree, up to 90cm/3ft high with wide-spreading pendulous branches); and 'Pygmy' (slow-growing, dwarf variety forming a tiny hummock of blue-green foliage; suitable for a rock or sink garden).
Cedrus libani (cedar of Lebanon), from Syria and Turkey, is a fairly slow-growing tree up to 7.5m (25ft) high and 6m (20ft) across. Its large, horizontal branches form a cone shape when young, though when mature it has a tiered, flat-topped appearance. The leaves are dark green or

Cedrus libani 'Nana'

Chamaecyparis
false cypress

Chamaecyparis obtusa 'Crippsii'

☐ Height at 25 years 3.5-9m (12-30ft)
☐ Mature height 12-15m (40-50ft)
☐ Spread 1-3.5m (3-12ft)
☐ Any well-drained soil
☐ Hardy conifer
☐ Features – form and foliage colour

banded with silver-blue. Cones are produced only on very old trees. Dwarf and weeping varieties, suited to small gardens, include 'Comte de Dijon' (slow-growing and of conical habit, with densely clothed branches, up to 1.5m/5ft high and across); 'Gold Dwarf' syn. 'Aurea Prostrata' (slow-growing, almost prostrate, yellow foliage); 'Nana' (compact conical shrub, slow-growing but eventually to 1.5m/5ft high and wide); and 'Sargentii' (syn. 'Pendula Sargentii', a slow-growing variety with blue-green foliage; it is weeping if the short trunk is staked, otherwise it retains a prostrate habit; suitable for a rock garden).

Cultivation
Cedars grow in any ordinary, well-drained soil. Plant container-grown specimens 30-45cm (1-1½ft) high, with a single, well-developed leading shoot, in early autumn or late spring. Stake young trees in exposed sites. Apply a general fertilizer in mid spring for a few years.

In frost-prone areas, *C. deodara* and its varieties do best in a lightly shaded site.

Pruning Prune to maintain a single leader. On older trees, remove lower branches when they begin to deteriorate, cutting them off flush with the bole from late winter to mid spring.

Pests and diseases Cedars may be killed by honey fungus.

Cedrus atlantica 'Glauca'

A fine specimen tree with a vast range of form and colour, false cypress is also excellent for screening, hedging or background planting in almost any situation.

The tiny leaves are borne in flattened sprays or plumes and come in shades of green, blue-green, grey-green and golden yellow. A false cypress tree may be open or close-set, or form a cone, pyramid or pillar shape.

For shrubby and dwarf forms of false cypress see pages 76-79.

Popular species
Chamaecyparis lawsoniana (Lawson cypress), a conical tree from Oregon and California, is up to 12m (40ft) high and 3.5m (12ft) across. It has drooping branches with fan-like sprays of dark green leaves with white marks beneath and bears clusters of red male flowers in mid spring. It is a fast-growing species, usually represented in gardens by numerous varieties which include: 'Allumii', (9m/30ft high, 2.4m/8ft across, columnar shape, blue-grey); 'Columnaris' (4.5m/15ft high, 1m/3ft wide and narrowly columnar, pale grey); 'Erecta', syn. 'Erecta Viridis' (9m/30ft high,

Chamaecyparis lawsoniana 'Lutea'

1.5m/5ft wide, pointed-topped columnar form with bright green upright branches; 'Fletcheri' (3.5m/12ft or more high, 1.5m/5ft across and usually with several main stems, columnar, grey-green foliage, bronze in winter, slow-growing); 'Grayswood Pillar' (9m/30ft high, 75cm/2½ft across, grey); 'Lanei' (6m/20ft high, 2.4m/8ft across, columnar, bright golden, feathery foliage); 'Lutea' (7.5m/24ft high, 2.4m/8ft across, columnar, golden); 'Pottenii' (7.5m/25ft high, 1.5m/5ft wide and narrowly columnar, pale green foliage); 'Stewartii' (7.5m/25ft high, 3m/10ft across, golden yellow); 'Triomphe de Boskoop' (12m/40ft high, 3m/10ft wide, vigorous and of dense conical habit, grey-blue); 'Winston Churchill' (7.5m/25ft high, 2.4m/8ft across, broadly columnar, rich golden); and 'Wisselii' (9m/30ft high, 2.4m/8ft across, slender column shape, blue-green).

Chamaecyparis nootkatensis (Nootka cypress), from western North America, is a conical tree up to 9m (30ft) high and 3m (10ft) across with drooping branches and flattened sprays of dark green foliage which smells pungent when crushed. 'Pendula' has upcurved branches with drooping branchlets.

Chamaecyparis obtusa (Hinoki cypress) is a Japanese tree up to 7.5m (25ft) high and 3m (10ft) across. It has upward-sweeping

branches and flattened sprays of bright green leaves with silvery undersides. 'Crippsii' is a pyramid-shaped, slow-growing variety up to 4.5m (15ft) high and 2.5m (8ft) across with young golden foliage turning dark green.

Chamaecyparis pisifera (Sawara cypress), a conical Japanese tree up to 6m (20ft) high and 2.5m (8ft) across, has horizontal sprays of bright green foliage with silver lines beneath. Older trees may lose their lower branches. Varieties, more commonly seen than the species itself, include: 'Filifera' (4.5m/15ft high, 3m/10ft across, pyramid shape, thread-like dark grey-green foliage); 'Filifera Aurea' (like 'Filifera', but slow-growing, and golden foliage); 'Plumosa' (7.5m/25ft high, 3m/10ft across, pale green, fluffy foliage); and 'Squarrosa' (9m/30ft high, 6m/20ft wide, broad and conical with upswept, blue-grey foliage).

Chamaecyparis nootkatensis 'Pendula'

Cultivation
False cypresses thrive in any ordinary well-drained but moisture-retentive garden soil in an open position or in moderate shade. Golden varieties retain their colour best in full sun. Plant young trees under 45cm (1½ft) high in mid autumn on light soils or in mid spring on heavy soils.

Pruning Rarely necessary except to maintain a single leading shoot if forking occurs. Long branches that spoil the shape can be cut back at any stage.

Pests and diseases Honey fungus may kill the trees.

CHRISTMAS TREE – see *Picea*
CHUSAN PALM – see
Trachycarpus
COLORADO RED CEDAR – see
Juniperus

Cryptomeria
Japanese cedar

Cryptomeria japonica 'Elegans'

□ Height at 25 years 6-12m (20-40ft)
□ Mature height 15-18m (50-60ft)
□ Spread 4.5-5m (15-16ft)
□ Hardy conifer
□ Acid, moist but well-drained soil
□ Features – elegant form, attractive foliage

An excellent specimen tree, Japanese cedar (*Cryptomeria japonica*) forms a neat cone when young, spreading into a more open form later. It has soft, stringy, orange-brown shredding bark and decorative sprays of tiny, round brown cones at the end of the shoots on mature trees. The tiny dark green or blue-green leaves are awl-shaped.

The species is a large, fast-growing tree up to 12m (40ft) high and 5m (16ft) wide after 25 years. Smaller, slower-growing varieties include 'Elegans' (to 6m/20ft high and 4.5m/15ft across, feathery blue-green foliage, bronze-red in winter) and 'Lobbii' (slow-growing to 9m/30ft high and 4.5m/15ft across, longer branchlets, deep rich green).

For dwarf and shrubby varieties see pages 87-88.

Cultivation
Japanese cedars do best in slightly acid, deep, moist but well-drained soil. Slow-growing in light shade, and the best results are obtained in a sunny sheltered site.

Plant young container-grown trees, up to 60cm (2ft) high, in early to mid autumn on light soils or in mid spring on heavier soils.

Apply an annual dressing of 75-100g (3-4oz) of general fertilizer over the root run in late spring to improve growth and colour. Keep young plants moist and clear of weeds.

Pruning Prune only to maintain a single leader in mid spring.
Pests and diseases Trouble free.

x *Cupressocyparis*
Leyland cypress

x *Cupressocyparis leylandii*

□ Height at 25 years 18m (60ft)
□ Mature height 30m (100ft)
□ Spread 4.5m (15ft)
□ Any well-drained soil
□ Hardy conifer
□ Features – fast-growing, tolerates wind-swept sites

The elegant Leyland cypress (x *Cupressocyparis leylandii*), a popular choice for hedging and screening, is one of the fastest-growing conifers. A cross between *Cupressus macrocarpa* and *Chamaecyparis nootkatensis*, it is up to 18m (60ft) high and 4.5m (15ft) across after the first 25 years, and can eventually achieve a height of 30m (100ft), though with frequent pruning it can be kept much smaller and trimmed into a formal shape.

As a specimen tree, the Leyland cypress forms a dense column and is the fastest-growing of all conifers, often adding 1.5m (5ft) annually to its height in the early years. Because of its extreme vigour, it is better suited for a wind screen than for a hedge in small gardens.

The dense foliage of scale-like leaves is held in flattened or irregular, slightly drooping sprays and is blue-green in the species. Mature trees bear small cones.

Several varieties are available, including 'Castlewellan Gold' syn. 'Galway Gold' (young plume-like foliage, golden-yellow maturing to bronze-green, slower-growing than green forms and suitable for hedging); 'Gold Rider' (outstanding golden-yellow form retains colour well even in full sun); 'Hag-

Cupressus
cypress

x *Cupressocyparis leylandii*
'Castlewellan Gold'

Cupressus macrocarpa 'Lutea'

Cupressus lusitanica

gerston Grey' (dark grey-green foliage in irregular sprays, rarely cones); 'Hyde Hall' (dwarf form with bright green foliage and suitable for small gardens); 'Leighton Green' (tall columnar tree, widely planted for screening, rich green foliage, cones freely); 'Naylor's Blue' (narrowly columnar, grey-green foliage, bluish-grey in winter); 'Robinson's Gold' (compact, broadly columnar, golden foliage, bronze in spring); and 'Silver Dust' (similar to 'Leighton Green' but foliage strongly speckled with cream-white).

Cultivation
Plant trees, preferably 45-60 cm (1½-2ft) high, in mid to late spring in any ordinary well-drained soil that allows deep-rooting and in sun or partial shade. They are tolerant of all soils and sites, including chalky soil and coastal exposure. On shallow soils these conifers may become unstable after a few years. Pull them back to the vertical and stake for two years. For hedging, space young trees 45-60cm (1½-2ft) apart.
Pruning Clip established hedges and screens annually in early autumn. Avoid cutting into old growth or die-back will occur.
Pests and diseases Trouble free.

☐ Height at 25 years 6-13.5m (20-45ft)
☐ Mature height 15-30m (50-100ft)
☐ Spread 75cm-5.5m (2½-18ft)
☐ Any well-drained soil
☐ Hardy conifer
☐ Features – decorative specimen tree

True cypress forms a stately pyramid or cone, densely clothed with irregular sprays of scaly leaves in shades of deep green to blue-green or gold. For dwarf cypresses, see page 88.

Popular species
Cupressus glabra (Arizona cypress), a conical tree up to 9m (30ft) high and 3m (10ft) across, is often incorrectly listed as *C. arizonica*. Its blistered purple bark peels off to reveal yellow patches. The blue-grey leaves are often white-spotted while the profuse male flowers are yellow. 'Pyramidalis' has silvery blue-grey leaves.

Cupressus glabra, cones

Cupressus lusitanica (Mexican cypress), up to 9m (30ft) high and 3m (10ft) across, is a graceful semi-hardy tree with grey-green foliage on drooping branchlets. 'Glauca Pendula' is a weeping blue-grey variety up to 6m (20ft) high and 5.5m (18ft) across.
Cupressus macrocarpa (Monterey cypress) from California is a fast-growing columnar species up to 15m (50ft) high and 3.5m (12ft) across, becoming flat-topped and open with age. The foliage is a rich dark green. Varieties include 'Donard Gold' (golden); 'Goldcrest' (rich yellow, feathery foliage) and 'Lutea' (yellow foliage, becoming green).
Cupressus sempervirens 'Stricta' (Italian cypress), syn. *C. s.* 'Fastigiata', forms a narrow, dark green column up to 7.5m (25ft) high and 75cm (2½ft) across.

Cultivation
Plant trees under 60cm (2ft) high in early autumn or mid spring in any well-drained soil in sun.
Pruning Prune to maintain a single leader in spring.
Pests and diseases Honey fungus may kill the trees.

CYPRESS – see *Chamaecyparis*, x *Cupressocyparis* and *Cupressus*
DEODAR – see *Cedrus*
DOUGLAS FIR – see *Pseudotsuga*
EUCALYPT – see *Eucalyptus*

Eucalyptus

eucalypt, gum tree

Eucalyptus glaucescens

Eucalyptus dalrympleana

- ☐ Height at 25 years 7.5-50m (25-165ft)
- ☐ Mature height 30-50m (100-165ft)
- ☐ Spread 3-15m (10-50ft)
- ☐ Near-hardy broadleaf
- ☐ Well-drained but moisture-retentive soil
- ☐ Features – graceful form; interesting foliage and bark

There are hundreds of different species of *Eucalyptus*, with an enormous range of sizes.

Renowned for their outstanding aromatic foliage and patterned bark, these fast-growing trees are graceful and versatile. They are naturally tall and narrow, but can be cut hard back annually to form small trees or shrubs.

The juvenile leaves, which grow on wood up to three years old, are generally round or oval and differ from the adult leaves, which are lance-shaped and range in colour from glistening silvery white to grey or pale to dark green. Unpruned trees flower when they are four to six years old. The fluffy, usually white flowers are sweetly scented.

Eucalyptus originates from Australia and Tasmania. They have poor wind resistance, but those described here are generally hardy in British gardens.

Popular species

Eucalyptus coccifera (Tasmanian snow gum, Mount Wellington peppermint) is up to 7.5m (25ft) high and 3m (10ft) across. Its bark peels away to reveal white patches underneath. The juvenile leaves are grey and the 6cm (2½in) long peppermint-scented adult leaves are silver-grey. The flowers appear in early summer.

Eucalyptus dalrympleana (mountain gum) can grow 30m (100ft) high and 7.5m (25ft) across or more, with patchwork-like cream, brown and pink bark. The oval juvenile leaves are dark green or blue-green; the pendulous, light green adult leaves are up to 23cm (9in) long and 2.5cm (1in) wide. The flowers appear in autumn.

Eucalyptus glaucescens is up to 12m (40ft) high and 4.5m (25ft) across with smooth red-brown bark peeling to reveal white underneath. The round juvenile leaves are brilliant blue-grey and the leathery grey adult leaves, sometimes tinged pink, are up to 15cm (6in) long and 2.5cm (1in) wide. The flowers appear in mid autumn.

Eucalyptus globulus (Tasmanian blue gum) is a semi to moderately hardy species with a dense crown. In mild areas it may reach a height of 50m (165ft) and a spread of 12-15m (40-50ft), but it is more often seen as a multi-stemmed shrub used in large bedding schemes in sheltered seaside gardens. The rounded juvenile foliage, which persists into the second and third year, clasps the stems and is silvery-grey in colour, while the adult leaves are narrowly lance-shaped, blue-green and up to 30cm (12in) long. The bark is smooth, bluish-white when newly exposed.

Eucalyptus gunnii (cider gum) is up to 30m (100ft) high and 12m (40ft) across. It is the most commonly grown species in Britain and is prized for its outstanding round, silvery-blue juvenile leaves. They are popular with flower arrangers. The leathery lance-shaped adult leaves are

Eucalyptus niphophila

Eucalyptus parvifolia, bark

Eucalyptus perriniana (spinning gum), is up to 7.5m (25ft) high and 4.5m (15ft) across with grey bark blotched brown. It is a fully hardy species, excellent for growing as an annually stooled shrub. The grey juvenile leaves grow in joined pairs, resembling discs with the stem growing through the centre. They remain on the shoots long after they have died, and spin in the wind. The silvery-green adult leaves are lance-shaped; white flowers are freely borne in mid and late summer.

Eucalyptus pulverulenta (powdered or silver-leaved mountain gum) is up to 12m (40ft) high and 7.5m (25ft) or more across with

blue-green or grey-green and up to 7.5cm (3in) long. The flowers appear in summer.

Eucalyptus niphophila (alpine snow gum), up to 9m (30ft) high and 4.5m (15ft) across, is correctly a subspecies of *E. pauciflora*. It has ornamental green, grey, cream and brown-red mottled and peeling bark. The sparse juvenile foliage is pale green and the leathery grey-green, lance-shaped adult leaves are about 7.5cm (3in) long. Clusters of white flowers appear in early summer. This tree is one of the hardiest of the genus.

Eucalyptus parvifolia (small-leaved gum), 9m (30ft) high and 6m (20ft) across, thrives on chalky soil. It has small, narrow blue-green juvenile and adult leaves. It flowers in mid summer.

Eucalyptus pauciflora, syn. *E. coriacea*, is known as cabbage gum. It can grow 9-12m (30-40ft) high, with a spread of 6m (20ft), but is usually seen as a stooled shrub – pruned to ground level annually in spring, it grows about 2m (7ft) high and 1.5m (5ft) across in a season. It is a hardy species, the trunk with flaking white and dark grey bark. The thick juvenile leaves are grey-green, the adult foliage bright green; stooled plants bear juvenile foliage only. White flower clusters are produced in early summer. The variety *E. pauciflora* var. *nana* is of slender, shrubby habit, up to 6m (20ft) high or 1.2m (4ft) as a stooled plant; it is particularly free-flowering.

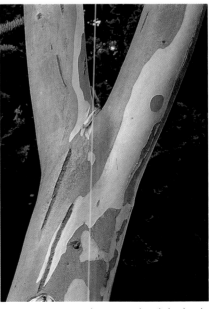

Eucalyptus niphophila, bark

33

Eucalyptus gunnii

Eucalyptus gunnii, juvenile foliage

Eucalyptus perriniana, adult foliage

attractive white and pale brown peeling bark. The silver-grey, stem-hugging oval juvenile leaves, which are good for cutting, are similar to the adult leaves. The flowers appear in spring. Hardy only in mild areas.

Eucalyptus urnigera (urn-fruited gum) is a hardy and vigorous species, to 15m (50ft) high and 6m (20ft) across, with drooping branches and pale green to cream-white bark that becomes mottled with red-brown in maturity. The rounded juvenile leaves and the adult lance-shaped foliage are dark glossy green. Small clusters of creamy-white flowers, borne in mid and late summer, are followed by glossy green, urn-shaped fruits. The variety 'Glauca' has blue-grey juvenile leaves and dark green adult foliage.

Cultivation
Plant trees 15-30cm (6-12in) high

in a sunny sheltered site from early to mid summer. They do best in moist, but well-drained, neutral to acid soil, which is of moderate fertility.

Stake securely for several years to prevent wind rocking. In cold areas protect the base of the stems during the first winter with straw or sacking. Alternatively, erect an open-topped wind screen of hessian or clear plastic.

Pruning Unchecked, most eucalyptus species rapidly form tall, narrow trees but they can be pruned to almost any size and shape. For a round-topped tree, cut out the tip of a young specimen in early summer to encourage the development of side-shoots.

Many eucalypts are pruned or stooled annually in order to produce a low thicket of stems which will bear juvenile foliage only. Cut them back almost to the ground

annually in spring just as growth begins.

Pests and diseases Silver leaf sometimes attacks mature trees. Leaves become silvered, shoots die back and wood may be stained.

Eucalyptus coccifera, bark

FALSE CYPRESS – see
Chamaecyparis
FIR – see *Abies*
FIR, DOUGLAS – see
Pseudotsuga

Ilex
holly

Ilex aquifolium 'Madame Briot'

Ilex aquifolium 'Bacciflava', berries

Ilex aquifolium, berries

☐ Height at 25 years 4.5-7.5m (15-25ft)
☐ Mature height 4.5-20m (15-65ft)
☐ Spread 3-4.5m (10-15ft)
☐ Ordinary soil
☐ Hardy broadleaf
☐ Features – foliage, berries

Grown for its glossy evergreen foliage and brilliant red or yellow berries, the holly tree provides year-round interest. The leaves are often spiny and many forms have interesting variegations. They are excellent as specimen trees and for hedging and screens.

In habit, hollies vary from shrubby species (see pages 118-119) to tall and dense trees, although they are slow-growing. In most species, male and female flowers are borne on separate trees, and for a female to produce berries a male species must be planted within pollination distance. Catalogues list the sexual orientation of all varieties.

Popular species
Ilex x *altaclarensis* is a group of vigorous, large-leaved hybrids with red berries. Many eventually form conical or columnar trees up to 7.5m (25ft) high and 3m (10ft) across; they include 'Mundyi' (male, spiny veined leaves) and 'Wilsonii' (female, spiny veined leaves, scarlet berries, domed form).
Ilex aquifolium (common English holly) grows up to 7.5m (25ft) high and 4.5m (15ft) across, with glossy, dark green spiny leaves. Varieties include 'Argentea Marginata' (silver holly, female, silver-edged leaves, red berries); 'Argentea Marginata Pendula' (similar, but with strongly weeping branches); 'Bacciflava' ('Fructo-luteo', female, yellow berries); 'J.C. van Tol' (self-fertile, spineless, red berries); and 'Madame Briot' (female, leaves mottled and margined yellow, purple stems, red berries).

Ilex latifolia is a handsome, moderately hardy Japanese tree up to 4.5m (15ft) high and 3m (10ft) across. It has large, glossy dark green leaves with serrated edges. The berries are orange-red.

Cultivation
Plant in mid to late spring or early autumn in sun or shade – variegated forms need sun; hollies prefer moist loamy soil but will grow in any good garden soil.
Pruning Clip to shape in summer.
Pests and diseases Birds eat the berries. Holly leaf miners tunnel into leaves and cause unsightly blotches. Honey fungus causes rapid death. Leaf spot shows as white or grey spots with dark brown edges.

JAPANESE CEDAR – see *Cryptomeria*

Ilex aquifolium 'Argentea Marginata Pendula'

Juniperus

juniper

Juniperus chinensis 'Aurea'

Juniperus recurva var. *coxii*

Juniperus scopulorum 'Blue Heaven'

- ☐ Height at 25 years 3-6m (10-20ft)
- ☐ Mature height 6-18m (20-60ft)
- ☐ Spread 30cm-2.4m (1-8ft)
- ☐ Any well-drained soil
- ☐ Hardy conifer
- ☐ Features – attractive shape and foliage, 'berries'

Junipers are versatile and useful conifers which thrive in most soils and situations, including dry and chalky soils. They range in form from creeping and prostrate types (see pages 121-123) to narrow pillar-shaped trees or broad pyramids. They are often used as focal points in heather gardens.

Junipers have two types of foliage – prickly, awl-shaped juvenile leaves and scale-like adult leaves. Some species may have both types at the same time, but many have only juvenile foliage.

The black or blue fleshy cones resemble hard, knobbly berries.

Popular species

Juniperus chinensis (Chinese juniper) is a conical and bushy tree up to 4.5m (15ft) high and 1.2m (4ft) across. It bears both dull green adult and bluish-green juvenile foliage. Male trees bear yellow flowers and females produce bright blue-black fruits. The species is rarely grown and has been superseded by named varieties including: 'Aurea' (Young's golden juniper, male, slow-growing, columnar, to 3m/10ft high, 1.2m/4ft across, golden foliage); 'Keteleeri' (narrow, 4.5m/15ft high, 1m/3ft across, vivid green adult leaves, profuse fruits); and 'Stricta' (slow-growing conical tree to 6m/20ft high, 1.2m/4ft across, blue-grey juvenile foliage).

Juniperus communis (common juniper) is a small tree or large shrub with aromatic, entirely juvenile foliage. It grows wild in many parts of the world from North America to Japan. The true species is rarely seen in gardens. Popular varieties include 'Hibernica' ('Stricta', Irish juniper, a slim, narrow column to 3.5m/12ft high, 75cm/2½ft across, grey-blue).

Juniperus recurva (drooping juniper) is a small conical tree or shrub from the eastern Himalayas. Up to 4.5m (15ft) high and 2.5m (8ft) across, it has grey-green adult foliage and drooping branchlets. Varieties include 'Castlewellan' (drooping branchlets in long sprays with soft, thread-like foliage) and *J. recurva* var. *coxii* (coffin juniper, to 6m/20ft high and 1.8m/6ft wide, longer, more pendulous branches, sage-green leaves).

Juniperus rigida (temple juniper) is a graceful, wide-branched, pyramid-shaped tree. Up to 6m (20ft) high and 2.5m (8ft) across, it has slender, pendent branches with juvenile, yellow-green foliage, bronze in winter.

Juniperus scopulorum (Rocky Mountain juniper, Colorado red cedar) is a conical cypress-like tree, sometimes with several

Juniperus scopulorum 'Skyrocket'

trunks, and up to 6m (20ft) high and 1.8m (6ft) across. It has light green to blue-green adult leaves. Varieties include: 'Blue Heaven' (narrow, bright silver-blue); 'Erecta Glauca' (columnar, silvery to grey foliage, purple in winter); 'Pathfinder' (narrowly conical, bluish grey); and 'Skyrocket' (narrow columnar tree, to 6m/20ft high, 30cm/1ft across, blue-grey). *Juniperus virginiana* (red cedar,

Juniperus communis 'Hibernica'

Juniperus virginiana

pencil cedar) is up to 6m (20ft) high and 1.8m (6ft) across. The pointed adult leaves are dark green. The tree also bears some greyish juvenile foliage. Varieties include: 'Burkii' (narrow pyramid shape, steel-blue, bronze-purple in winter); 'Canaertii' (conical, bright green foliage, shiny blue fruits); 'Glauca' (columnar, silvery grey); and 'Pendula' (to 6m/20ft high, 2.5m/8ft across, drooping branchlets, green).

Cultivation
Junipers thrive in any ordinary well-drained garden soil in full sun or light shade. Coloured forms need full sun. Plant seedlings 60-90cm (2-3ft) high in mid spring.
Pruning None required, but straggly shoots can be pruned back to the main stem.
Pests and diseases Scale insects encrust stems and leaves. Caterpillars of the juniper webber moth eat the leaves and spin the foliage together. Rust produces horn-like yellow-orange spores in spring.

LEBANON CEDAR – see *Cedrus*
MADRONA – see *Arbutus*

Magnolia
magnolia

Magnolia delavayi

- ☐ Height at 25 years 3-4.5m (10-15ft)
- ☐ Mature height 14m (46ft)
- ☐ Spread 3-6m (10-20ft)
- ☐ Well-drained loamy soil
- ☐ Near-hardy broadleaf
- ☐ Features – flowers, attractive leaves

Evergreen magnolias reach impressive proportions in their native habitats, though in Britain they attain more modest sizes. They do best when grown against sunny, sheltered walls; in mild areas they also survive in the open garden when given full sun.

These trees are magnificent when their exquisite chalice-shaped flowers open in late summer, but they are imposing at any time with their large glossy evergreen leaves.

Tree magnolias do not flower before they reach maturity, but most varieties are grafted and these flower at an earlier age.

Popular species
Magnolia delavayi, a bushy, lime-tolerant species from China, can eventually reach a height of 7.5m (25ft) and a spread of 6m (20ft) under ideal, sheltered conditions. It bears huge, leathery leaves, as much as 30cm (1ft) long, matt sage-green above and bluish-white beneath. The creamy white cup-shaped flowers, as much as 20cm (8in) across, appear in late summer; they have a spicy fragrance, but each bloom lasts only a couple of days.

Magnolia grandiflora (bull bay) from the south-eastern United States, is a lime-tolerant tree up to 4.5m (15ft) high and 3m (10ft) wide. With age it develops into a round-headed tree, with branches sweeping to the ground. The thick, leathery glossy leaves are

Magnolia grandiflora 'Exmouth'

rich green with red-brown felting beneath. It bears huge, bowl-shaped flowers, up to 25cm (10in) across, in late summer and autumn; they are creamy-white and fleshy, with a rich spicy fragrance. Varieties which flower when young include 'Exmouth' ('Exoniensis' or 'Lanceolata', 25cm/10in long, glossy, soft green leaves and large, exceptionally fragrant flowers); 'Goliath' (broad, dark glossy green leaves, large globular flowers); 'Samuel Summer' (dark, glossy green leaves, brown-felted underneath, flowers up to 35cm/14in across from an early age, the hardiest variety); and 'Undulata' (glossy green, oblong leaves with pronounced wavy margins and prominent veins).

Cultivation
Plant container-grown specimens in mid spring, keeping the graft union slightly above ground. Evergreen magnolias need moist but well-drained loamy soil and are tolerant of lime. They are best grown against sheltered south- or west-facing walls in all but the mildest gardens. Top-dress annually in spring with organic matter and give a protective winter mulch to young trees for a couple of years until established.

Pruning No pruning is necessary. However, on wall-trained

Magnolia grandiflora, flower

specimens, remove forward-facing shoots from the base in spring. On mature trees set in open ground, the lower branches can be pruned back flush with the trunk to create a shade tree.

Pests and diseases Grey mould may appear as a brown-grey coating on frost-damaged shoots, causing die-back. Honey fungus kills trees. Leaf spot shows as irregular pale spots.

MIMOSA – see *Acacia*
PENCIL CEDAR – see *Juniperus*

Picea

spruce

Picea engelmannii 'Glauca'

Picea abies, cones

Picea orientalis, cones

☐ Height at 25 years 4.5-12m (15-40ft)
☐ Mature height 12-35m (40-115ft) or more
☐ Spread 1.2-5.5m (4-18ft)
☐ Hardy conifer
☐ Deep moist, ideally acid soil
☐ Features – graceful form, range of foliage colour, cones

Spruces are trees of great natural beauty, with their almost perfectly symmetrical form and dense foliage in a wide range of colours.

The branches of these conical or pyramid-shaped trees grow in neat whorls, and the needle-like leaves range from dark green to grey, blue-grey, silver and yellow. The woody-scaled pendent cones are often highly ornamental.

Spruces make excellent specimen trees and are good for forming screens and shelter belts in large gardens. Slow-growing and dwarf varieties are suitable for more restricted areas, even for rock and sink gardens.

Popular species

Picea abies (common or Norway spruce, Christmas tree), syn. *P. excelsa*, from northern and central Europe, is up to 12m (40ft) high and 4.5m (15ft) across, eventually growing to 35m (115ft) or more. It has glossy, dark green leaves and bears cones up to 15cm (6in) long. Varieties include 'Acrocona' (up to 4.5m/15ft high, with drooping branches, large cones) and 'Pyramidata' (narrow, 9m/30ft high, 1.2m/4ft across). Dwarf forms include 'Clanbrassiliana (slow-growing to 90cm/3ft high and wide); 'Nidifermis' (flat-topped, to 30cm/12in, spreading to 90cm/3ft); and 'Will's Zwerg' (rich green, pyramid shape, 90cm/3ft high and wide).

Picea breweriana (Brewer's weeping spruce) is up to 6m (20ft) high and 2.5m (8ft) across, eventually growing up to 15m (50ft) high. This beautiful, slow-growing species has spreading branches with pendent, curtain-like branchlets and dark grey-green leaves. The pointed cones are purple-brown when ripe.

Picea engelmannii 'Glauca', up to 6m (20ft) high and 3m (10ft) across, but eventually up to 18m (60ft) high, forms a dense pyramid with blue-grey foliage.

Picea glauca (white spruce), syn. *P. alba*, from Canada and the north-eastern United States, is a conical tree up to 9m (30ft) high and 2.4m (8ft) across, and eventually up to 20m (65ft) high. The foliage is grey-green. 'Caerulea'

Picea omorika

Picea orientalis 'Aurea'

Picea abies

Picea pungens 'Hoopsii'

Picea breweriana, flowers

Picea abies 'Acrocona', cones

Picea breweriana

has silvery leaves; 'Echiniformis' is 60cm/2ft high, clothed with blue-grey and green foliage.

Picea likiangensis, from western China, is up to 9m (30ft) high and 5.5m (18ft) across, eventually reaching 20m (65ft) high or more. This broad, conical tree with slightly upswept branches has pale blue-green foliage and profuse red flowers. The cones are red when young.

Picea omorika (Serbian spruce), a lime-tolerant, narrow tree, is up to 10m (33ft) high and 1.8m (6ft) across. It has glossy dark green leaves and deep purple cones. 'Nana' is slow-growing to 90cm

(3ft), with bright green foliage.

Picea orientalis (oriental spruce) is up to 9m (30ft) high and 4.5m (15ft) across, but eventually grows to 30m (100ft) or more. It is a broad, dense tree with glossy dark green foliage. Varieties include 'Aurea' (slow-growing, yellow young growth turning green) and 'Pendula' (slow-growing, weeping branches).

Picea pungens (Colorado spruce) is a large pyramid-shaped tree with cylindrical cones. Varieties, usually 4.5-6m (15-20ft) high and 1.8-4.5m (6-15ft) across, include: 'Hoopsii' (grey-blue); 'Koster's' (intense silver-blue); 'Moerheimii' (narrow, light grey-blue); 'Pendula' (grey-blue, pendent branches); and 'Spekii' (grey-blue). 'Globosa' is silvery-blue, 60cm (2ft) high.

Picea smithiana (Himalayan weeping spruce), up to 10m (33ft) high and 3m (10ft) across, eventually reaches 30m (100ft) or more. An imposing specimen tree with horizontal branches with pendent, curtain like branchlets and glossy dark green foliage. Purple cones up to 15cm (6in) long are borne on old trees.

Cultivation

Spruces thrive in deep, moist, preferably acid soil. Plant young trees 60-90cm (2-3ft) tall from late autumn to mid spring in sun or partial shade and in a sheltered position. On heavy soils, delay planting until spring.

Pruning Prune only to maintain a single leader.

Pests and diseases

Adelgids eat leaves and stems and produce galls on young shoots.

Aphids cause yellowing foliage.

Grey mould appears as a sparse web of grey fungal growth. Young succulent shoots may collapse and wither.

Honey fungus kills trees.

Mites cause premature needle-drop.

Rust shows as golden yellow pustules on the needles in spring.

Stem canker, which often follows frost damage, causes dead, slightly sunken patches.

PINE – see *Pinus*
PINE, UMBRELLA – see *Sciadopitys*

Pinus

pine

Pinus ayacahuite

Pinus parviflora, cones

Pinus nigra maritima, bark

- ☐ Height at 25 years 3-15m (10-50ft)
- ☐ Mature height 12-30m (40-100ft) or more
- ☐ Spread 1-9m (3-30ft)
- ☐ Hardy conifer
- ☐ Well-drained acid or alkaline soil
- ☐ Features – graceful form, cones

The majestic symmetry of pine trees is best appreciated on a large, open lawn. Most are broadly conical, making excellent screens or windbreaks. The lower branches often drop off as the trees age and become rounded or flat-topped.

The needle-like, 2.5-25cm (1-10in) long leaves are held in twos or clusters of three to five and range from green to blue, silver and yellow. The woody cones are short and wide or long and banana-shaped.

Most pines eventually reach a height of 20-30m (65-100ft). They are slow-growing, and dwarf and shrubby types are suitable for rock gardens (see pages 145-6).

Popular species

Pinus aristata (bristlecone pine), from the south-western United States, is a very slow-growing tree up to 3m (10ft) high and 1.5m (5ft) across after 30 years. The grey-green leaves are carried in bunches, and the cones are bristly.

Pinus ayacahuite (Mexican white pine), from Mexico and central America, is up to 12m (40ft) high and 9m (30ft) across. It has a narrow crown and broad base and bears long blue-green leaves. The banana-shaped cones are up to 38cm (15in) long.

Pinus bungeana (lace-bark pine), from China, is up to 3.5m (12ft) high and 1.5m (5ft) across, but eventually grows to 20m (65ft) or more. It has dark green leaves and bark that peels off to reveal yellow, green and brown patches.

Pinus cembra (Arolla pine), from the mountains of central Europe and northern Asia, is up to 6m

(20ft) high and 1.8m (6ft) across. It is slow-growing and of conical form, with dense blue-green leaves held in groups of three.

Pinus contorta latifolia (lodgepole pine), a pyramid-shaped, lime-hating tree from the mountains of western North America, is up to 7.5m (25ft) high and 2.4m (8ft) across with long, dull green leaves. Good in coastal areas.

Pinus leucodermis (Bosnian pine), a lime and drought-tolerant tree from Italy and the Balkan Peninsula, is up to 9m (30ft) high and 4.5m (15ft) across. It has dense, dark green leaves, attractive bark and pointed blue-purple cones ripening to dull brown.

Pinus montezumae (Montezuma pine), from the mountains of Mexico, is up to 6m (20ft) high and 3m (10ft) across. It has a broad crown, deeply fissured bark and grey-blue leaves up to 25cm (10in) long.

Pinus wallichiana, cones

Pinus patula

Pinus sylvestris 'Fastigiata'

Pinus nigra, from Europe, is up to 10.5m (35ft) high and 6m (20ft) across. It grows well in chalky soils and exposed sites. It has stiff, almost black leaves and broad yellow cones ripening to brown. The variety *maritima* (Corsican pine) has grey-green foliage.

Pinus parviflora (Japanese white pine) usually grows 5.5m (18ft) high and 3m (10ft) across. It has a wide-spreading crown, purple bark and bunches of twisted, blue-grey leaves with silvery inner surfaces. It bears clusters of oval, upright cones. 'Breviflora' is smaller with blue-green foliage.

Pinus montezumae

Pinus wallichiana

Pinus sylvestris 'Aurea'

shaped and often takes on an attractive gnarled appearance with age. Varieties include: 'Aurea' (to 4.5m/15ft high, 2.5m/8ft across, young foliage yellowish, golden in winter); and 'Fastigiata' (narrowly columnar, to 7.5m/25ft high, 1m/3ft across).

Pinus thunbergii (Japanese black pine), up to 7.5m (25ft) high and 4.5m (15ft) across, has twisted, spreading branches, black bark and rich green foliage.

Pinus wallichiana, syn. *P. excelsa* (Himalayan or Bhutan pine), up to 15m (50ft) high and 9m (30ft) across, has graceful drooping blue-green leaves up to 25cm (10in) long. It is conical when young, but develops a broad-headed crown with age.

Cultivation

Pines need full light and well-drained acid or alkaline soil. When established, most tolerate some drought; they dislike polluted air.

Plant young trees up to 60cm (2ft) high in autumn or spring.

Pruning Prune to maintain a single leader; pinch out shoot tips to restrict growth.

Pests and diseases

Adelgids feed on stems and foliage, producing tufts of waxy white wool.

Caterpillars of the pine shoot moth kill young growth.

Grey mould may attack seedlings of *P. contorta latifolia*, covering needles with a sparse web of grey fungal growth.

Honey fungus kills trees.

Rust affects two-needled pines; needles become twisted and die.

Sawfly larvae feed on leaves.

Pinus pinea

Pinus patula (Mexican yellow pine) is a beautiful but only moderately hardy species up to 7.5m (25ft) high and 4.5m (15ft) across and rarely growing to more than 15m (50ft). The bright green foliage is held in drooping clusters up to 30cm (1ft) long. Intolerant of lime.

Pinus pinea (umbrella pine, stone pine), from the Mediterranean, is up to 6m (20ft) high and 3.5m

(12ft) across and eventually reaches 15m (50ft) or more. Shaped like an umbrella, it has stiff, grey-green leaves and glossy oval cones bearing edible seeds (pine nuts). It flourishes on sandy soils and by the sea.

Pinus sylvestris (Scots pine), the only pine native to Britain, is up to 12m (40ft) high and 4.5m (15ft) across. The young tree is pyramid

Podocarpus

podocarpus

Podocarpus macrophyllus

Podocarpus nivalis

- ☐ Height at 25 years 1-6m (3-20ft)
- ☐ Mature height up to 12m (50ft)
- ☐ Spread 1-3m (3-10ft)
- ☐ Moist, well-drained soil
- ☐ Hardy and half-hardy conifers
- ☐ Features – foliage, fleshy fruits

Podocarpus trees are related to the yews (*Taxus*) and resemble them in appearance, although, coming chiefly from the Southern Hemisphere, they are less hardy. In Britain, they succeed in southern gardens and can also be grown in tubs and large containers on patios in sheltered and sunny sites.

They are slow-growing trees, with soft, needle-like foliage studded with fleshy fruits.

Popular species

Podocarpus andinus (plum-fruited yew, Chilean yew) is extremely slow-growing, to 5.5m (18ft) after 25 years, with a spread of 3m (10ft). In habit, it is yew-like, with bright green foliage, which is bluish-green underneath. The fruits resemble small black plums.

The species is generally hardy and thrives on good chalky soil.

Podocarpus gracilior (fern podocarpus) is an elegant small tree, growing up to 6m (20ft) high and 3m (10ft) wide in mild, frost-free gardens. It is half-hardy but is suitable for growing in a tub that can be moved under glass in winter. The drooping branches are densely clothed with grey-green adult foliage interspersed with glossy dark green juvenile leaves.

Podocarpus macrophyllus (yew podocarpus) is one of the hardier species, growing to 4.5m (15ft) high and 90cm (3ft) wide, eventually to 12m (40ft) high. It is an excellent specimen and tub tree, with attractive dark green leaves set in spiral clusters along the branches. The variety 'Argenteus' is very slow-growing, with narrower, silver-marked leaves. Both dislike lime.

Podocarpus nivalis (alpine totara), a mountain species from New Zealand, is hardy through-out Britain and does well on chalky soil. It is low-growing, seldom more than 1m (3ft) high but spreading to 1.8m (6ft), and good for ground cover; the branches are crowded with leathery, olive-green foliage.

Cultivation

Plant young pot-grown specimens in autumn or mid spring. They do best in moist but well-drained, loamy soil which is acid or alkaline, except for *Podocarpus macrophyllus*. A sunny and sheltered position is ideal.

Pruning None required but straggly shoots can be cut back to the base in spring.

Pests and diseases Generally trouble free.

Pseudotsuga
Douglas fir

Pseudotsuga menziesii

☐ Height at 25 years 9-24m (30-80ft)
☐ Mature height 50m (164ft)
☐ Spread 4.5-6m (15-20ft)
☐ Hardy conifer
☐ Any good moist soil
☐ Features – imposing tree, cones

The Douglas fir (*Pseudotsuga menziesii*), listed with various synonyms including *P. taxifolia* and *Abies douglasii*, is neither a hemlock (*Tsuga*) nor a fir (*Abies*), but is a distinctive, vigorous conifer of stately habit. It is suitable only for large gardens and for screening, though smaller and more slow-growing varieties are also available.

Douglas fir is of broad columnar shape, 9m (30ft) or more high and 6m (20ft) wide, with soft, aromatic foliage, dark green above and silvery beneath. Mature trees bear pendent brown cones and have corky, resin-blistered trunks. Ornamental varieties include 'Fletcheri' (2.4m/8ft high, shrubby, blue-green foliage); and 'Glauca' (slow-growing to 10.5m/35ft high and 3m/10ft wide, blue-grey foliage, lime-tolerant).

Cultivation
Plant young trees, up to 60cm (2ft) high, in early spring in good, deep, well-drained but moisture-retentive soil.
Pruning None is essential except to prune out any competing leading shoots. These conifers tolerate hard pruning, and branches and main stems can be cut back at any time of year to control growth.
Pests and diseases Adelgids may feed on the foliage and stems of young trees.

Quercus
oak

Quercus coccifera

☐ Height at 25 years 1.2-7.5m (4-25ft)
☐ Mature height up to 18m (60ft)
☐ Spread 3-6m (10-20ft)
☐ Any ordinary garden soil
☐ Near-hardy broadleaf
☐ Features – foliage, attractive form

The stately oaks found in parks and landscapes are usually thought of as deciduous trees whose late-opening leaves mature to fine colours before falling in autumn. However, several oak species are evergreen and they are as imposing as their deciduous relatives; they are generally slow-growing and often seen as multi-stemmed shrubs rather than trees. Most originate from the Mediterranean regions and the south-eastern states of North America and are therefore not recommended for cold northern gardens.

Evergreen oaks make splendid specimen trees, casting welcome shade on hot summer days and adding colour to the winter garden.

Popular species
Quercus coccifera (Kermes oak), from the Mediterranean region, is extremely slow-growing, taking several decades to reach a height of 2.5m (8ft) and a spread of 1.5m (5ft). It forms a dense, multi-stemmed shrub clothed with glossy green leaves, some of which are prickly while others are smooth. The species takes its name from the kermes insect, for which it is the host, and from

Quercus suber

Sciadopitys

umbrella pine

Sciadopitys verticillata

☐ Height at 25 years 4.5-6m (15-20ft)
☐ Mature height 7.5-9m (25-30ft)
☐ Spread 4.5m (15ft)
☐ Moist, lime-free soil
☐ Hardy conifer
☐ Features – form, foliage

Quercus ilex

which the red dye, cochineal, was formerly obtained. It is hardy in southern gardens and thrives on poor, stony soils.

Quercus ilex (evergreen or holm oak) is up to 6m (20ft) high and wide and may eventually reach a height of 18m (60ft). It is a majestic tree with deeply furrowed bark and a round-headed crown, the branches of which become pendulous with age. The leathery leaves, entire or toothed, are dark glossy green above, and greyish-green on the undersides. The species is highly wind-resistant and excellent for coastal gardens; it is not recommended for inland, frost-prone areas. It responds well to pruning and can be grown as a tall hedge or windbreak.

Quercus suber (cork oak), also from the Mediterranean, is a moderately hardy, round-headed tree up to 7.5m (25ft) high and almost as much wide. It has dark green, oval and lobed leaves that are silvery underneath. The thick and spongy bark is the commercial source of cork. The species thrives in dry, gravelly soil; though generally frost-resistant it does not do well in exposed northern gardens.

Cultivation

Evergreen oaks thrive in any ordinary well-drained garden soil, preferably in an open site in full sun, though they tolerate partial shade. They do well on deep chalky soils. Plant in early to mid autumn or mid to late spring. During the first few years apply an annual mulch of well-rotted organic matter in spring.

Pruning Prune as little as possible and merely to direct growth; this should be done in mid to late spring. Trim established hedges of *Q. ilex* in mid spring – clip again if necessary in early autumn.

Pests and diseases Various caterpillars and chafer beetles feed on the leaves, and honey fungus kills the trees, but the most common damage is caused by severe frosts which injure the foliage and cause cracking of the stems. Oak phylloxera insects, which form colonies on the undersides of leaves, may cause extensive discoloration and leaf fall.

The umbrella pine (*Sciadopitys verticillata*) is an ultra-hardy conifer from Japan. Pyramidal in shape, it makes a choice specimen tree for a lawn and is extremely slow-growing – after 50 years it reaches a maximum height of 9m (30ft). It takes its common name, umbrella pine, from the arrangement of the soft, dark green needle-like leaves which are densely grouped on the branchlets like the spokes of an umbrella.

The bark on the trunk peels away to reveal the new reddish bark underneath. Mature trees bear erect oval cones, 7.5-12.5cm (3-5in) long; they ripen in the second year from green to brown.

Cultivation

Plant young trees from mid autumn to mid spring. They thrive in neutral to acid, moist soils and dislike hot, dry situations and air pollution. A site in sun or light shade and sheltered from strong winds is ideal.

Pruning None required, but competing leading shoots should be reduced to the strongest, at any time of year.

Pests and diseases Scale insects may infest the stems. Yellowing of the foliage occurs on poorly drained soils. It can also be due to lack of nutrients; apply a general fertilizer in spring.

Taxus
yew

Taxus baccata 'Fastigiata Aureomarginata'

Taxus baccata 'Lutea', fruits

☐ Height at 25 years 3.5-4.5m (12-15ft)
☐ Mature height up to 12m (40ft)
☐ Spread 60cm-4.5m (2-15ft)
☐ Any well-drained soil
☐ Hardy conifer
☐ Features − dense foliage; colourful fruits; good hedging plant

The common yew (*Taxus baccata*) was a sacred symbol before the days of Christianity. Later, it was often planted in churchyards where fine specimens as much as 500 years old may sometimes be seen. Though also known as the English yew, it grows wild in other parts of Europe and in Iran and Algeria.

This long-lived bushy tree or shrub is slow-growing and grows no more than 4.5m (15ft) high and across after 25 years. When fully grown it is about 12m (40ft) high, often with a trunk of remarkable girth. It also makes a good hedge and is ideal for topiary.

Common yew has almost horizontal branches covered with red and brown scaly bark. The feathery, needle-like leaves are dark green. Male and female flowers are borne on separate trees; the small globular, pale yellow male flowers are carried in clusters on the previous year's shoots. The single green female flowers are scarcely visible, but are followed later by tiny, fleshy red cup-shaped fruits. All parts of the tree are poisonous.

For shrubby and dwarf yews, see pages 169-70.

Popular varieties
'**Dovastoniana**' (Westfelton yew) is up to 3.5m (12ft) high and 4.5m (15ft) across. It has long, horizontal branches with weeping branchlets.
'**Dovastonii Aurea**' is similar to 'Dovastoniana' but with golden foliage.
'**Fastigiata Aureomarginata**' (golden Irish yew), a columnar tree up to 3.5m (12ft) high and 60cm (2ft) across, has golden foliage.
'**Lutea**' is a large shrub or a small tree with yellow to orange fruits.

Cultivation
Plant 30-60cm (1-2ft) high trees from mid autumn to mid spring in any type of soil, except one that is waterlogged, and in sun or shade.

For hedges, set 38cm (15in) high young plants at intervals of 38-45cm (15-18in). Pinch out leading shoots to encourage bushy growth.
Pruning Cut any sprouts and suckers from the trunk at any time. Hedges should be trimmed or clippped into shape in early spring.
Pests and diseases Scale insects may encrust the stems. Gall mites attack the ends of young shoots and produce conspicuous galls. Mites also infest buds and distort the foliage. Honey fungus may kill some of the roots but not necessarily the trees. Waterlogging causes yellowing of the foliage.

Thuja
thuja, arbor-vitae

Thuja plicata 'Aurea'

☐ Height at 25 years 4.5-12m (15-40ft)
☐ Mature height 6-30m (20-100ft) or more
☐ Spread 75cm-3.5m (2½-12ft)
☐ Any moist garden soil
☐ Hardy conifer
☐ Features − form and colour, aromatic foliage

Thujas include fast-growing species suitable for large gardens and for hedging and windbreaks, as well as slow-growing specimen trees and shrubby and dwarf types for rock gardens (see also page 171). The scale-like leaves, borne in soft fan-like sprays, are usually aromatic when crushed and the upright cones are small, with the tips of the scales curving outwards.

Popular species
Thuja occidentalis is a slow-growing columnar tree ideal for screening. Up to 7.5m (25ft) high and 2.5m (8ft) across after 25 years, it eventually grows to about 15m (50ft). The dull green, apple-scented leaves often turn bronze in winter. Varieties include: 'Fastigiata' (narrowly conical); 'Europe Gold' (narrowly conical, up to 6m/20ft high and 1.2m/4ft across, golden); 'Malonyana' (nar-

Trachycarpus
windmill palm, Chusan palm

Thuja occidentalis 'Europe Gold'

Trachycarpus fortunei

rowly columnar, 7.5m/25ft high, 1m/3ft across, rich green); and 'Spiralis' (narrowly columnar, up to 6m/20ft high and 75cm/2½ft across, rich dark green foliage in spiralling sprays).

Thuja orientalis (Chinese thuja), a large shrub or small tree, is conical or columnar when young and becomes gaunt with age. It is up to 3m (9ft) high and 1.2m (4ft) across with mid green foliage, turning bronze in winter. 'Elegantissima' has golden-yellow foliage, green in winter.

Thuja plicata (western red cedar), syn. *T. lobbii*, is a fast-growing, long-lived tree. Up to 12m (40ft) high and 3.5m (12ft) across after 25 years, it eventually reaches 30m (100ft) or more. It has peeling, light brown bark, a fluted trunk and shiny rich green aromatic foliage; it is good for hedging and screening. Varieties include: 'Aurea' (rich gold); 'Fastigiata' ('Stricta', narrow, dense branches); 'Semperaurescens' (yellow-green); and 'Zebrina' (yellow-banded foliage).

Cultivation
Thujas will grow in any garden soil but thrive in deep, moist soil. Plant trees under 60cm (2ft) high, in a sheltered position in full sun, from late autumn to early spring.

For hedges, space plants 45cm (1½ft) high at intervals of 45-60cm (1½-2ft). Pinch out the growing tips for bushy growth.

Pruning None required. Clip hedges in summer or early autumn.
Pests and diseases Honey fungus may kill the roots of *T. plicata*.

- ☐ Height at 25 years 2.4-3m (8-10ft)
- ☐ Spread 1.8-2.4m (6-8ft)
- ☐ Any well-drained soil
- ☐ Near-hardy broadleaf
- ☐ Features – interesting foliage

Windmill palm (*Trachycarpus fortunei*, syn. *Chamaerops excelsa* and *C. fortunei*) is an exotic-looking tree for British gardens except those in the north-east. Its large fan-like leaves rise from sharply toothed stalks, about 90cm (3ft) long, above a thick, rough trunk scarred by old leaf bases and fibres.

The leaves measure 90cm (3ft) or more across and are mid green; they last for years before being replaced by young foliage, and fall off to leave the trunk with characteristic palm-like leaf scars. Mature trees in mild, sheltered gardens may produce small yellow flowers in dense sprays up to 60cm (2ft) long. The flowers, in early summer, are occasionally followed by small blue-black globular fruits.

The moderately hardy windmill palm makes a fine specimen tree for smaller gardens, where it looks best planted in the middle of a lawn.

Cultivation
Plant young pot-grown specimens in late spring in ordinary, well-drained soil. Choose a sunny or lightly shaded position sheltered from north and east winds and from frost pockets.

Pruning Remove wind-damaged leaves flush with the trunk.
Pests and diseases Trouble free.

Trachycarpus fortunei

Tsuga

hemlock

Tsuga canadensis, foliage and cones

☐ Height at 25 years 3-15m (10-50ft)
☐ Mature height 15-45m (50-150ft)
☐ Spread 1.8-6m (6-20ft)
☐ Moist, lime-free soil
☐ Hardy conifer
☐ Features – graceful form

For gardeners with deep moist soil, the genus *Tsuga* provides a range of fine specimen trees grown for their graceful form, with sweeping branches and drooping or gently arching branchlets.

These handsome trees have needle-like leaves in shades ranging from mid to dark green, often with white bands beneath. The small cones, which measure about 2.5cm (1in) long, droop from the tips of the shoots.

Hemlocks make fine specimen trees for large gardens and are also useful for hedging, providing a dense bushy screen. Dwarf types (see page 172) are suitable for small gardens.

Popular species

Tsuga canadensis (eastern hemlock), from eastern North America, is up to 9m (30ft) high and 6m (20ft) across. It has a broad crown above a trunk with rough, ridged, grey-brown bark; the leaves are dark green with white-marked undersides twisted upwards. This species tolerates lime. 'Fremdii' is a slow-growing broadly conical variety.
Tsuga caroliniana (Carolina hemlock), from the south-eastern United States, rarely grows more

than 3m (10ft) high in British gardens. It bears yellowish green, white-banded foliage.
Tsuga diversifolia (northern Japanese hemlock), a slow-growing species, is up to 6m (20ft) high and 4.5m (15ft) across. It has horizontal branches and often more than one trunk. The bark is orange-brown and the leaves are glistening deep green.
Tsuga heterophylla (western hemlock) is a conical, slender tree up to 15m (50ft) high and 6m (20ft) across, with dense dark green foliage hanging from slightly upward-sweeping branches. It has dark brown furrowed bark, a fluted trunk and profuse cones. A good specimen or hedging tree. 'Greenmantle' has pendulous branches.
Tsuga mertensiana, syn. *T. pattoniana,* from western North America, is a slow-growing tree up to 7.5m (25ft) high and 1.8m (6ft) across. The grey-blue leaves grow spirally round the shoots; the pur-

Tsuga mertensiana

ple cones are up to 7.5cm (3in) long. The dark red-brown bark is rough and scaly.

Cultivation

Hemlocks thrive in deep moist acid soils, although *T. canadensis* tolerates lime. Plant trees under 60cm (2ft) high from mid autumn to mid spring in partial shade in a site sheltered from east winds.

For hedges of *T. heterophylla,* set 30-45cm (1-1½ft) high plants at intervals of 45-60cm (1½-2ft). Pinch out the growing tips to promote bushy growth.
Pruning Clip established hedges in early summer or early autumn.
Pests and diseases Trouble free.

UMBRELLA PINE – see
Sciadopitys
WATTLE, SILVER – see *Acacia*
WINDMILL PALM – see
Trachycarpus
YEW – see *Taxus*

Woodland shrubs In late spring, rhododendrons and azaleas come into their full glory.

A-Z of evergreen shrubs

Evergreens have special virtues in garden planning schemes, the chief of which is their year-round colourful foliage. Green plants in a winter garden suggest security and a comforting assurance that spring will arrive; in summer they offer shade and relief from the glare and heat of the sun. Evergreen is a slight misnomer as foliage colour veers from shades of green to grey and silver, blue or purple-black, and all of these basic colours may be splashed or edged with markings and variegations of yellow, pink or white.

Foliage and plant size are the usual factors governing the choice of evergreen shrubs. Most are flowering plants for the shrub or mixed border – rhododendrons, camellias and sun roses are but a few examples – but however spectacular the seasonal display, it is brief compared with the year-round display of leaf colour, shape and texture.

The ornamental value of an evergreen also influences choice. There are shrubs for planting as backgrounds to flowering plants – Portuguese and spotted laurels for example – while others are ideal for hedging and screening, along boundary lines or as internal divisions between garden compartments – spiny green holly or flowering escallonias, for example, and dwarf box or sweet lavender. Yet other evergreens demand a position of prominence, as specimen plants on their own or in groups, like the strawberry tree, the colourful pieris or the imposing yuccas. Prostrate shrubs will cover the ground with evergreen carpets, such as ling and heathers, aromatic Christmas box or bright-berried pernettya. On a different plane, there are evergreen climbers, such as passion flower, potato vines and ivies to clamber up walls and fences.

Few evergreens are as versatile as the shrubby conifers. There are literally hundreds of varieties, differing widely in shape and size, in foliage colours and growth habit. Tall and medium-sized conifers serve the same purposes as broad-leaved evergreen shrubs, while dwarf and miniature types are tailor-made for rockeries and trough gardens.

BROAD-LEAVED EVERGREENS

**Evergreen shrubs and trees furnish a garden
with permanent colour and life, and generously add
magnificent flowers and brilliant berries.**

Among garden plants, the broad-leaved evergreens – trees, shrubs and climbers – work hardest to earn their keep, and it is well worth including a selection of them in the garden. In late autumn, winter and early spring, broad-leaved evergreens give green and variegated colour when deciduous shrubs are dormant; and in the growing season, they provide the perfect backdrop for colourful – but often shorter-lived – perennials and annuals.

An evergreen plant keeps its foliage all year round. Evergreens do shed old leaves and replace them with young ones, but gradually – never as dramatically as the autumnal leaf fall of deciduous trees and shrubs. Broad-leaved evergreens have flat leaves, which range in size from the tiny ones of *Lonicera nitida* to the enormous ones of *Rhododendron sinogrande* – 75cm (2½ft) or more in length.

Though many broad-leaved evergreens have round, oval or elliptical leaves, not all do. Some, such as yucca, have long, sword-like leaves; others, such as fatsia, have fan-shaped or palmate leaves. Many broad-leaved evergreens are green, but there are also numerous varieties with grey, silver, gold or variegated leaves.

The category excludes conifers, most of which are evergreen but have thin, needle-like leaves.

Trees and shrubs
Evergreen trees are especially valuable for the mass of year-round foliage they provide. The largest broad-leaved evergreen tree in cool temperate climates is the holm oak (*Quercus ilex*). Given enough time and space, it makes a magnificent tree, with the rounded shape and acorns of an oak but greyish evergreen foliage. It grows too large for the average garden, but there are other, more suitable choices, such as holly and the magnificent tree magnolias. Though holly is often grown as a hedge, it makes a splendid specimen tree or large shrub, especially attractive in winter with its dark green or variegated shiny leaves and red or yellow berries.

For mild, sheltered gardens, delightful mimosa (*Acacia*) is clothed with silver-grey, fern-like leaves and, in spring, a glorious mass of sweet-scented yellow blossom. There is also the much hardier, picturesque strawberry tree (*Arbutus unedo*), which combines evergreen foliage with attractive red bark, flowers which resemble lily-of-the-valley, and bright red fruits. Other options are the different species and varieties of eucalyptus, graceful trees with aromatic grey leaves and silvery bark.

Most broad-leaved evergreens are shrubs, grown as specimen plants, included in mixed borders or pruned as hedges. There are hundreds of species and cultivated varieties, including bay, box, camellia, Mexican orange, escallonia, pyracantha, elaeagnus, mahonia, pieris, skimmia, *Garrya elliptica* and many barberries, viburnums and cotoneasters. Sizes range from huge Portugal laurels to ground-hugging and spreading *Cotoneaster congestus* and *Gaultheria procumbens*.

There are plain green and variegated forms of many broad-leaved evergreen shrubs and they

◀ **Shade lover** One of the best broad-leaved evergreens for dark town gardens, *Aucuba japonica* also thrives in industrial sites. The variety 'Picturata' is boldly splashed with bright yellow.

▲ **Berry colour** The low, wide-spreading branches of *Cotoneaster horizontalis* are laden with bright red berries in autumn. In mild winters, the shrub is semi-evergreen; spells of hard frost cause it to drop its tiny leaves.

◄ **Variegated holly** Tolerant of close clipping, hollies, and especially the variegated types, make admirable specimen trees. They can be trained as standards with a clear trunk or grown as multi-stemmed shrubs or hedging plants.

serve different purposes. For example, the all-green forms of spotted laurel – *Aucuba japonica* 'Crassifolia', 'Hillieri', 'Lance Leaf' and 'Salicifolia' – can be visually more restful than the yellow spotted laurel (*A. japonica* 'Variegata'). And though the gold or silver variegated forms of elaeagnus are strikingly colourful, the cool greeny grey foliage of *E.* x *ebbingei* can make a welcome change.

Evergreen climbers

The most common evergreen climber is ivy, which comes in a wide range of all-green cultivars: the arrow-shaped *Hedera helix* 'Sagittifolia'; the bright green, frilly-edged 'Green Ripple'; the deeply cut 'Green Feather'; and

▲ **Canary Island ivy** The plants offered as *Hedera canariensis* are almost invariably the Algerian ivy (*Hedera algeriensis*). This is a vigorous species suitable for covering walls and ground space if sheltered from hot sun and strong, drying winds.

▼ **Dwarf rhododendrons** Gardeners on alkaline soil must forego the pleasure of rhododendron glades. As recompense, dwarf and compact types, like the small-leaved, deep waxy-red 'Baden Baden' cultivar, can be grown in pots of ericaceous compost on shady patios.

▲ **Dependable firethorn** Utterly hardy and undemanding, the firethorns (*Pyracantha* species) are among the most popular of broad-leaved evergreens. Frequently grown against shady walls, their moment of glory comes when bright berries appear in autumn.

the large-leaved Irish ivy, 'Hibernica'. In addition there are numerous attractive variegated forms, such as the cream marbled *H. colchica* 'Dentata Variegata' and the gold-centred *H. helix* 'Goldheart'.

Among the most beautiful evergreen clematis are *C. armandii*, with large, glossy leaves and creamy white flowers; and *C. cirrhosa*, the fern-leaved clematis with its greenish-yellow winter flowers and silky seed heads. Both need sun and shelter in order to flourish. Other evergreen climbers needing a sheltered spot include the primrose jasmine (*Jasminum mesnyi*) and the purple-blue potato vines (*Solanum* species).

Flowers, berries and fruits

All broad-leaved evergreens flower, and some of the showiest blooms – rhododendrons, camellias and magnolias, for example – are produced by evergreens. Others, including box and privet (*Ligustrum*), have flowers of such modesty as to be insignificant, and such evergreens are grown solely for their foliage.

Many broad-leaved evergreens flower in winter, when there is a shortage of colour. Camellia, daphne, garrya, *Viburnum tinus*, mahonia and sarcococca are winter-flowering, as are some of the evergreen clematis.

Some evergreens, including aucuba, holly, pernettya, skimmia, pyracantha, cotoneaster and gaultheria, produce handsome berries or fruit – again, often in late autumn and winter. In some cases male and female forms are needed for fruits to form.

Using evergreens

Flowers and fruit are a welcome bonus, but year-round greenery is the main advantage of broad-leaved evergreens. Many are shade-tolerant and especially useful in town gardens and under trees. They include aucuba, box, camellia, daphne, elaeagnus, euonymus, fatsia, gaultheria, holly, honeysuckle, ivy, laurel, leucothoë, mahonia, osmanthus, pachysandra, periwinkle, rhododendron, sarcococca, skimmia and viburnum.

As a seasonal bonus, a few broad-leaved evergreens turn red, crimson or russet in winter; these include several of the *Hedera helix* cultivars and the mahonias. Others, such as photinia and

▲ **Persian ivy** Sometimes known as elephant's ears from the shape of its large leathery leaves, the fast-growing and ultra-hardy Persian ivy (*Hedera colchica*) is an ideal climber for walls, fences and banks. It is just as suitable for large-scale ground cover. The variety 'Dentata Variegata' is bright green with wide margins of creamy-yellow maturing to near white.

◄ **Chusan palm** In mild frost-free gardens, the Chusan or windmill palm (*Trachycarpus fortunei*) makes a spectacular focal point in a sheltered border. The huge leaf fans measure as much as 1.5m (5ft) across and persist for many years before dropping off to leave conspicuous fibrous scars on the trunk.

pieris, have bright red young spring growth – as colourful as any flower.

Broad-leaved evergreens – and many conifers – are ideal for boundary hedges as they usually have a dense growth habit and remain clothed in foliage all year round. They are also suitable, for the same reason, for camouflaging or concealing unpleasant views.

Broad-leaved evergreens with dramatic foliage or habits of growth make good specimen plants or focal points – a holly in the centre of a lawn, for example, or a yucca in the centre of a bed or border. Others are excellent in pots – fatsia, camellia and ivy, for example. All provide a suitable background for lighter-leaved plants and bright flowers, and most can be used to fill in awkward gaps in shady corners where few other plants could survive.

Caring for evergreens

Broad-leaved evergreens grown as hedges need regular pruning to keep them dense and, in the case of flowering hedges such as escallonia, to encourage the production of flowering wood. They also benefit from an annual feed and moisture-retentive mulch.

▲ **Winter cheer** The glorious *Camellia japonica* starts to flower in late winter, unfolding its brilliant blooms even in the shade of a north-facing wall. Hundreds of varieties are available – single, double or peony-like and in a range of pastel and vibrant colours.

Like other plants, broad-leaved evergreens vary in hardiness and frost tolerance. Some plants, such as box, are ultra-hardy, able to withstand the worst of winter weather without harm, while others, such as *Carpenteria californica*, need a sheltered sunny site.

Many, such as aucuba, will tolerate almost any growing conditions, while a few, such as fremontodendron, can be temperamental and demand extra attention. As with any other plant group it is a question of choosing the right plant for the right place.

◄ **Tropical touches** The glossy bright green leaves of *Fatsia japonica* lend a tropical air to a shrub border. It thrives in semi-shade and is ideal for dark town gardens, with its year-round greenery and dramatic autumn display of creamy white flowers.

◄ **Winter sunshine** The glossy-leaved mahonias are particularly valuable for their winter flowers. In frost and snow they open their sprays and clusters of sunshine-yellow, often scented blooms; wind and rain cannot wash the gloss from their deeply divided foliage, and in time these hardy shrubs reach near tree-like proportions, thriving in sun or shade and in any type of soil.

▼ **Winter clematis** To most people, the large-flowered, brightly coloured clematis hybrids belong to summer. Evergreen clematis, however, bloom in winter and spring, and unlike the deciduous clematis remain attractive in leaf throughout the year. *Clematis cirrhosa* is hardy in most winters and drapes its purplish stems with wide, yellow-white bells during the winter months. In the variety *balearica*, the flowers are spotted with red-purple on the inside.

Abelia

abelia

Abelia x grandiflora

☐ Height 1.5-2.4m (5-8ft)
☐ Spread 1.2-2m (4-7ft)
☐ Flowers late spring to early autumn
☐ Ordinary garden soil
☐ Sunny, sheltered position

Evergreen abelias are prized for their late flowering display, often into autumn, and for their handsome glossy foliage. They bear an abundance of drooping clusters of tubular flowers whose red sepals remain attractive for several weeks after the petals have fallen. The small, broadly ovate leaves are bronze-green in spring, dark green in summer and bronze in autumn. These easily grown shrubs are semi-evergreen in all but the mildest districts.

Popular species
Abelia floribunda, from Mexico, is the least hardy of the species and needs the protection of a sunny and sheltered wall. It grows 1.5m (5ft) high, and more in favourable sites,

with a similar spread. From late spring until well into summer, the branches are clothed with brilliant rose-pink flower clusters.
Abelia x *grandiflora* has a spreading habit – 90cm-1.2m (3-4ft) wide and 1.5-1.8m (5-6ft) high. The slightly fragrant, pink and white flowers appear from mid summer to early autumn.

Cultivation
Plant in early autumn or mid spring in ordinary garden soil in a sunny, sheltered position.

Regular pruning is unnecessary, although overgrown shoots can be thinned after flowering to encourage new growth. Frost-damaged shoots should be cut out from the base in spring.
Propagation Take 7.5-10cm (3-4in) long cuttings of the current season's wood in mid summer. Root in a cold frame and plant out the following spring.
Pests and diseases Trouble free.

Abutilon

abutilon

Abutilon vitifolium 'Tennant's White'

☐ Height 1.8-2.4m (6-8ft)
☐ Spread 1.5-2.4m (5-8ft)
☐ Flowers late spring to mid autumn
☐ Any well-drained soil
☐ Sunny sheltered wall

Two species of these half-hardy South American shrubs can be grown outdoors in Britain, though they require a sunny site against a sheltered wall. So enchanting are the flowers, however, that the shrubs fully deserve such prized positions.

Although evergreen, abutilons are likely to lose much of their bright green vine-like foliage during a hard winter.

Popular species
Abutilon megapotamicum has conspicuous, drooping yellow and red tubular flowers from late spring to early autumn. It is a slender-stemmed, spreading shrub, reaching 1.8-2.4m (6-8ft) high and across, with bright green, oval, toothed leaves.
Abutilon vitifolium is the hardier species. It bears clusters of mauve or lavender-blue, mallow-like flowers from late spring to mid autumn. It reaches 2.4m (8ft) high and 1.5m (5ft) across and has green lobed leaves covered with short white hairs. 'Tennant's White' has large, freely borne pure white flowers, and 'Veronica Tennant' bears dark blue blooms.

Cultivation
Plant abutilons in late spring against a sheltered sunny wall in ordinary well-drained soil. Alternatively, grow abutilons as pot

Akebia
akebia

Andromeda
bog rosemary

Andromeda polifolia

Akebia quinata

Abutilon megapotamicum

plants and move them under cover for the winter.

Protect both species with straw during winter. Remove frosted or dead shoots in mid spring.

Propagation Take 7.5-10cm (3-4in) cuttings of half-ripe lateral shoots in summer and root in a propagating frame at 15-18°C (59-64°F). Pot the rooted cuttings and grow on before hardening them off in a cold frame. Plant out in late spring.

Pests and diseases Generally trouble free.

☐ Height 4.5m (15ft)
☐ Flowers mid to late spring
☐ Any well-drained soil
☐ Sunny or lightly shaded position

Hardy, vigorous and easily grown, *Akebia quinata* is an attractive climber, valued for the spreading rich green tapestry of leaves that it quickly weaves. The small round green leaflets which cover its slender twining stems generally persist through all but the coldest winters. In early spring they are joined by purple-flushed young leaves and later by small strings of flower buds that open into three-petalled, fragrant and reddish-purple blooms.

Cultivation
Plant in autumn or spring in any deep, moisture-retentive but well-drained soil in sun or light shade. Train up trees, pergolas, walls, or trellis, with wires or string for the twining stems. After flowering, prune out weak shoots and, if space is restricted, cut other side-shoots hard back.
Propagation Layer long shoots in autumn, or root cuttings under glass in late summer.
Pests and diseases Trouble free.

☐ Height 45cm (18in)
☐ Spread 38cm (15in)
☐ Flowers late spring to early summer
☐ Acid moisture-retentive soil
☐ Shady site

In the wild, bog rosemary (*Andromeda polifolia*) grows in marshes and on wet moorland; in gardens it is an excellent low-growing shrub for peat gardens or cool, shady corners in a rockery.

Its slender, wiry stems are covered in small grey-green and leathery leaves – resembling those of rosemary – throughout the year. Clusters of pink, urn-shaped flowers appear at the tips of the stems in late spring to early summer. 'Compacta' is a popular variety, smaller and denser, with bright pink flowers; 'Alba' is a white-flowered form; and 'Macrophylla' bears rich pink flowers.

Cultivation
Plant from autumn to spring, in moist, acid, humus-rich soil, in a cool shaded site.
Pruning is not necessary.
Propagation Increase stock by layering the plants in autumn or spring, or by division or hardwood cuttings in autumn.
Pests and diseases Trouble free.

Abutilon vitifolium 'Tennant's White'

Arbutus
strawberry tree

Arbutus unedo, fruits

☐ Height 2.4m (8ft) or more
☐ Spread 1.5m (5ft) or more
☐ Flowers in autumn
☐ Any well-drained soil
☐ Sunny position sheltered from cold
   winds

Among the loveliest of all evergreens is the strawberry tree (*Arbutus unedo*). Its red or orange fruits, resembling strawberries in shape and size, stand out brilliantly against the lustrous dark green foliage. They are edible and hang on the branches from one year to the next, often ripening in the company of the current year's flowers. These are borne in mid and late autumn, in pendulous clusters of tiny, creamy white or pale pink blooms.

In south-western Ireland, where the strawberry tree grows wild, the species reaches tree-like proportions (see page 26), but in gardens elsewhere the maximum height is likely to be 2.4m (8ft). When mature it takes on a splendid gnarled appearance with deep brown, peeling bark on older wood. It is usually grown as a multi-stemmed shrub, but can also be pruned to a single trunk.

Several named varieties include the following: 'Elfin King' (shrubby, fruiting at an early stage); and 'Rubra' (red-tinged flowers).

Cultivation
Plant in autumn or spring in full sun and in a site sheltered from north and east winds. Although a member of the acid-loving heather family, the strawberry tree will tolerate some lime in the soil, provided this is well drained.

Arbutus unedo, flowers

It does well in mild coastal gardens.

Protect young plants in winter with straw or bracken (once established they become hardier). Prune straggly shoots back to the main stems in mid spring. On established shrubs, the lower shoots can be cut out flush with the main stems to expose the flaking bark.
Propagation Take 7.5-10cm (3-4in) long heel cuttings in summer and root in a propagating unit at a temperature of 18°C (64°F). Cuttings are often difficult to root, but when successful, pot them up singly and grow on for a couple of years in a cold frame.
Pests and diseases Leaf spot shows as small brown spots on the foliage.

Arctostaphylos
bearberry

Arctostaphylos uva-ursi 'Point Reyes'

☐ Height 15cm (6in)
☐ Spread 1.2m (4ft) or more
☐ Flowers late spring
☐ Moist acid soil
☐ Full sun or light shade

The ultra-hardy bearberry (*Arctostaphylos uva-ursi*) is an excellent ground-cover shrub for banks with stony or poor soil. It forms an evergreen, near-prostrate but rapidly spreading mat of short-pointed, oval, dark green, leathery leaves on wiry stems that root where they touch the ground.

In late spring, bearberry produces pendulous sprays of tiny pale pink flowers, but it is particularly attractive in autumn when the foliage takes on a bronzy sheen, and the shoots glisten with clusters of bright red berries that last through the winter. 'Point Reyes' bears blush pink flowers.

Cultivation
Plant container-grown specimens in early autumn or mid spring. Bearberries do best in cool moist climates and thrive in coastal gardens with sandy or poor, acid soil. They prefer full sun, but they will also grow, though with fewer berries, in light shade. Pruning is unnecessary when the plants are grown for ground cover; wayward shoots can be cut back at any time of year.
Propagation Layer long shoots in spring and separate from the parent plant after one or two years. Alternatively, take heel cuttings in late summer and root in a cold frame.
Pests and diseases Trouble free.

Arundinaria

bamboo

Arundinaria japonica

Arundinaria variegata

- ☐ Height 1.2-4.5m (4-15ft)
- ☐ Spread 90cm-2.4m (3-8ft)
- ☐ Foliage plant
- ☐ Any moist soil
- ☐ Sunny or partially shaded site sheltered from cold winds

These elegant, hardy grasses make excellent evergreen screens and windbreaks in gardens with plenty of space, though they can also be grown as specimen plants. Being moisture-lovers they look particularly effective planted by water.

All have long grass-like leaves, some of which are pale green while others are variegated. Their woody stems are gracefully arched and jointed. They rarely flower – and when they do, the flowers are inconspicuous.

Popular species

Arundinaria anceps, syn. *Sinarundinaria anceps*, forms a dense thicket of bright green stems, 3-4.5m (10-15ft) high and topped with narrow, glossy green leaves. It is a good screening species and is highly invasive. Set the plants 1.8-2.4m (6-8ft) apart.

Arundinaria humilis, syn. *Pleiblastus humilis*, is a particularly rampant species forming a low clump 60cm (2ft) high and 1.2m (4ft) across. Its slender, dark green stems carry light green leaves which are downy on the underside. This bamboo makes excellent ground cover and will grow beneath trees.

Arundinaria japonica, syn. *Pseudosasa japonica*, is ideal for screening, being invasive and reaching 2-4.5m (7-15ft) high. It has olive-green stems and glossy green leaves and is the most commonly planted bamboo in Britain. Set the plants 1.8-2.4m (6-8ft) apart.

Arundinaria murielae, syn. *Thamnocalamus spathaceus*, makes an excellent specimen plant as it forms clumps and does not spread. Its fresh mid green leaves are carried on yellow-green stems which arch gracefully. This species grows 1.8-2.4m (6-8ft) high and should be set 90cm (3ft) apart.

Arundinaria nitida, syn. *Sinarundinaria nitida*, is a non-invasive species with dark purple canes and bright green leaves, which are grey-green underneath. It makes a good specimen plant, and thrives in a tub. Best in light shade, where it can reach 3m (10ft) high. Set the plants 1.2m (4ft) apart.

Arundinaria vagans, syn. *Sasa ramosa*, is an invasive, carpet-forming species. It reaches 30cm (1ft) and is excellent as ground cover in a wild garden. The narrow leaves, 10cm (4in) long, are mid green and the thin canes are bright green, becoming darker with age. Set the plants 45cm (18in) apart.

Arundinaria variegata, syn. *A. fortunei*, forms a dense thicket up to 1.2m (4ft) high. It has pale green canes and dark green leaves striped with white. Plant 1.8m (6ft) apart.

Arundinaria viridistriata, syn. *A. auricoma*, is a non-invasive, clump-forming species with rich yellow and green variegated foliage borne on purple canes. It grows 1.2m (4ft) high, and should be set 45-60cm (18-24in) apart.

Cultivation

Plant bamboos in mid to late spring in ordinary moist garden soil, and in a sunny or lightly shaded position, sheltered from cold winds.

Pruning is unnecessary, but old dead canes can be cut out at ground level in early autumn; they make fine garden canes.

Propagation Divide and replant in mid spring or autumn. Or remove rooted suckers at the same time and replant.

Pests and diseases Trouble free.

Arundinaria viridistriata

Aucuba
spotted laurel

Aucuba japonica

- ☐ Height 1.8-3.5m (6-12ft)
- ☐ Spread 1.5-2m (5-7ft)
- ☐ Flowers early to mid spring
- ☐ Ordinary garden soil
- ☐ Sunny or shaded position

Its decorative leaves and handsome scarlet berries made the spotted laurel (*Aucuba japonica*) so popular among Victorians that a good plant in fruit could cost a huge sum of money. Today this hardy evergreen is more often relegated to the back of a shrubbery – but it deserves better.

Spotted laurel grows in all soils and in any position, though for the best foliage it needs partial shade and good soil.

Insignificant olive-green star-shaped flowers in spring are followed by scarlet berries on female plants in autumn. Male and female shrubs are essential for berry production.

Popular varieties
Named varieties are listed as male or female:
'Crassifolia', male, large glossy, deep green leaves.
'Crotonifolia', male, large green leaves speckled gold.
'Longifolia', female, narrow bright green willow-like leaves.
'Variegata' ('Maculata'), female, green leaves blotched yellow.

Cultivation
Plant in autumn or spring in any soil in sun or shade. Tolerant of town pollution.
Propagation Take 10-15cm (4-6in) heel cuttings in late summer and root in a cold frame.
Pests and diseases Trouble free.

BAMBOO – see *Arundinaria*
BARBERRY – see *Berberis*
BAY LAUREL – see *Laurus*
BEARBERRY – see *Arctostaphylos*

Aucuba japonica 'Variegata'

Berberis
berberis, barberry

Berberis julianae

- ☐ Height 45cm-3m (1½-10ft)
- ☐ Spread 45cm-3.5m (1½-12ft)
- ☐ Flowers mid to late spring
- ☐ Ordinary soil
- ☐ Sunny or lightly shaded position

The evergreen berberis are ornamental shrubs, which are hardy and easy to grow as specimen plants or as barrier hedges. With their handsome glossy green and spiny leaves – which often take on bronze hues in winter – their fiercely thorny stems, yellow or orange flower clusters in spring, and their decorative, long-lasting berries, berberis repay a minimum of care with year-round interest.

Popular species
Berberis buxifolia, syn. *B. dulcis*, has dark green, leathery and spine-tipped leaves with grey undersides. It grows 1.8m (6ft) high and wide; in early and mid spring it bears yellow flower clusters followed in autumn by blue-black berries with a waxy bloom. The variety 'Nana' rarely grows more than 45cm (18in) high and is suitable for a rock garden or as a low ledge; it seldom flowers or fruits.
Berberis calliantha is a compact shrub, 90cm (3ft) high and wide, with holly-like, dark green leaves, waxy white beneath; the young stems are red-tinged. Clusters of pale yellow flowers in late spring are followed by blue-black berries.
Berberis darwinii is one of the most popular species. Of bushy habit and with dark green, glossy holly-like leaves, it makes an excellent hedge. It produces an abundance of rich yellow-orange

Berberis gagnepainii lanceifolia

Berberis darwinii

flowers in mid to late spring followed by blue autumnal berries. It grows to a height and spread of 2.4-3m (8-10ft).

Berberis x *frikartii* is a dense, slow-growing shrub, rarely more than 90cm (3ft) high and wide. It bears glossy dark green, spiny leaves, conspicuously blue-white on the undersides. Large yellow flowers are borne singly or in pairs in late spring and early summer. The berries are blue-black.

Berberis gagnepainii grows 1.8m (6ft) high, with a spread of 1.5m (5ft). It is of dense, erect habit, with narrow, lance-shaped, crinkle-edged leaves. It forms an impenetrable hedge. The yellow flowers in late spring are followed by black berries.

Berberis insignis is an outstanding foliage shrub, 1.5m (5ft) high and up to 1.8m (6ft) across. It is of dense, erect habit with yellowish shoots and large, lance-shaped leaves which are prominently toothed; they are dark green above, glossy yellow-green under-neath. Large showy clusters of yellow flowers, borne in late spring, are followed by black berries.

Berberis julianae bears leathery, lance-shaped leaves which are tinted copper when young. Reaching 3m (10ft) high and 1.8m (6ft) across, with strongly spiny stems, it makes an excellent screening or hedging shrub. Its yellow, slightly scented flowers appear in early summer and are followed by large clusters of black berries.

Berberis linearifolia is an erect, slow-growing species, up to 3m (10ft) high and 1.2m (4ft) across. It is one of the best berberis for flowering, bearing clusters of rich orange flowers in mid spring; they are particularly fine in the form 'Orange King'. The variety 'Jewel' opens bright orange from scarlet buds.

Berberis x *stenophylla* grows vigorously, making it an excellent hedging shrub up to 2.4-3m (8-10ft) high and 3-3.5m (10-12ft) across. The arching stems are clothed with narrowly, lance-shaped deep green leaves that are bluish-white on the undersides. Sweetly scented golden-yellow flowers are borne from mid to late spring and are followed by purple berries.

Several dwarf varieties, with a height and spread of 1.2m (4ft), have been developed and include 'Autumnalis' (flowers in spring and autumn); 'Coccinea' (red flower buds opening to orange blooms); 'Corallina Compacta' (red buds and orange flowers, only 30cm (1ft) high; 'Cream Show-ers' (creamy-white flowers, unusual in berberis); 'Pink Pearl' (pale yellow, pink or orange flow-ers all on the same plant and pink or cream variegated leaves); and 'Semperflorens' (red-budded and orange-flowered over a particular-ly long period).

Berberis verruculosa grows slowly to 90cm-1.5m (3-5ft) in height, with a similar spread. The arching stems are set with tiny warty growths and small, spiny-toothed leaves that are dark green above, white beneath. The golden-yellow flowers, borne singly or in pairs, appear in late spring and early summer; they are followed by black berries. Good hedging shrub.

Cultivation

Plant in autumn or in spring, in sun or light shade. Any ordinary garden soil – including a poor or shallow one – is suitable. For hedging and screening, set young plants 45-60cm (1½-2ft) apart and cut them back by a quarter to encourage bushy growth.

Little pruning is necesary, but old or wayward shoots can be cut

Berberis x stenophylla

back to ground level or to healthy young shoots after flowering. Hedges should be trimmed to shape when flowering has finished; they will not produce berries.

Propagation Take heel cuttings from lateral shoots in late summer and early autumn and root in a cold frame. The following spring pot up the cuttings singly and plunge them in an outdoor nursery bed until ready for planting in their permanent positions two years later.

Pests and diseases Honey fungus can kill berberis.

BLUEBERRY – see *Vaccinium*
BOG ROSEMARY – see
Andromeda
BOX – see *Buxus*
BUCKTHORN – see *Rhamnus*

Berberis gagnepainii

Buddleia
orange ball tree

Buddleia globosa

- Height 3m (10ft)
- Spread 3m (10ft)
- Flowers late spring
- Any well-drained soil
- Sunny site

The evergreen orange ball tree (*Buddleia globosa*), from Chile, is quite distinct from the other, deciduous buddleias, the butterfly bushes. It is less hardy but usually survives most winters in all but the coldest and most exposed gardens, though it may lose some of its foliage.

It is of vigorous, upright habit, with a height and spread of 3m (10ft) and bears lance-shaped, dark green, wrinkled leaves with tawny undersides. In late spring and early summer, the shrub is covered with clusters of globular orange-yellow flower heads that are sweetly scented. The variety 'Lemon Ball' has lemon-yellow flowers.

Cultivation
Plant in autumn or spring in any fertile, well-drained soil and in full sun; in exposed gardens, the shrubs are best grown against sheltered west-facing walls.

This buddleia flowers on shoots of the previous season; after flowering, prune away the faded clusters with about 7.5cm (3in) of stem.
Propagation Take 10cm (4in) heel cuttings of half-ripe side-shoots in late summer and root in a cold frame. In spring, transfer the rooted cuttings to an outdoor nursery bed and grow on for about a year before transplanting.
Pest and diseases Trouble free.

BUTCHER'S BROOM – see *Ruscus*

Buxus
box

Buxus sempervirens 'Aurea Marginata'

- Height up to 3m (10ft)
- Spread 1.2-1.8m (4-6ft)
- Foliage shrub
- Ordinary garden soil
- Sunny or lightly shaded site

Common box (*Buxus sempervirens*) is one of Britain's few native broad-leaved evergreens. In its dwarf form, it has been part of the English garden for centuries – as a surround for medieval herb plots, or forming

Buxus sempervirens

the basic pattern of the Elizabethan knot garden. Box is one of the most suitable shrubs for topiary work, and for formal hedging.

Popular varieties
'Aurea Marginata' has leaves edged with yellow.
'Elegantissima' is slow growing, compact, leaves edged silver-white.
'Suffruticosa' is commonly used for edging and can be trimmed to 15cm (6in) above ground; glossy green leaves.

Cultivation
Plant in autumn or spring in any type of soil, in sun or shade. For hedges, space 23-30cm (9-12in) high plants at 30-38cm (12-15in) intervals. Clip hedges and topiary specimens in late summer and early autumn.
Propagation Take cuttings in late summer and early autumn.
Pests and diseases Box suckers may feed on the leaves, and rust can be a problem.

CABBAGE PALM – see *Cordyline*
CALICO BUSH – see *Kalmia*
CALIFORNIAN LILAC – see *Ceanothus*

Calluna

heather, ling

Calluna vulgaris 'Anne Marie'

Calluna vulgaris 'Silver Queen'

☐ Height 15-60cm (6-24in)
☐ Spread 30-60cm (1-2ft)
☐ Flowers late summer and early
   autumn
☐ Any lime-free soil
☐ Sunny open site

From late summer on, vast tracts of acid moorland, heath and bog in Britain are covered with the purple flower spikes of *Calluna vulgaris*, Britain's native heather.

Although only one hardy evergreen species exists, hundreds of varieties displaying a wide range of colours in both flower and leaf have been developed for garden decoration. The spikes of closely set bell flowers may be purple, mauve, pink, red or white while the scale-like leaves are green, gold, silver-grey or bronze, though they sometimes change colour with the seasons.

Heathers look effective as ground cover for conifers, in a bed of their own or as individual dwarf shrubs. The flower spikes are excellent for cutting; they keep their colours well and are good dried for winter decoration.

Popular varieties
'Anne Marie' has flower spikes that open pale pink and gradually turn deep carmine-rose. It reaches 25cm (10in) high.
'County Wicklow' bears double shell-pink flowers; it grows 25cm (10in) high and spreads widely.
'Darkness' has dark green foliage and short dense spikes of

rich purple-red flowers. It reaches 30cm (1ft) high.
'Gold Haze' is white-flowered, with bright golden foliage; it grows to 60cm (2ft) high.
'Kinlochruel' has bright green foliage and dense spikes of double white flowers. It grows about 25cm (10in) high.
'H.E. Beale' has long sprays of double rose-pink flowers and reaches 60cm (2ft) high.
'My Dream' has double white flowers tinged pink with age. It is 60cm (2ft) high.
'Nana Compacta' is of compact habit, up to 20cm (8in) high, and

Calluna vulgaris 'My Dream'

Calluna vulgaris 'Kinlochruel'

Calluna vulgaris 'Nana Compacta'

Calluna vulgaris 'County Wicklow'

Calluna vulgaris 'Schurig's Sensation'

Calluna vulgaris 'Silver Knight'

bears a profusion of purple-pink flowers.

'Orange Queen' has golden young foliage that turns deep orange as it matures. Purple-pink flowers. It grows 45cm (1½ft) high.

'Robert Chapman' has purple flowers and gold foliage that deepens to bronze-red in winter. It reaches 45cm (1½ft) high.

'Schurig's Sensation' bears dark green leaves and long spikes of crimson-rose flowers. It grows up to 45cm (1½ft) high.

'Silver Knight' has woolly silver foliage and pink flowers and grows 30cm (1ft) high.

'Silver Queen' has woolly silver foliage and pale mauve flowers. It is 25cm (10in) high.

Cultivation

Plant in autumn or spring in an open sunny position. A peaty, acid soil provides perfect growing conditions, but heathers thrive in all but alkaline soils, including poor and sandy types.

In spring cut off dead flower stems close to the foliage. Prune tall varieties lightly with shears after flowering or before new growth starts, to prevent legginess.

Propagation Take cuttings from young side-shoots between mid summer and mid autumn.

Large plants can be increased by layering in early spring. The layers should have rooted after a year.

Pests and diseases Honey fungus may attack and heather dieback can be a problem, but they are generally trouble free.

Calluna vulgaris 'Robert Chapman', 'Gold Haze'

Calluna vulgaris 'Darkness'

Camellia
camellia

Camellia japonica 'Rubescens Major'

Camellia japonica 'Alba Simplex'

- ☐ Height 1.8-4.5m (6-15ft)
- ☐ Spread 1.2-1.8m (4-6ft)
- ☐ Flowers late winter to mid spring
- ☐ Fertile lime-free soil
- ☐ Lightly shaded site, and shelter

The beautiful camellias are prized as much for their rich green, usually shiny foliage as for their flowers, which range from white through all shades of pink to reds of varying intensity. The spectacular blooms, single, semi-double, double, rose-shaped, anemone or peony-shaped, are borne in late winter and early spring.

Camellias are hardy and ideal for woodland conditions as they thrive in dappled shade. They are also excellent grown against west- or north-facing walls and as free-standing tall specimen shrubs. Camellias, and especially those that flower in late winter, do well as pot and container plants.

Popular species and varieties
Camellia varieties have been developed from three species.
Camellia japonica and its varieties have a height and spread of 1.8-3.5m (6-12ft). They include:

'**Adolphe Audusson**', semi-double blood-red flowers with golden stamens; early.
'**Alba Simplex**', large white single flowers, yellow stamens; mid season.
'**Apple Blossom**' (syn. 'Joy Sander'), pale blush-pink, semi-double flowers; mid season.
'**Betty Sheffield Pink**', semi-double, deep pink flowers; mid season.
'**Brushfield's Yellow**', creamy white anemone-shaped flowers; compact; mid season.
'**C.M. Wilson**', pale pink, anemone-shaped flowers; early to mid season.
'**Elegans**', salmon-rose, anemone-shaped flowers occasionally marbled white; early.
'**Lady Clare**', deep peach-pink semi-double flowers; early.
'**Lady Vansittart**', semi-double pinkish-white flowers streaked rose-pink; mid to late.
'**Magnoliiflora**', blush-pink semi-double medium-sized flowers; mid season.
'**Mathotiana Rubra**', crimson rose-shaped double flowers; mid season.

'**Nagasaki**', semi-double blush-pink flowers marbled white; mid season.
'**Nobilissima**', cream-white, peony-shaped flowers; early.
'**Rubescens Major**', double, crimson flowers with darker veining; mid season.
'**Tricolor**', white semi-double flowers streaked with carmine pink; mid season.
Camellia reticulata has a more open habit than other camellias and is less hardy; it is best trained against a wall. It is renowned for its large flowers which may reach 15cm (6in) across. The shrubs have a height of 3-4.5m (10-15ft) and a spread of 2.4-3.5m (8-12ft). Popular varieties, which flower from late winter to mid spring, include:
'**Captain Rawes**', carmine-pink, semi-double flowers; early.
'**Inspiration**', semi-double, deep pink flowers; mid season.
'**Robert Fortune**', double rose-red flowers; early.
'**Shot Silk**', semi-double, with brilliant pink wavy petals; early.
Camellia x williamsii is an early flowering camellia. Its blooms – which are more profuse than those of *C. japonica*, one of its parents – drop as they fade. The shrubs grow 1.8-2.4m (6-8ft) high and have a spread of 1.2-1.8m (4-6ft). Flowering begins in winter and continues until mid spring.

Camellia reticulata 'Inspiration'

Camellia reticulata 'Shot Silk'

Camellia japonica 'Mathotiana Rubra'

'Anticipation', large deep rose-pink peony-shaped flowers.
'Brigadoon', semi-double, bright rose-pink flowers.
'Daintiness', large salmon-pink semi-double flowers.
'Debbie', clear-pink peony-shaped flowers.
'Donation', large semi-double, soft pink flowers.
'Francis Hanger', single white flowers.
'J.C. Williams', bright pink flowers.

Cultivation
Camellias grow in any good lime-free soil – enrich light soils with organic matter. A site in dappled shade is ideal, and they will also thrive against west-facing or north-facing walls. Avoid an east-facing site as morning sun after night frost damages developing buds; avoid exposed sites.

Plant in early to mid spring or early to late autumn. Staking may be necessary until the shrubs are established. In mid spring give a mulch of well-rotted manure, peat substitute or lime-free compost.

Dead-head all camellias except varieties of *C.* x *williamsii*.
Propagation Take cuttings of half-ripe lateral shoots in summer. Alternatively, layer large plants in early autumn, and separate 18 months later.
Pests and diseases Birds may damage the flowers and bud drop may occur on dry soils.

Camellia japonica 'Tricolor'

Camellia japonica 'C.M Wilson'

Camellia japonica 'Betty Sheffield Pink'

Camellia japonica 'Brushfield's Yellow'

Camellia japonica 'Apple Blossom'

Carpenteria

carpenteria

Carpenteria californica

□ Height 3m (10ft)
□ Spread 1.8-2.4m (6-8ft)
□ Flowers early to mid summer
□ Any fertile soil
□ Sunny sheltered site

Sometimes known as the tree anemone, *Carpenteria californica* is a moderately hardy, bushy shrub, with lance-shaped leaves that are rich glossy green, grey-green beneath. It is the flowers that make it an outstanding shrub; resembling anemones, the glistening white blooms appear from early to mid summer and have a sweet fragrance. 'Ladham's Variety' is even more free-flowering, with blooms about 7.5cm (3in) across.

Cultivation
Plant in mid to late spring. Carpenterias will thrive in any fertile and well-drained soil including those that are rich in lime. The site should be in full sun – preferably against a south or west wall where the plants will be protected from cold winds.

Shorten straggly shoots after flowering. Otherwise no pruning is required.

Propagation Seed propagation is the most suitable method; it is a slow process.

Pests and diseases Trouble free.

Ceanothus

Californian lilac, ceanothus

Ceanothus dentatus

□ Height 10cm-6m (4in-20ft)
□ Spread 1.8-3m (6-10ft)
□ Flowers late spring to mid autumn
□ Good well-drained soil
□ Sheltered sunny position

The blue-flowered, evergreen ceanothus are nearly all native to California. Many are of hybrid origin and generally hardier than the species; they thrive in seaside gardens, and do best inland and in cold areas when grown in the shelter of sunny walls.

Ceanothus, which range from tall shrubs to prostrate and creeping types, are prized for their dense clusters or nodding panicles of star-shaped flowers, all in shades of blue, which are borne in great abundance in late spring and early summer and/or in autumn. The evergreen foliage is ovate to lance-shaped and usually glossy green.

Popular species and hybrids
Ceanothus arboreus is a half-hardy tree-like species reaching 3-6m (10-20ft) high. The most commonly grown form is 'Trewithen Blue' which has panicles of deep blue flowers in late spring and early summer.
Ceanothus 'Autumnal Blue' is the hardiest of the evergreen ceanothus; it grows about 2m (7ft) high and wide, with bright glossy green foliage. In late summer and early autumn, and sometimes in spring as well, the shrub is laden with panicles of rich sky-blue flowers.
Ceanothus 'Burkwoodii' reaches 1.8-3m (6-10ft) high and 1.8-2.4m

Chamaecyparis
false cypress

Chamaecyparis lawsoniana 'Pembury Blue'

☐ Height 30cm-1.8m (1-6ft)
☐ Spread 30cm-1.8m (1-6ft)
☐ Coniferous shrub
☐ Ordinary well-drained soil
☐ Sun or light shade

Ceanothus thyrsiflorus

(6-8ft) across and is one of the hardier hybrids. It is also one of the few evergreens to flower from mid summer until autumn. The flowers are bright blue and the leaves glossy green.

Ceanothus 'Cascade' grows 3m (10ft) high, and its arching branches reach a similar spread. It blooms in late spring, with clusters of rich blue flowers, and needs to be grown near a wall for protection against harsh weather in all but the mildest gardens.

Ceanothus dentatus is near-hardy and grows 2.4m (8ft) high and wide. Its clusters of dark blue flowers appear in late spring and early summer.

Ceanothus gloriosus is a prostrate creeping shrub, forming an evergreen carpet, 3m (10ft) wide, of dark glossy green and toothed leaves studded in late spring with lavender-blue flower clusters.

Ceanothus thyrsiflorus is hardy, with pale blue flowers in late spring and early summer. It is a popular ceanothus for covering a wall as it reaches more than 3m (10ft) high. 'Repens', a shorter, more compact form, grows into a dome 90cm-1.2m (3-4ft) high.

Cultivation

Plant container-grown young shrubs in mid or late spring in fertile, well-drained soil. Although generally lime-tolerant, evergreen ceanothus do not thrive on shallow, chalky soils. In mild parts of the country, hardy species and hybrids can be grown in an open sunny position, but elsewhere they are best grown against south-facing or west-facing walls.

Evergreen ceanothus need no pruning, though if necessary, shoots can be shortened and dead wood pruned out after flowering.

Propagation Take heel cuttings of firm, non-flowering side-shoots in mid summer and insert in a propagating frame. Pot rooted cuttings in containers of potting compost and overwinter in a cold frame. Pot on in late spring, plunge outdoors, and transplant to the permanent sites the following spring.

Pests and diseases Chlorosis may occur on strongly alkaline soils.

This genus of hardy evergreen conifers contains several species and varieties that grow so slowly that they are usually treated as shrubs and are commonly known as dwarf cypresses. They are ideal for growing in rock gardens and among heathers, and miniatures can provide winter interest in window-boxes and sink gardens.

Chamaecyparis conifers can be distinguished from other conifers by their leaves – formed of small flat overlapping scales carried in pairs on either side of the shoots. The leaves are arranged in sprays flattened into one plane and come in an enormous range of colours – dark, light and mid green, golden-yellow and blue. After a few years' growth, small round cones appear.

C. lawsoniana 'Pygmaea Argentea'

Chamaecyparis obtusa 'Crippsii'

Chamaecyparis lawsoniana 'Green Pillar'

The shape of dwarf cypresses varies according to species – columnar, conical, prostrate and round being some of the forms available.

Popular species and hybrids
Most popular dwarf cypresses have been developed from one of three species.
Chamaecyparis lawsoniana, Lawson's cypress, has given rise to numerous varieties whose only common feature is the fan-like arrangement of their scaly leaves.
'Aurea Densa' has bright golden-yellow foliage and grows into a dense dome 30-45cm (1-1½ft) high.
'Chilworth Silver' is slow-growing and broadly columnar with silver-blue foliage. Maximum height is 1.8m (6ft).
'Ellwoodii' has grey-green foliage and slowly forms a dense pyramidal shape, eventually reaching 1.8m (6ft) tall. A gold-leaved form 'Ellwood's Gold' and a variegated form, 'Ellwoodii Variegata' ('Ellwood's White') are also available.
'Ellwood's Pillar' is a miniature, narrow form of 'Ellwoodii', reaching 60-75cm (2-2½ft) high. It has blue-grey foliage and is ideal

Chamaecyparis obtusa 'Nana Aurea'

for a rock garden.
'Fletcheri' is a popular variety, broadly column-shaped. It is extremely slow-growing but eventually reaches a height of 3.5m (12ft). Its grey-green foliage turns bronze in winter.
'Green Globe' is a bun-shaped miniature, 30cm (1ft) high and across, with short sprays of bright green foliage.
'Green Pillar' is of conical and upright shape, with bright green foliage that is gold-tinted in spring.

It is slow-growing, but eventually grows as tall as 'Fletcheri'.
'Little Spire' forms a tall, thin, green column up to 1.8m (6ft) high.
'Minima Aurea' has golden soft foliage and forms a rounded pyramid 90cm (3ft) high and across. A blue-green variety, 'Minima Glauca' is also available.
'Pembury Blue' is of conical shape with silver-blue foliage. It reaches 45-60cm (1½-2ft) high.
'Pygmaea Argentea' has blue-green foliage tipped white and forms a rounded shrub with a height of 30-45cm (1-1½ft).
Chamaecyparis obtusa, the Hinoki cypress, has horizontal branches and flattened sprays of foliage. The leaves are arranged in unequal pairs and have blunt tips.
'Crippsii' is a bright golden form with an open graceful habit, slowly forming a loose conical shrub. Eventual height is 4.5m (15ft).
'Fernspray Gold' is of open bushy habit, with golden foliage in fern-like sprays. It can reach tree-like proportions, but pruning can restrain it to 1.5m (5ft).
'Nana Aurea' has golden-green foliage and forms a flat-topped miniature 60-75cm (2-2½ft) high.
'Nana Gracilis' is a conical shrub with shiny dark green foliage. It eventually grows 2.4m (8ft) high.
'Spiralis' forms an upright, dark green spire with twisted branchlets; it grows 75cm (2½ft) high.

Chamaecyparis pisifera 'Filifera Nana'

Chamaecyparis lawsoniana 'Fletcheri'

Chamaecyparis lawsoniana 'Minima Aurea'

Choisya
Mexican orange blossom

Choisya ternata 'Sundance', foliage

☐ Height 1.5-1.8m (5-6ft)
☐ Spread 1.8-2.4m (6-8ft)
☐ Flowers mid to late spring
☐ Any well-drained soil
☐ Sheltered site in full sun or partial
  shade

For a shrub from Mexico, *Choisya ternata* is surprisingly hardy. Though appreciating protection from north-east winds in late winter, and not always surviving in extreme northern gardens unless given wall protection, it is of easy cultivation. The Mexican orange blossom is particularly suitable for small gardens, being of compact and neat growth and taking many years to reach its ultimate height of 1.8m (6ft). The glossy evergreen leaves are three-lobed and highly aromatic when crushed.

Grow Mexican orange blossom in a mixed border, close to a path or beneath a window so that its sweet scent can be easily appreciated. In mild coastal gardens, it is suitable for informal hedging and needs only light trimming.

The blossom resembles orange blossom and is similarly sweetly scented. The white flowers are borne in clusters along the branches, even on young plants, and appear in late spring and early summer; often there is a second, smaller display in autumn, following warm summers.

'Sundance' is a popular, recent variety, notable for its bright golden-yellow foliage, especially on young unfolding leaves. It is slow-growing and rarely exceeds 90cm (3ft) in height and spread.

Chamaecyparis lawsoniana 'Chilworth Silver'

Chamaecyparis lawsoniana 'Green Globe'

Chamaecyparis pisifera has spreading horizontal branches and sharply pointed leaves.
'Boulevard' forms a broad pyramidal shrub with silver-blue foliage, best in light shade. It can be pruned to 1.2m (4ft) high.
'Filifera Nana' has mid green leaves and grows into a dense flat-topped dome 60cm (2ft) high.
'Nana' is bun-shaped and flat-topped, 30cm (1ft) high with dark green foliage.
'Plumosa Aurea' grows into an irregularly shaped shrub 1.5m (5ft) high. Its young growth is bright yellow, which deepens with age to yellow-green.
'Plumosa Aurea Compacta' forms a dense conical shrub 60cm (2ft) high, with bright yellow leaves fading to green-yellow.
'Squarrosa Sulphurea' has spreading branches on a broadly conical shrub 90cm (3ft) high. The foliage is sulphur-yellow and particularly intense in spring.
'Sungold' has golden-yellow foliage on a rounded, flat-topped shrub up to 60cm (2ft) high.

Cultivation
Dwarf cypresses grow in any well-drained soil in an open position or in light shade. The golden varieties are best grown in full sun as this preserves their colouring. Avoid siting cypresses where they will be exposed to drying winds.

Caption for middle photo: *Chamaecyparis pisifera* 'Boulevard'

Plant in mid autumn on light soils or in mid spring on heavy soils. An application of nitrates in mid spring helps to improve their leaf colour.

Pruning is not necessary except where a leading shoot forks. Remove the weaker shoot in spring. Dwarf cypresses can also be pruned to restrict growth and spread at any time during the growing season.
Pests and diseases Honey fungus may kill dwarf cypresses.

CHECKERBERRY – see *Gaultheria*
CHERRY LAUREL – see *Prunus*
CHINESE SACRED BAMBOO – see *Nandina*

Choisya ternata

Cistus

sun rose, rock rose

Cistus ladanifer

☐ Height 45cm-2.4m (1½-8ft)
☐ Spread 60cm-2.7m (2-9ft)
☐ Flowers late spring to mid summer
☐ Any well-drained soil
☐ Open sunny position

Cultivation

Plant container-grown young specimens in mid to late spring in any type of soil provided that it is well drained. Choisyas do best in sites which are sheltered from cold winds, and in northern gardens they should preferably be grown against south- or west-facing walls. Choisyas revel in full sun though they will tolerate light shade.

'Sundance' is suitable for growing in a container on a sunny patio; in winter protect the roots against frost by covering with a straw mulch, or move the container into a cold greenhouse.

Choisyas do not require much pruning, but any frost-damaged shoots should be cut back to the base in early spring so that new shoots can develop. When the main flowering display has finished, cut out any wayward shoots in order to maintain the bushy shape.

Propagation Take 7.5cm (3in) long cuttings of half-ripened side-shoots in late summer. Root the cuttings in a propagator unit with a temperature of 16-18°C (61-64°F); pot the rooted cuttings singly in 7.5cm (3in) pots of a proprietary potting compost and overwinter them in a cold frame.

In late spring, move them on to larger pots and plunge in a sheltered outdoor nursery bed. Leave them to grow on until the following late spring, then plant out in permanent sites.

Pests and diseases Few pests trouble these shrubs. Frost may damage and kill entire shoots, but they usually sprout again from the base. Honey fungus has been known to kill the shrubs.

CHRISTMAS BOX – see *Sarcococca*

To smell the aromatic leaves of *Cistus*, even in winter, is to be transported from an English garden to a sun-baked hillside in the Mediterranean. These so-called sun or rock roses are only moderately hardy, although they do well in mild coastal gardens when given conditions as near as possible to their native lands. All cistus species and the numerous hybrids have exquisite, usually white, flowers resembling single roses, with petals like crumpled silk that surround a prominent boss of colourful stamens. The individual blooms last only a single day, but they are produced in such abundance that the flowering display extends from late spring to mid summer.

Popular species and hybrids
Cistus x aguilari reaches 1.2-1.5m (4-5ft) high and across. It has pure white flowers which, in the variety 'Maculatus', are blotched with crimson. The green lance-shaped leaves have wavy margins.
Cistus x corbariensis is a low, spreading hybrid, which reaches 90cm-1.2m (3-4ft) high and 1.8-2.7m (6-9ft) across. Its reddish buds open into white flowers blotched with yellow. The leaves are dull green and oval.
Cistus crispus is low-growing (60cm/2ft high and across), grey-leaved and with purple-pink flowers. The variety 'Sunset' has cerise-pink flowers.

Cistus x cyprius

Cistus crispus 'Sunset'

Cistus x *cyprius*, one of the taller hybrids reaching 2.4m (8ft) high and across, has sticky olive-green leaves and clusters of white flowers blotched crimson-maroon.

Cistus ladanifer (gum cistus) grows 1.8m (6ft) or more high, spreading to 1.2m (4ft). Its erect stems are clothed with narrowly lance-shaped, dull green leathery leaves that exude a fragrant gum. The large white flowers, up to 10cm (4in) across, have bright yellow stamens and crimson blotches at the base of the petals. The species is the parent of numerous hybrids.

Cistus laurifolius is 2m (7ft) high and 1.8m (6ft) across and has leathery, dark green leaves and white flowers with yellow centres. It is the hardiest of the sun roses.

Cistus x *lusitanicus*, syn. *C.* x *dansereaui*, is a dwarf sun rose, rarely growing more than 45cm (1½ft) high or 60cm (2ft) across. It bears narrow, dark green, wavy-edged leaves and white flowers prominently marked with crimson blotches. The variety 'Decumbens' is similar but spreads to 1.2m (4ft).

Cistus populifolius reaches 1.8m (6ft) high and has a spread of 1.2-1.5m (4-5ft). The oval leaves are light green and the white flowers have a yellow stain at the base of each petal. It is one of the hardier species.

Cistus x *purpureus* grows into a vigorous, upright shrub 1.2-1.5m (4-5ft) high and across. It has

lance-shaped, grey-green leaves and carmine-pink flowers with maroon blotches.

Cistus 'Silver Pink' is a hardy hybrid with a height and spread of 60-90cm (2-3ft). The clear pink flowers have golden stamens, and the lance-shaped leaves are dark green above and grey beneath.

Cistus x *skanbergii* is a naturally occurring hybrid. It grows 90cm-1.2m (3-4ft) high and as much across, with narrow grey-green leaves. Clear pink flowers are borne in clusters during early and mid summer.

Cultivation

Cistus do not transplant well and should be purchased as young container-grown shrubs. Plant in mid or late spring in any, even poor, well-drained soil in an open sunny site sheltered from east and north winds. Avoid pruning as the shrubs often die back after the shoots have been cut.

Propagation Take 7.5-10cm (3-4in) long heel cuttings of half-ripened, non-flowering shoots in mid to late summer. Root in a propagating unit and overwinter in a cold frame.

Pests and diseases Frost damage may cause die-back.

Cistus x *purpureus*

Clematis

clematis

Clematis armandii 'Apple Blossom'

Clematis cirrhosa

☐ Height 3-7.5m (10-25ft)
☐ Flowers mid spring to mid summer, and winter
☐ Well-drained alkaline soil
☐ Sunny and sheltered site

Most of the climbing clematis species and large-flowered hybrids are deciduous and popular for their displays of stunning blooms in spring and summer. In winter they can look rather dreary, with their long bare stems seemingly lifeless. However, several species are evergreen and remain attractive in leaf throughout the year.

Evergreen clematis species are slightly less hardy than deciduous types, but given a sunny and sheltered wall or fence they usually survive all but the most severe of winters.

Popular species

Clematis armandii is a vigorous species that climbs up to 7.5m (25ft) or more on a sunny wall and can spread to 15m (50ft), clinging by exceptionally strong tendrils. The three-lobed leaves are dark green with prominent veins. The large saucer-shaped flowers, with pointed petals, are creamy-white and appear in mid spring; they are followed by silky seed heads. The variety 'Apple Blossom' is tinged with pink, and 'Snowdrift' is pure white.

Clematis cirrhosa grows 3-4.5m (10-15ft) high and bears ovate to heart-shaped or three-lobed leaves. The creamy-white, bell-shaped flowers, up to 6cm (2½in) across, open in winter and are succeeded by fluffy seed heads.

Clematis hookeriana is up to 3m (10ft) high, with attractive fern-like, glossy green foliage. The yellow-green, star-shaped flowers are strongly fragrant and silky in texture; they are freely borne in late spring and early summer.

Clematis uncinata is the least hardy of the evergreen species. On a warm and sheltered wall it will reach a height of 4.5m (15ft), with large deeply lobed leaves that are greyish-green on the undersides. In early and mid summer the foliage is almost hidden by large sprays of pure white, fragrant flowers.

Cultivation

Plant container-grown specimens in spring when all danger of hard frost has passed, in well-drained, slightly alkaline soil. The ideal site is a warm and sheltered position in sun, with shade over the root area. Keep the plants well watered during dry spells and tie the stems to the trellis supports until growth is well developed.

Pruning is generally unnecessary. Frost may damage some stems, but new ones will usually grow again from the base. Cut back frosted shoots in late spring; overlong stems that have outgrown their allotted space can be pruned back by up to two-thirds at the same time, or after flowering.

Propagation Take stem cuttings of young, non-flowering shoots in summer and root in a propagator unit. Alternatively, layer young, long shoots in late spring and sever them after one year, when they should have rooted.

Pests and diseases Aphids, snails and slugs can be troublesome. Clematis wilt is the most common disease though rarely fatal.

CONNEMARA HEATH – see *Daboecia*

Convolvulus

convolvulus

Convolvulus cneorum

□ Height 60-90cm (2-3ft)
□ Spread 60-90cm (2-3ft)
□ Flowers late spring to early autumn
□ Ordinary well-drained soil
□ Sunny site

The large genus of *Convolvulus* includes many herbaceous annuals and perennials, some of which are weeds. One species, *Convolvulus cneorum,* is a neat evergreen shrub which, though only moderately hardy, will thrive in a sunny sheltered position in well-drained soil – a rock garden or drystone wall would be ideal.

It grows as a bushy shrub 60-90cm (2-3ft) high and across, and its narrow lance-shaped leaves, covered in hairs, give it a silvery appearance. Clusters of pink buds open into funnel-shaped white flowers between late spring and early autumn.

Cultivation
Plant in mid to late spring in any well-drained soil in a sunny sheltered position. Pruning is not necessary – but growth can be cut back to shape in late spring.

Propagation Take 3-7.5cm (1½-3in) long heel cuttings of basal shoots or lateral growths between early and mid summer. Root in a cold frame, pot the rooted cuttings singly in pots of compost and overwinter in a frost-free cold frame. Plant out in late spring.

Pests and diseases Trouble free.

Cordyline

cabbage palm

Cordyline australis

□ Height 60-90cm (2-3ft)
□ Spread 60-90cm (2-3ft)
□ Foliage shrub
□ Well-drained soil
□ Sun or light shade

Most palms are too tender to be grown outdoors in Britain, but one species, *Cordyline australis* from New Zealand and Australia, succeeds in mild southern gardens where frosts are rare. It is often grown as a pot plant that can be moved under cover during winter.

As a pot plant, the cabbage palm reaches about 90cm (3ft) in height. It is slow-growing, with an erect stem from which sprout clusters of long, strap-shaped, grey-green leaves. The variety 'Purpurea' has purple-flushed leaves. In favoured sites, mature shrubs may bear sprays of scented, creamy-white flowers in early summer.

Cultivation
In the open, plant cabbage palms in late spring in any good well-drained soil, in full sun or light shade. They are tolerant of strong winds and thrive in mild coastal gardens. Elsewhere, grow the shrubs in 15-20cm (6-8in) pots of a proprietary potting compost; move them outdoors when all danger of frost has passed and bring them under frost-free cover in autumn. Pruning is unnecessary.

Propagation Detach suckers in spring, pot them up and grow on.

Pests and diseases Leaf spot disease may disfigure the leaves.

CORNISH HEATH – see *Erica*

Corokia

wire-netting bush

Corokia cotoneaster

- ☐ Height 1.5m (5ft)
- ☐ Spread 1.2m (4ft)
- ☐ Flowers late spring to early summer
- ☐ Fertile well-drained soil
- ☐ Sheltered sunny site

Corokia cotoneaster is the one species from this genus of New Zealand shrubs which can be grown in this country. Being only moderately hardy, it usually succeeds in coastal gardens and warm sheltered spots in mild areas.

The wire-netting bush grows into a dense shrub 1.5m (5ft) high and 1.2m (4ft) across. The rigid wiry branches twist and twine, a feature responsible for its common name.

In late spring to early summer small star-shaped yellow flowers appear. The sparse, dark green, spoon-shaped leaves are felted white underneath.

Cultivation

Plant in fertile well-drained soil in a sunny and sheltered site in late spring. It is best to avoid pruning as this spoils the attractive growth habit. However, if thinning is essential, prune after flowering in mid summer.

Propagation Take 7.5cm (3in) long heel cuttings of semi-ripe lateral shoots in late summer. Root in a cold frame, pot on as necessary and plant out one or two years later in spring.

Pests and diseases Trouble free.

Coronilla

coronilla

Coronilla glauca

- ☐ Height 1.8m (6ft)
- ☐ Spread 1.5m (5ft)
- ☐ Flowers early to mid spring
- ☐ Any well-drained soil
- ☐ Sunny sheltered position

Easy to grow, but only moderately hardy, the evergreen *Coronilla glauca* (syn. *C. valentina glauca*) is prized for its elegant, deeply divided foliage of small grey-green leaves. In a warm and sheltered site, it bears a profusion of bright yellow pea-like flowers in mid spring, though the shrub may bloom intermittently throughout the year. The variety 'Citrina' has lemon-yellow flowers, and 'Variegata' has leaves heavily variegated with cream; it is slightly smaller than the species.

Cultivation

Plant in mid spring in any well-drained garden soil, including alkaline types, in a warm sheltered position – ideally against a south-facing wall.

Prune out frost-damaged shoots in spring and shorten any long shoots if necessary.

Propagation Take semi-ripe cuttings in late summer and root in a cold frame. Pot on as necessary and grow on under glass for at least one year before planting out in mid spring.

Pests and diseases Trouble free.

Cotoneaster

cotoneaster

Cotoneaster frigidus 'Rothschildianus'

- ☐ Height 5cm-4.5m (2in-15ft)
- ☐ Spread 30cm-4.5m (1-15ft)
- ☐ Flowers late spring to mid summer
- ☐ Ordinary garden soil
- ☐ Sunny position

The hardy evergreen cotoneasters are among our most accommodating garden shrubs. They are easy to grow in any type of soil, need the minimum of attention and are particularly valued in winter when the glossy leaved branches are studded with bright berries.

In growth habit, cotoneasters range from creeping prostrate species suitable for ground cover to tall dense shrubs ideal for hedging and screening.

Popular species

Cotoneaster congestus is a dwarf species which forms a dense mound of tightly packed branches 5-15cm (2-6in) high and 30-90cm (1-3ft) across. It has tiny bright green leaves and small pink flowers which appear in early summer. The autumn berries are red. The shrub is ideal for a rock garden.

Cotoneaster conspicuus forms a dense mass of arching stems 1.8-2m (6-7ft) high and 1.5-1.8m (5-6ft) across. The white early-summer flowers conceal the small glossy dark green leaves, and are followed in autumn by bright red berries. 'Decorus' is a low-growing, free-fruiting variety, 60-90cm (2-3ft) high and across and suitable for covering sunny banks.

Cotoneaster dammeri is another ground-hugging shrub, 5-7.5cm

Cotoneaster dammeri

(2-3in) high, but with a spread of 1.5-2m (5-7ft). It bears small, glossy dark green leaves, white flowers and red berries. It is perfect for carpeting banks and bare ground under trees.

Cotoneaster franchetii has a graceful arching habit. Reaching 1.8-2.4m (6-8ft) high and 1.5-1.8m (5-6ft) across, it bears oval greygreen leaves, pink and white blooms in early summer and orange-red berries. A good hedging shrub.

Cotoneaster frigidus itself is sometimes semi-evergreen or even deciduous, but several varieties remain evergreen. Most of these reach 3.5-4.5m (12-15ft) high and across. 'Cornubia' is semi-evergreen with a profusion of large red berries; 'Hybridus Pendulus' has long branches with abundant

Cotoneaster horizontalis

bright red berries; it is of prostrate habit but is often grafted and trained as a small weeping tree; 'John Waterer' is vigorous, with large clusters of red berries. The varieties 'Exburiensis', 'Fructo-luteo' and 'Rothschildianus' all bear large clusters of creamyellow fruits.

Cotoneaster horizontalis, deciduous or semi-evergreen, is conspicuous with its branches arranged in an attractive herringbone fashion. It grows 60cm (2ft) high and

1.8-2m (6-7ft) across; against a wall it easily reaches a height of 2.4m (8ft). Pink flowers appear in early summer and are followed by red berries. 'Variegatus', a slow-growing form, has small creamwhite variegated leaves tinged pink in autumn.

Cotoneaster lacteus is an excellent hedging shrub. Reaching 3-4.5m (10-15ft) high and 2.4-3.5m (8-12ft) across, it has large leathery, deep green leaves which are grey and hairy below. The cream-white flowers appear in summer and are followed by dense clusters of red berries. These ripen late and last well into winter.

Cotoneaster microphyllus, a 15cm (6in) high species spreading 1.8-2.4m (6-8ft) across, has glossy dark green leaves that are grey and hairy beneath. White flowers appear in late spring and early summer, and in autumn scarlet berries crowd the branches. Suitable as ground cover and for covering banks and walls.

Cotoneaster salicifolius grows to a height and spread of 3.5-4.5m (12-15ft). It bears glossy green narrow willow-like leaves. In early summer, white flowers are carried in downy clusters, and red berries appear in autumn. Popular varieties include 'Autumn Fire'

Cotoneaster lacteus

Cotoneaster salicifolius 'Gnom'

(orange-red berries), and 'Gnom' (a low mound-forming variety).

Cultivation

Plant at any time between autumn and late winter in any well-drained soil, ideally in a sunny situation. For hedging, space the shrubs 60-90cm (2-3ft) apart and cut them back by a quarter to encourage bushy growth.

Pruning is not essential, though vigorous forms can be pruned hard back in spring. Trim hedges to shape after flowering.

Propagation Layer long shoots in autumn – the layers should root within a year. Alternatively, take 7.5-10cm (3-4in) long heel cuttings of ripe shoots in late summer.

Pests and diseases Aphids may make the plants sticky and sooty. Honey fungus, fireblight and silver leaf can occur.

COTTON LAVENDER – see *Santolina*

Cotoneaster conspicuus

Crinodendron
lantern tree

Crinodendron hookerianum

Cryptomeria
Japanese cedar

Cryptomeria 'Sekkan Sugi'

☐ Height 45cm-1.8m (1½-6ft)
☐ Spread 30cm-1.5m (1-5ft)
☐ Coniferous shrub
☐ Moist but well-drained acid soil
☐ Sunny sheltered position

The Japanese cedar, *Cryptomeria japonica*, is a handsome conifer (see page 30). It is too tall and fast-growing for the average garden, but numerous dwarf forms have been developed from it. These are ideally suited for specimen planting in small gardens as they rarely exceed 1.8m (6ft) in height, and some are compact enough to warrant a place in the rock garden.

These hardy shrubby conifers are easy to grow and valued for their attractive foliage which often takes on rich colours in autumn and winter.

Popular varieties
'Compressa' grows slowly to a height and spread of 90cm (3ft). It forms a flat-topped compact globe of dense foliage which turns reddish-purple in winter. It is suitable for a rock garden.
'Elegans Compacta' has soft, blue-green, plume-like foliage and forms a shrub 2m (7ft) high and 1.5m (5ft) across. In winter the leaves are bronze-red.
'Elegans Nana' grows into a compact shrub 90cm (3ft) high and 1.5m (5ft) across. Its blue-green leaves turn bronze in winter.
'Globosa Nana', syn. 'Lobbii Nana', is a compact domed shrub

☐ Height 3-4.5m (10-15ft)
☐ Spread 1.8-3m (6-10ft)
☐ Flowers late spring and early summer
☐ Rich, moist, lime-free soil
☐ Partially shaded and sheltered site

In early autumn the lantern tree (*Crinodendron hookerianum*, syn. *Tricuspidaria lanceolata*) puts out a mass of small long-stalked buds. The following year, in late spring and early summer, the buds swell until they resemble crimson lanterns. Like masses of unopened fuchsia buds, the flowers droop from the branches on long slender stalks in festoons.

This semi-hardy shrub was introduced to Britain from Chile in 1848 by the plant collector William Lobb. Since then it has become one of the most valued plants for mild, sheltered gardens in the south-west of England and Ireland. It is not sufficiently hardy to be grown outdoors in cold northern gardens.

The 3-4.5m (10-15ft) high and dense shrub bears narrow leaves that are dark green and slightly toothed, with a leathery texture.

Cultivation
Plant in mid to late spring in rich, moist, lime-free soil. The site should be partially shaded and, ideally, sheltered by a west-facing wall.

Regular pruning is not necessary; remove any dead or frost-damaged stems in late spring.
Propagation Take 7.5-10cm (3-4in) long heel cuttings of half-ripe shoots in mid to late summer and root in a propagating unit at a temperature of 16°C (61°F). Pot the rooted cuttings in containers of a proprietary potting compost and overwinter in a frost-free frame or greenhouse. Pot on into 10-12cm (4-5in) pots and plunge in a well-ventilated cold frame. Leave the young plants in the cold frame for another winter before planting out.
Pests and diseases Honey fungus can kill the shrubs.

Cryptomeria 'Globosa Nana'

Cupressus

dwarf cypress

Cupressus macrocarpa 'Golden Cone'

☐ Height 60cm-2.4m (2-8ft)
☐ Spread 60cm-3m (2-10ft)
☐ Coniferous shrub
☐ Ordinary well-drained soil
☐ Sunny position

This well-known group of hardy conifers includes such favourites as the Monterey and Italian cypress (see page 31) as well as several dwarf varieties.

Popular varieties

Cupressus glabra 'Compacta', a dwarf form of the Arizona cypress, forms a rounded conical shrub 60cm (2ft) high and across with grey-green foliage.
Cupressus macrocarpa 'Gold Spread' has a low spreading habit 90cm (3ft) high and 3m (10ft) across, and golden foliage. 'Golden Cone', with a conical habit, can be kept clipped to 2.4m (8ft).
Cupressus sempervirens 'Swane's Golden' grows into a narrow golden column 1.8m (6ft) high.

to 90cm (3ft) high and 1.5m (5ft) across. Its rich green leaves, borne on arching branchlets, are blue-green in winter. A good specimen conifer.

'Sekkan Sugi' has an upright tree-like habit and reaches 1.5-1.8m (5-6ft) high. In winter the foliage is a cream colour tinged with bronze.

'Spiralis' is also known as granny's ringlets because of the bright green foliage which is twisted spirally around the branches. It is of dense and spreading habit and grows slowly to a height of about 90cm (3ft).

'Vilmoriniana' forms a compact globular shrub just 45cm (1½ft) high and 60cm (2ft) across. In winter the foliage turns a dull bronze colour. Popular dwarf conifer for a rock garden.

Cultivation

Plant in mid to late autumn on light soils and in spring on heavy soils. These conifers do best in moist but well-drained and slightly acid soil. Choose a sunny and sheltered site.

Do not allow young plants to dry out, and keep them clear of weeds. In late spring, apply a dressing of general fertilizer over the root run. Pruning is unneces-

sary, but cut out any forking at the main stem in mid spring.
Propagation Take 5-10cm (2-4in) long cuttings in early autumn and root in a cold frame. When rooted, pot the cuttings individually and plunge them outdoors. Set them out in a nursery bed in autumn and grow on for a couple of years before moving to permanent sites.
Pests and diseases Trouble free.

CURRY PLANT – see
Helichrysum
CYPRESS, FAKE – see
Chamaecyparis

Cultivation

Plant in any well-drained soil in autumn or early spring in a sunny position. Pruning is unnecessary though competing leading shoots should be reduced to one.
Propagation Take heel cuttings in early autumn and root in a cold frame.
Pests and diseases Honey fungus can kill the shrubs.

Daboecia

St. Dabeoc's or Connemara heath

Daboecia cantabrica 'Bicolor'

- ☐ Height 45cm (1½ft)
- ☐ Spread 45cm (1½ft)
- ☐ Flowers early summer to early winter
- ☐ Rich acid, moisture-retentive soil
- ☐ Full sun or light shade

This dwarf hardy shrub is one of the loveliest of Britain's wild flowers. A heath-like shrub 45cm (1½ft) high, it carries long one-sided spikes of bright rose-purple urn-shaped flowers from late spring until early winter.

Daboecia cantabrica is ideal for rock gardens and for ground cover; it makes suitable under-planting for rhododendrons, provided these do not cast too much shade.

Popular varieties
'Alba' has attractive white flowers.
'Atropurpurea' has deep purple flowers.
'Bicolor' bears a mixture of white, pink, purple and bicoloured flowers.
'Porter's Variety', only 15cm (6in) high and of compact habit, has crimson-purple flowers.

Cultivation
Plant in spring or autumn in full sun or partial shade. The soil should be acid, rich and moisture-retentive. Set the plants 45cm (1½ft) apart.

Dead-head in spring and lightly shear in late autumn to prevent legginess.
Propagation Layer large plants in early spring. Allow a year for the layers to root.
Pests and diseases Trouble free.

DAISY BUSH – see *Olearia*

Daphne

daphne

Daphne laureola

Daphne x burkwoodii 'Somerset'

- ☐ Height 15cm-1.8m (6in-6ft)
- ☐ Spread 60cm-1.8m (2-6ft)
- ☐ Flowers any time of year
- ☐ Good well-drained soil
- ☐ Sunny or partially shaded site

The evergreen daphnes, like their deciduous relatives, are mainly grown for their richly scented flowers which appear in winter or spring, summer or autumn, depending on species. They are generally hardy and easy to grow.

Daphnes grow into small or medium-sized shrubs, making them suitable for rock gardens or the front of borders.

Popular species
Daphne bholua is a winter-flowering shrub, its purplish blooms appearing in profusion in the depth of winter. Though the species is evergreen, 'Gurkha' – the variety usually grown – is deciduous and has white flowers flushed purple. It is an upright open shrub with a height of 1.8m (6ft) and a spread of 1.5m (5ft).

Daphne blagayana is a mat-forming species with a height of just 15cm (6in) but a spread of 1.8m (6ft). It has mid green leaves, and cream-white flowers which appear in mid and late spring. It grows best in light shade.
Daphne x burkwoodii grows into a neat, well-branched bushy shrub, about 90cm-1.2m (3-4ft) high and across. A semi-evergreen, it bears

Daphne cneorum

clusters of soft pink flowers in late spring and early summer. 'Somerset', a popular variety, has pale mauve-pink flowers.

Daphne cneorum, garland flower, is a deservedly popular species although it is sometimes difficult to establish. It only grows 15cm (6in) high, with a spread of 60-90cm (2-3ft). It has deep green leaves and highly scented, rose-pink flowers which are borne in dense clusters in late spring and early summer. Varieties include 'Alba' (white flowers); 'Eximia' (crimson buds opening to rose-pink flowers); and 'Ruby Glow' (deep pink).

Daphne collina, syn. *D. sericea*, grows 75-90cm (2½-3ft) high and wide. It is of compact habit, the shoots clothed with ovate, glossy dark green leaves and terminating in late spring and early summer with clusters of scented, rose-purple flowers. It is ideal for a rock garden.

Daphne x hybrida is 90cm (3ft) or more high and bears lance-shaped, dark green glossy leaves. It flowers from late autumn through winter with exceptionally fragrant red-purple blooms. One

of its parents is *D. odora*, but it is hardier than that species.

Daphne laureola, spurge laurel, is native to Britain. It makes a useful evergreen ground-cover plant (60cm-1.2m/2-4ft high and 90cm-1.5m/3-5ft across) and bears tiny green-yellow flowers between late winter and early spring.

Daphne odora grows into a bushy shrub 1.5-1.8m (5-6ft) high and across. It bears lance-shaped, glossy green leaves and pale purple flowers between mid winter and mid spring. As this species is only moderately hardy, it should be grown under the protection of a wall. 'Aureo-marginata' has leaves with yellow edging and is slightly hardier.

Daphne retusa is a 90cm (3ft) high shrub with a spread of 45-60cm (1½-2ft). Its rose-purple flowers appear in late spring to early summer and are followed by bright red berries. The dark green, thick leaves are shiny.

Daphne tangutica, from China, flowers in early and mid spring, and usually again in late summer. It grows 90cm (3ft) high and spreads to 60cm (2ft). The foliage is glossy green, and the sweetly

scented flowers are white, tinged rose-purple on the outside.

Cultivation

Plant in early autumn or in mid spring in good well-drained garden soil. The site can be in sun or partial shade. Set out container-grown plants as daphnes dislike root disturbance.

Regular pruning is not necessary but straggly growth can be removed in early spring.

Propagation Take 5-10cm (2-4in) long heel cuttings of lateral non-flowering shoots from mid summer to early autumn. Root them in a cold frame. The following spring pot up the rooted cuttings singly and plunge them in an outdoor nursery bed. Transplant to the permanent positions one or two years later.

Pests and diseases Aphids may infest young growth and leaf spot can occur, showing as small brown spots, particularly on leaves at the base. The foliage eventually shrivels and falls off.

Desfontainia

desfontainia

Desfontainia spinosa

☐ Height 3m (10ft)
☐ Spread 3m (10ft)
☐ Flowers in summer
☐ Fertile acid soil
☐ Light shade and shelter

The one species in this genus, *Desfontainia spinosa*, is a magnificent shrub from South America which will succeed outdoors in Britain in all but the coldest regions. It is valued for its late-summer flowers – long slender trumpets, waxy in texture and scarlet and yellow in colour – that droop singly or in pairs from the leaf axils.

Desfontainia is a slow-growing, compact shrub, eventually reaching up to 3m (10ft) in height and spread. Its erect branches are clothed with small, holly-like leaves which are dark green and shiny. The variety 'Harold Comber' bears 5cm (2in) long trumpet flowers in varying shades of red.

Cultivation

Plant in early autumn or in mid spring. Desfontainias are lime-haters and require a cool acid soil, rich in organic matter and well drained. They thrive, like rhododendrons, in woodland conditions with dappled shade and shelter from winds. They also make excellent wall shrubs, ideally in west-facing positions.

Desfontainia spinosa

Pruning is rarely necessary; frost-damaged shoots should be cut back to healthy wood in mid spring.

Propagation Take 10cm (4in) long heel cuttings in late summer from non-flowering side-shoots and root in a propagator unit at a temperature of 16-18°C (61-64°F). Pot up the rooted cuttings and overwinter in a frost-free greenhouse. Pot on as necessary during spring or summer and grow on for another year before moving the young plants to their permanent sites, in mid spring.

Pests and diseases Trouble free.

Drimys

winter's-bark

Drimys winteri

☐ Height 1.8-7.5m (6-25ft)
☐ Spread 1.8-4.5m (6-15ft)
☐ Flowers in spring
☐ Fertile, moist soil
☐ Sunny and sheltered site

In favoured situations, winter's-barks will grow into handsome specimen shrubs or even small trees. They originate from South America and Australia and are therefore not recommended for cold and exposed gardens. They generally survive most winters if given a site in a warm, sheltered border or positioned against a sunny wall.

Popular species

Drimys lanceolata, syn. *D. aromatica*, is a slow-growing shrub, 1.8-2.4m (6-8ft) high and wide. It is of upright, slender habit and highly aromatic, with purple-red shoots. The leathery leaves are oval to lance-shaped, glossy dark green above, pale green on the undersides; they are copper-tinted when young. Numerous clusters of small white flowers are produced in mid and late spring; they are followed by small fruits on female plants.

Drimys winteri grows much taller, to 7.5m (25ft) in height and 4.5m (15ft) across, as a conical shrub or a small tree. It has aromatic bark and large leathery, oval leaves, soft green above and bluish-grey beneath. It flowers when quite young, bearing loose clusters of attractive, fragrant, creamy-white flowers in late spring.

Elaeagnus
elaeagnus

Drimys lanceolata

Cultivation
Plant in mid autumn, in good loamy soil that is always moisture-retentive. The shrubs need a warm and sheltered site, protected from cold winds and away from frost pockets; they thrive in woodland conditions. Shallow chalky soils are not suitable. Pruning is rarely necessary, but any frost-damaged shoots should be cut out in spring.

Propagation Take 15-20cm (6-8in) hardwood cuttings in autumn and root in a cold frame. In late spring, transfer the rooted cuttings to a sheltered nursery bed outdoors and grow them on for a couple of years before moving to permanent sites. Long shoots can also be layered in spring; they should have rooted by the following year.

Pests and diseases Generally trouble free.

Elaeagnus pungens 'Maculata'

- [ ] Height 2.4-4.5m (8-15ft)
- [ ] Spread 1.8-4.5m (6-15ft)
- [ ] Foliage shrub
- [ ] Ordinary, even poor, well-drained soil
- [ ] Full sun or partial shade

The evergreen elaeagnus are ultra-hardy shrubs grown chiefly for their handsome foliage and for their ability to tolerate shade, wind and salty sea sprays. They make fine accent plants in shrub borders and are particularly useful for hedging and screening in exposed sites.

Most bloom in autumn, and although the flowers are small, they are sweetly scented and freely produced when little else is in bloom.

Popular species
Elaeagnus x ebbingei is a fast-growing shrub with leathery silver-grey leaves. Silvery flowers appear in mid to late autumn followed by small red or orange fruits. It grows 3-4.5m (10-15ft) high and across. 'Gilt Edge' has gold-margined leaves; and 'Limelight' has green leaves with broad deep yellow markings.

Elaeagnus macrophylla has broad leathery leaves which are silver-green when young but become mid green with age. Silver flowers appear on the 1.8-3m (6-10ft) high shrub in mid and late autumn followed by red berries.

Elaeagnus glabra resembles *E. x ebbingei* but is less vigorous, growing 3-3.5m (10-12ft) high and wide. The leathery, elliptic to ovate leaves are silvery-grey – a handsome background for the clusters of silvery, fragrant flowers that are borne in late autumn. They are followed in spring by orange-red, egg-shaped berries.

Elaeagnus pungens is a vigorous, spreading shrub with leathery leaves glossy green above and dull white below. The silver flowers, which appear in mid to late autumn, are sometimes followed by small red or orange fruits. With a height and spread of 2.4-3m (8-10ft), this species is excellent for hedging. Popular varieties include 'Dicksonii' (slow-growing and erect, gold-edged leaves); 'Frederici' (slow-growing, narrow creamy-yellow leaves edged bright green); 'Goldrim' (glossy deep green leaves margined bright yellow); 'Maculata' (leaves splashed with gold in the centre); and 'Variegata' (vigorous, cream-edged leaves).

Elaeagnus x ebbingei 'Gilt Edge'

Embothrium
fire bush

Embothrium coccineum

☐ Height 4.5-6m (15-20ft)
☐ Spread 2-3m (7-10ft)
☐ Flowers late spring to early summer
☐ Lime-free, moisture-retentive soil
☐ Sunny site against a west-facing or south-facing wall

Erica
heath, heather

Erica vagans 'Lyonesse'

☐ Height 23cm-6m (9in-20ft)
☐ Spread 23cm-2.4m (9in-8ft)
☐ Flowers throughout the year
☐ Moist, but well-drained acid soil
☐ Sunny open site

Cultivation
Plant in mid spring or early autumn in any, even poor and shallow, chalky or sandy soils. Evergreen elaeagnus do equally well in sun and partial shade.

For hedges, space young plants 45cm (1½ft) apart, for screens 60-90cm (2-3ft) apart. After planting, cut all shoots back by at least one-third to promote bushy growth from low down.

Regular pruning is not necessary, though long straggling shoots can be shortened in mid to late spring. Variegated varieties of *E. pungens* often revert to green-leaved shoots; these should be removed immediately, cutting right back to their base.

Propagation Take 10cm (4in) long heel cuttings in late summer or early autumn and root in a cold frame. Pot the rooted cuttings singly in spring, and plunge them in an outdoor nursery bed until autumn when the young plants can be moved to their permanent positions.

Pests and diseases Leaf spot can cause brown blotches on the leaves.

The fire bush (*Embothrium coccineum*) from Chile and Argentina can be grown outdoors only in the mild, south-western regions of Britain – and even there it requires a sunny, sheltered site.

Under favoured conditions, the fire bush grows into a magnificent shrub, with stiff upright stems to a height of 4.5-6m (15-20ft) and a spread of up to 3m (10ft) from numerous suckers. The shiny, oval mid green leaves provide year-round interest, and in late spring and early summer the shrub bears numerous clusters of brilliant scarlet flowers.

'Lanceolatum' has long lance-shaped leaves and is hardier than the species; it is usually semi-evergreen.

Cultivation
Plant in mid to late spring in good lime-free and moist soil in a sunny site, ideally near a west-facing or south-facing wall. Until the plants are well established, protect them with straw or bracken in winter.

Pruning is not required, though straggly growth can be shortened after flowering.

Propagation Increase by detaching suckers from the base and growing on in pots.

Pests and diseases Trouble free.

Ericas are chiefly grown for their flowers – at any time of year at least one species or variety is producing spikes of white, pink, purple or bicoloured bell-shaped blooms at the end of the stems. They are excellent for cutting and drying for winter decoration.

The neat, needle-like foliage is composed of dense green whorls, though some varieties have handsome leaves in shades of orange, red or yellow.

The hardy ericas, which are closely related to true heathers (*Calluna*), range in height from 23cm (9in) to 6m (20ft). Low-growing types make excellent ground cover while the taller ones can be treated as specimen plants or grown as hedges. All associate particularly well with conifers.

Popular species and varieties
Erica arborea, tree heath, generally reaches 3.5m (12ft) high and 1.8-2.4m (6-8ft) across, though in mild conditions it may grow to a height of 6m (20ft). It has mid green leaves and ash-white slightly fragrant flowers which appear in early to mid spring. The species itself is slightly tender, but 'Alpina', with bright green foliage, is fully hardy.
Erica australis is a tree heath from southern Europe, hardy in Britain in all but the coldest areas. It grows up to 1.2m (4ft) across and 1.8m (6ft) high, though

Erica arborea 'Alpina'

Erica carnea 'Aurea' in winter

trained against a wall or other support it can reach a height of double that. It flowers from mid spring to early summer, with dense spikes of rich rose-pink flowers. The variety 'Mr Robert' is pure white; and 'Riverslea' is pink. *Erica carnea* (syn. *E. herbacea*), a dwarf compact species flowering from early winter to late spring, is parent to a large number of garden varieties. With a height of 30cm (1ft) and a spread of 60cm (2ft), it makes excellent ground cover. The species and its varieties tolerate alkaline soils. The following popular varieties all have mid green leaves unless otherwise stated: 'Aurea' (deep pink flowers fading to white, golden foliage in spring and early summer); 'December Red' (purple-red); 'Foxhollow' (pale pink flowers, golden foliage in summer); 'Heathwood' (rose-purple flowers and dark green or bronze leaves); 'King George' (carmine-pink);

'Myretoun Ruby' (ruby-red flowers, dark green leaves); 'Pink Spangles' (abundant pink flowers); 'Ruby Glow' (ruby-red flowers in spring, bronze foliage); 'Springwood Pink' (rose-pink); 'Springwood White' (pure white, dense flowers, dark green leaves); and 'Vivellii' (red flowers and bronze leaves in winter, dark green leaves in summer).
Erica ciliaris (Dorset heath) is native to Britain and ultra-hardy. It forms a low, pale green shrub, 30-38cm (12-15in) high, spreading to 60cm (2ft). The flower spikes, in shades of pink, rose and purple as well as white, appear in mid summer and continue until winter. Popular varieties include 'Corfe Castle' (salmon-pink flowers, bronze winter foliage); 'David McClintock' (pink, white-tipped flowers, grey-green leaves); 'Mrs C.H. Gill' (clear red flowers, dark green foliage); and 'Stoborough' (pure white).

Erica cinerea, bell heather, grows wild in Britain. It has a height and spread of 23-30cm (9-12in) and is an excellent ground-cover plant. The flowers, which appear between early summer and mid autumn, are white or striking shades of deep pink, red, maroon or mahogany. When they fade in autumn they resemble russet-brown bells. The following popular varieties all have mid green foliage unless otherwise stated: 'Alba Minor' (white flowers and light green leaves); 'Atrorubens' (ruby-red); 'Atrosanguinea Smith's Variety' (bright scarlet flowers and dark green leaves); 'C.D. Eason' (rose-red); 'Cindy' (bright pink flowers and bronze-green foliage); 'Eden Valley' (bicoloured lavender and white flowers); 'Golden Drop' (pale purple flowers and coppery yellow leaves which turn bronze-red in winter); 'Pink Ice' (pink flowers and bright dark green foliage); and 'Velvet Knight' (dark purple flowers and dark green leaves).
Erica x darleyensis is a hybrid between *E. carnea* and *E. mediterranea*. It grows 60cm (2ft) high with a spread of 90cm (3ft) or more, and grows well on limy soils. The leaves are usually mid green, and the white, pink or purple flowers appear between early winter and late spring – though they are at their finest in early and mid spring. Popular varieties include 'Arthur Johnston' (rose-coloured flowers); 'Darley Dale' (abundant pale pink flowers);

Erica carnea 'Aurea' in spring

'Jack H. Brummage' (deep pink flowers and greenish-yellow leaves tinged red in winter); and 'White Perfection' (pure white flowers, bright green foliage).

Erica mediterranea, syn. *E. erigena,* is a tall species capable of reaching 3m (10ft) or more high and 1.2m (4ft) across. Not suitable for the colder, eastern parts of Britain, it is lime-tolerant though not recommended for shallow chalky soils. Popular varieties include 'Brightness' (low-growing, rose-purple flowers and bronze-green leaves); 'Irish Dusk' (clear pink flowers and dark green foliage); 'Rubra' (compact ruby-red flowers, dark green leaves); and 'W.T. Rackliff' (cream-white flowers and dark green leaves).

Erica terminalis, syn. *E. stricta,* grows wild in northern Ireland. Reaching 2.4m (8ft) high and 1.2m (4ft) across, it makes a good hedging shrub and grows on alkaline soils. The pink or purple flowers appear in abundance in early summer and continue until winter. The leaves mature from bright to dark green.

Erica tetralix, cross-leaved heath, grows in boggy places in the wild, though in gardens it will thrive in any lime-free soil. With a height and spread of 23-30cm (9-12in), it has grey, often hairy leaves. Soft pink flowers are produced in summer. Popular varieties include 'Alba Mollis' (white flowers and silver-grey foliage); 'Con Underwood' (crimson flowers and grey-green foliage); and 'Hookstone

Erica vagans

Erica cinerea 'Atrorubens'

Erica vagans 'Lyonesse'

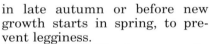

Erica x darleyensis 'Darley Dale'

Pink' (clear rose-pink flowers and light silver-grey foliage).

Erica vagans, Cornish heath, is a vigorous species native to Britain, with a height of 1.2m (4ft) and a spread of 2.4m (8ft). Its pale pink or purple flowers are borne between mid summer and winter, and are set off by mid green leaves. Varieties include: 'Cream' (cream-white flowers); 'Lyonesse' (white flowers); 'Mrs D.F. Maxwell' (cerise-pink flowers); 'St. Keverne' (clear salmon-pink); and 'Valerie Proudley' (white flowers and bright yellow foliage).

Cultivation

Plant in an open sunny position in mid to late spring or mid to late autumn. Most species and varieties are lime-haters and require acid, well-drained soil. However, *E. carnea*, *E. x darleyensis*, *E. mediterranea*, *E. terminalis* and *E. tetralix* tolerate alkaline soils.

Winter and spring-flowering ericas rarely need pruning, but faded flower spikes should be trimmed off with scissors. The spikes of summer and autumn-flowering types remain ornamental as they fade, and dead-heading can be delayed until spring.

With age, summer and autumn-flowering ericas can become straggly and produce inferior flowers. Cut old woody stems hard back in spring. Tree heaths should be pruned lightly

in late autumn or before new growth starts in spring, to prevent legginess.

Propagation All ericas are easily increased. Layer low-growing types in spring or autumn; they usually root within a year when they can be severed from the parent plants and set out. Alternatively, take 2.5-5cm (1-2in) cuttings of non-flowering side-shoots in late summer or early autumn and root in a cold frame.

Pests and diseases Honey fungus and heather die-back – a grey discoloration of the foliage which is caused by a fungus – may affect the plants. Chlorosis may occur on strongly alkaline soils.

Erica mediterranea 'W.T. Rackliff'

Eriobotrya

loquat

Eriobotrya japonica

Eriobotrya japonica

□ Height 3-5.5m (10-18ft)
□ Spread 4.5m (15ft)
□ Flowers in autumn
□ Any moisture-retentive soil
□ Sunny or lightly shaded, sheltered site

The loquat tree (*Eriobotrya japonica*) thrives in Mediterranean regions where it is cultivated for its tart, edible fruits. In Britain it succeeds only in mild sheltered gardens, preferably against a sunny wall, and is usually grown as a multi-stemmed shrub about 3m (10ft) in height.

The fragrant white flowers, which resemble hawthorn clusters, appear from autumn onwards, but in Britain hot summers are necessary for flower production, and the globular fruits are rarely seen in the open.

Most loquats are grown for the architectural beauty of their foliage. The firm, leathery leaves are 30cm (12in) or more long, and have corrugated surfaces and sawtooth edges. They are oblong, glossy dark green above, and coated with a fuzzy brown wool on the undersides.

Cultivation

Plant in early autumn or mid spring in ordinary moisture-retentive but well-drained soil. The site can be in full sun or light shade and should be sheltered from cold winds; mild maritime positions are ideal. Loquats are best grown as wall shrubs and can be trained flat in espalier fashion. Little pruning is necessary, unless the shrubs are grown as espaliers, but frost-damaged shoots should be cut back to healthy wood in early spring.

Propagation Take 10-15cm (4-6in) long heel cuttings of semi-ripe young shoots in late summer and root in a propagator unit. When rooted, pot up the cuttings singly and overwinter in a frost-free greenhouse. Plunge the pots outdoors in a sheltered, lightly shaded spot in late spring, and grow the young plants on, with winter protection, until they are large and strong enough to be planted out.

Pest and diseases Loquats are sometimes affected by fireblight disease which shows as a browning of leaves and shoots.

Eriobotrya japonica, fruits

Escallonia

escallonia

Escallonia 'C.F. Ball'

☐ Height 1.5-2.4m (5-8ft)
☐ Spread 1.5-1.8m (5-6ft)
☐ Flowers late spring to mid autumn
☐ Any well-drained soil
☐ Sunny position

Escallonias are slightly tender shrubs, although they grow well in southern and western areas, particularly by the sea, where they are much used for informal hedging. Elsewhere, they need a sunny site beside a south-facing wall. They bear clusters of small tubular flowers between late spring and mid autumn, set among small lance-shaped, mid to deep green glossy leaves.

Most garden escallonias have been raised from the hardier species and have largely superseded the South American species.

Popular varieties

'Apple Blossom' is a slow-growing compact shrub 1.5m (5ft) high and across, with cup-shaped pink and white flowers.

'C.F. Ball' has large tubular crimson flowers. Its dark green leaves are aromatic when crushed. This is a vigorous variety reaching 2.4m (8ft) high and 1.8m (6ft) across.

Escallonia 'Apple Blossom'

Eucryphia
eucryphia

Escallonia 'Donard Gem'

Eucryphia x nymansensis

'Donard Brilliance' is a bushy shrub 1.8m (6ft) high and across. Its arching branches carry bright rose-red flowers intermittently between early summer and early autumn.

'Donard Gem' is a bushy shrub 1.8m (6ft) high and across, with pale pink, sweetly scented flowers and toothed leaves.

'Donard Seedling' forms a graceful shrub with its 1.8m (6ft) long cascading branches. It has white-budded, flesh-pink flowers in early to mid summer, and makes a good hedging plant.

'Peach Blossom' grows into an upright bushy shrub 1.8-2.4m (6-8ft) high and 1.5-1.8m (5-6ft) across. The flowers are peach-pink.

'Slieve Donard' is a compact shrub clothed with apple-blossom-pink flowers. A particularly hardy variety, with a height of 1.8m (6ft) and a spread of 1.5m (5ft), it makes an excellent hedging plant.

Cultivation
Plant in mid autumn or in early to mid spring in any ordinary well-drained soil. In mild gardens, the site should be sunny and open; in colder gardens, grow escallonias as wall shrubs. Trim flowering shoots when the blooms have faded; large straggly shoots can be pruned hard back to shape at the same time.

Propagation Take 7.5-10cm (3-4in) long heel cuttings of half-ripe non-flowering shoots in late summer and early autumn and root in a cold frame.

Pests and diseases Silver leaf can cause die-back.

☐ Height 4.5m (15ft)
☐ Spread 2m (7ft)
☐ Flowers late summer to early autumn
☐ Well-drained neutral or acid soil
☐ Sheltered sunny or lightly shaded position

There comes a time in late summer when a fresh effect is needed in the garden. *Eucryphia x nymansensis*, whose glossy dark foliage sets off to perfection its cream-coloured blooms, is admirably suited. Borne from late summer to early autumn, these delicately fragrant flowers are cup-shaped, with a satiny sheen.

The shrub is hardy throughout the south and west except in the severest winters. It is vigorous, with an upright habit, and quickly reaches 4.5m (15ft) high and 2m (7ft) across.

Cultivation
Plant in autumn or spring, in well-drained, neutral to acid soil with a cool root run (this can be provided by shading the roots with a low-growing shrub). Eucryphias need a sunny or partially shaded site, ideally in the shelter of light woodland or a west-facing wall.

During the winter protect young plants from frost by covering the

Eucryphia x nymansensis

roots with straw or bracken. No pruning is required, though the growing tips of young plants should be pinched out to encourage branching. Remove any frost-damaged shoots in late spring.

Propagation Take 7.5-10cm (3-4in) long heel cuttings of lateral non-flowering shoots in late summer to early autumn. Root in a propagating case at a temperature of 16-18°C (61-64°F).

Pot the rooted cuttings singly in pots of a proprietary compost, and overwinter in a frost-free greenhouse or cold frame. Pot on and plunge outdoors in late spring; overwinter in a cold frame and plant out in permanent positions the following spring.

Pests and diseases Trouble free.

Euonymus
euonymus

Euonymus fortunei 'Silver Queen'

Euonymus fortunei 'Emerald 'n' Gold'

☐ Height 15cm-4.5m (6in-15ft)
☐ Spread 30cm-2.4m (1-8ft)
☐ Foliage shrubs
☐ Any kind of soil
☐ Sun or partial shade

The evergreen euonymus are invaluable in garden planning for year-round interest. They are generally hardy and flourish in all kinds of conditions. Some provide close ground cover, in shades of glossy green or gold and silver variegations, while upright and climbing types are useful for hedging and wall covering.

Chiefly grown for their handsome foliage of small oval and leathery leaves, evergreen euonymus do bloom – in summer – but the clusters of small pale green to white flowers are less conspicuous than the pink or orange fruits in autumn.

Popular species and varieties
Euonymus fortunei is a variable species, creeping and prostrate in the young stages and shrubby or climbing in the adult form, rather like ivy (*Hedera*). At ground level the long stems sprawl to 1.8m (6ft), rooting where they touch the soil; as a self-clinging climber on a wall the species easily reaches a height of 3m (10ft). Only adult forms produce flowers, in early

summer, followed by orange seeds enclosed in pink capsules.

Numerous varieties have been bred from *E. fortunei*; they include the following: 'Carrierei' (large-leaved glossy shrub up to 2.5m/9ft against a wall and bearing flowers and fruit); 'Coloratus' (glossy green leaves tinged red-purple in winter; trails or climbs to 8m/26ft against a wall); 'Emerald Charm' (upright shrub to 3m/10ft with glossy green leaves and yellowish seed capsules); 'Emerald Cushion' (prostrate, mound-forming shrub with rich green leaves); 'Emerald Gaity' (bushy shrub 60cm/2ft high and 90cm/3ft across with deep green leaves edged with white which turns pinkish in winter); 'Emerald 'n' Gold' (dense dwarf shrub, 45cm/1½ft high and 60cm/2ft wide, with glossy green leaves

Euonymus fortunei 'Emerald 'n' Gold'

margined broadly with yellow, turning pink in winter; given support, the shrub will climb).

'Gold Tip' ('Golden Prince', upright shrub 45cm/1½ft high with dark green leaves tipped golden yellow); 'Kewensis' (prostrate shrub 15cm/6in high with miniature green leaves, suitable for a rock garden); 'Sarcoxie' (upright shrub to 1.8m/6ft high, with glossy dark green leaves and large white fruit tinted pink); and 'Silver Queen' (small compact shrub, as adult reaching 3m/10ft against a wall; young leaves creamy-yellow becoming green with broad creamy-white margins).

Euonymus japonicus is a densely branched shrub reaching 3-4.5m (10-15ft) in height, with a spread of 1.5m (5ft). It bears narrowly ovate, shallow-toothed leaves that are leathery and glossy dark green. Small clusters of green-white flowers are borne in late spring and occasionally followed by pink and orange fruits. Although the species is not reliably hardy in cold eastern areas, it thrives in coastal gardens in the south and west and is much used for hedging.

Numerous forms have been raised from *E. japonicus* and include: 'Albomarginatus' (pale green young leaves ageing to blue-green with narrow white edges); 'Aureus' (syn. 'Aureopictus', green leaves with broad yellow centres, often reverts); 'Duc d'Anjou' (pale green leaves with dark green central blotches);

Fabiana
fabiana

Euonymus japonicus 'Aureus'

Fabiana imbricata

☐ Height 2m (7ft)
☐ Spread 2m (7ft)
☐ Flowers in early summer
☐ Neutral or acid soil
☐ Sunny sheltered site

'Latifolius Albomarginatus' (syn. 'Macrophyllus Albus', outstanding variegated form with broad white edges to the leaves); 'Microphyllus Variegatus' (small and slow-growing, of dense habit, with small narrow leaves margined with white; similar to box in appearance); 'Ovatus Aureus' (syn. 'Aureovariegatus', compact and slow-growing, with leaves edged and suffused with creamy-yellow; it needs a site in full sun to retain its bright leaf colours); and 'Robustus' (stiff and upright, compact growth, thick and rounded leaves).

Euonymus kiautschovicus, syn. *E. patens*, is a wide-spreading shrub, 2.4m (8ft) high and wide, with bright green pointed leaves. It bears comparatively large, yellow-green flower clusters in early autumn, followed by pink seeds in orange capsules in early winter.

Cultivation
Plant euonymus in early to mid autumn or in mid spring. They thrive in any kind of soil, moist or dry, and do particularly well on chalk; the site can be in full sun or partial shade. Varieties of *E. japonicus*, and especially variegated forms, require sheltered sites against walls or beneath trees in most gardens.

For hedging, use young plants about 30cm (12in) high and space them 38-45cm (15-18in) apart. After planting and during the first year of growth, pinch out the tips of leading shoots to encourage branching.

Specimen shrubs need little regular pruning, though they can be trimmed to shape with shears at any time. Prune established hedges in mid spring and, if necessary, again in late summer.

Propagation Take 7.5-10cm (3-4in) heel cuttings in late summer or early autumn and root in a cold frame. The following late spring, set out the cuttings in an outdoor bed and grow on for a couple of years before planting out.

Pests and diseases Scale insects and caterpillars may infest stems and leaves. Powdery mildew is common on *E. japonicus* and shows as a white coating. Honey fungus causes rapid death of the shrubs.

EVERLASTINGS – see *Helichrysum*

Fabiana imbricata, the species grown in Britain, is easily confused with the tree heaths. It is, however, a member of the potato family.

The shrub is only moderately hardy and requires a warm sheltered spot – seaside gardens are ideal. It is well worth growing for its dense plumes of white flowers in early summer. The variety *F. i. violacea* has lavender-blue flowers, and 'Prostrata', hardier and smaller than the species, bears mauve-tinted flowers. The green leaves are small and needle-like.

Cultivation
Plant in good, moist but well-drained soil in a sheltered sunny site. The shrub thrives in acid to neutral soil although it is tolerant of lime.

Pruning is not necessary, but the shrub can be trimmed to shape in mid summer.

Propagation Take semi-ripe cuttings in summer and root in a propagating case.

Pests and diseases Trouble free.

FALSE CASTOR OIL PLANT – see *Fatsia*
FALSE CYPRESS – see *Chamaecyparis*

x *Fatshedera*

fatshedera

x *Fatshedera lizei*

☐ Height 1.2-2.4m (4-8ft)
☐ Spread 90cm-1.2m (3-4ft)
☐ Foliage shrub
☐ Any well-drained soil
☐ Sunny or partially shaded site

x *Fatshedera lizei* is a hybrid between *Fatsia* and *Hedera* (ivy). A hardy sprawling shrub, it can be used for ground cover, allowed to trail over low walls, or it can be trained up vertical surfaces as a climber – it has no way of clinging to the support and needs tying in.

Fatshedera is grown for its handsome foliage – shiny, deep green leathery leaves which are palmate with five deep lobes. Pale green flowers (borne in mid to late autumn, indoors) rarely open outside. The form 'Variegata', has cream-white markings on the leaves.

Cultivation

Plant in early to mid autumn or early to mid spring in ordinary well-drained soil in a sunny or partially shaded site.

Though regular pruning is not necessary, lateral growths can be shortened in early to mid spring. If growing fatshedera as ground cover, peg upright shoots down into the soil when they are 45cm (1½ft) high.

Propagation Take 10-12cm (4-5in) long cuttings of tip or side-shoots in mid to late summer. Root the cuttings in a cold frame.

Pests and diseases Trouble free.

Fatsia

false castor oil plant

Fatsia japonica

☐ Height 2.4-4.5m (8-15ft)
☐ Spread 2.4-4.5m (8-15ft)
☐ Foliage shrub
☐ Good moist soil
☐ Sheltered sunny or shaded site

Despite its exotic appearance, this Japanese relation of ivy (*Hedera*) is hardy in southern gardens; it is frequently grown as an indoor pot plant. *Fatsia japonica* is an erect shrub, with strong stems that rarely branch, supporting glossy hand-shaped leaves often more than 30cm (1ft) across. The leaves are mid green above and paler green on the undersides. In autumn each stem bears a multiple head of creamy-white, ivy-like flower clusters, sometimes followed by black berries.

Fatsia is a dramatic plant. To show it off to best effect set it against a wall to provide a backdrop of greenery throughout the year. It thrives in town gardens, being tolerant of pollution and shade.

Cultivation

Plant in early to mid autumn or in mid spring in any kind of moist but well-drained soil. Choose a sheltered position in sun or shade. In cold areas plant the shrub against a south-facing or west-facing wall.

Pruning is not essential, but hard cutting back in mid spring of straggly shoots will force lush new growth.

Fatsia japonica, flowers

Propagation Detach suckering shoots in early to mid spring. Pot singly in potting compost and root in a cold frame. Pot on as necessary and plant out in the permanent positions in mid spring the following year.

Pests and diseases Frost damage may distort the leaves, making small holes in them.

FIRE BUSH – see *Embothrium*
FIRETHORN – see *Pyracantha*
FLANNEL BUSH – see
Fremontodendron

Fremontodendron

flannel bush

Fremontodendron californicum
'California Glory'

Fremontodendron californicum

☐ Height 4.5-7.5m (15-25ft)
☐ Spread 2.4-4.5m (8-15ft)
☐ Flowers summer and autumn
☐ Good well-drained soil
☐ Sunny and sheltered site

Native to California, fremontodendrons are magnificent tall shrubs for south-facing walls. When established, they are in almost continuous bloom from late spring until well into autumn, the tall stiff stems smothered with large cup-shaped flowers of glistening bright yellow.

Fremontodendrons in the open garden are reliably hardy only in mild, frost-free regions in the south; they will survive most winters elsewhere if grown against sheltered walls in full sun and are rarely killed completely.

Popular species

Fremontodendron californicum is the most commonly grown species. It is a vigorous grower, eventually up to 7.5m (25ft), with a spread of 4.5m (15ft). The slender stems are set with dark green, three-lobed leaves that are covered with a pale brown felt on the undersides. From late spring on, and throughout summer and early autumn, the shrub bears a profusion of yellow flowers that open out flat to 5cm (2in) across. 'California Glory' is hardier than the species and flowers even more profusely, with blooms up to 6cm (2½in) wide.

Fremontodendron mexicanum resembles *F. californicum*, but has five-lobed glossy foliage and narrower flowers that open out to stars. They are lemon-yellow flushed with red on the outside.

Cultivation

Plant in early autumn or in mid spring, in any fertile, well-drained soil; fremontodendrons are drought-resistant and thrive on chalky soils. They require full sun and shelter from cold winds; they are best trained against trellis or sunny walls.

Pruning is rarely necessary, but any straggly shoots and frost-damaged stems should be cut back to healthy buds in early spring.

Propagation Take heel cuttings, 7.5-10cm (3-4in) long in late summer and root in a propagator unit at a temperature of 16°C (61°F). Pot up the rooted cuttings singly and overwinter in a frost-free greenhouse. In late spring, plunge the pots outdoors in a sunny and sheltered spot for the summer. Move them under frost-free cover for the winter and plant out in the permanent sites the following spring or early autumn.

Pests and diseases Trouble free.

GARLAND FLOWER – see *Daphne*

Garrya

silk tassel bush

Garrya elliptica

□ Height 2.4-4.5m (8-15ft)
□ Spread 1.8-3.5m (6-12ft)
□ Flowers mid winter to early spring
□ Well-drained garden soil
□ Sunny or partially shaded site

Few plants have such splendid catkins as the male *Garrya elliptica*. Great festoons of silvery lime-green, up to 23cm (9in) long, sway in the breeze from mid winter to early spring. Female shrubs have smaller, less attractive silver-grey catkins, but they are followed by round clusters of silky purple-green berries. For such fruits to be produced, both male and female shrubs must be grown to ensure cross pollination.

Garryas can become massive – up to 4.5m (15ft) high and almost as much across. Thinned regularly, however, they are suitable for small gardens. The leaves are thick, oval and leathery and have a grey-green appearance. They are prone to frost damage in cold and exposed sites.

Cultivation

Plant container-grown garryas in mid spring in any well-drained soil. A sunny or lightly shaded site is suitable, though they produce better catkins in sun. In exposed sites, plant the shrubs against a west-facing or south-facing wall. During the winter, protect young plants with a straw covering.

Pruning is not necessary, but straggly and crowded shoots can be shortened and thinned out after flowering. Garryas dislike root disturbance, and established shrubs should not be moved.

Propagation Take 7.5-10cm (3-4in) long heel cuttings of semi-ripe side-shoots in late summer to early autumn. Root in a cold frame and pot up the rooted cuttings singly the following spring. Plunge the pots outdoors and transplant to permanent positions the following spring. Alternatively, layer long shoots in early autumn.

Pests and diseases Trouble free.

x Gaulnettya

gaulnettya

x Gaulnettya wisleyensis

□ Height 90cm (3ft)
□ Spread 90cm (3ft)
□ Flowers late spring to early summer
□ Well-drained lime-free soil
□ Sunny or partially shaded site

By crossing *Gaultheria shallon* with *Pernettya mucronata,* plant breeders have produced another shrub to join the small collection of acid-loving plants.

Reaching just 90cm (3ft) high and 90 cm (3ft) across, this hardy bushy shrub spreads by means of suckers. It is a useful plant for winter interest – as well as being evergreen, it is laden with clusters of dark wine-red fruits through the coldest months of the year.

Gaulnettyas have ovate, dark green, leathery leaves and sprays of small, white or pink flowers which appear between late spring and early summer.

Popular varieties

Two favourite varieties have been developed from x *Gaulnettya wisleyensis*.
'Pink Pixie', dwarf and suckering, has white flowers tinged with pink, and purple-red berries.
'Ruby', a vigorous, thicket-forming shrub, flowers profusely in late spring and early summer with white blooms, followed by ruby-red fruits.

Cultivation

Plant in early to mid autumn, or mid to late spring, in well-drained acid soil in sun or partial shade. Thin out old wood in early spring.
Propagation Detach and replant rooted suckers in early autumn.
Pests and diseases Trouble free.

Gaultheria
gaultheria

Gaultheria procumbens

☐ Height 7.5cm-1.8m (3in-6ft)
☐ Spread 90cm-1.8m (3-6ft)
☐ Flowers late spring and summer
☐ Moist acid soil
☐ Partially shaded site

Gaultherias are hardy shrubs characterized by their habit of spreading through underground stems. They are suitable for large-scale ground cover on lime-free soils and are particularly handsome in spring and early summer with their sprays of small urn-shaped flowers, followed by large clusters of fleshy berries.

Popular species
Gaultheria procumbens, commonly called checkerberry, wintergreen or partridge berry, is a prostrate shrub only 7.5-15cm (3-6in) high, but spreading to 90cm (3ft) or more. It has tufts of shiny, dark green leaves, oval and toothed. The small, white or pink flowers appear in mid to late summer and are followed by round bright red berries.
Gaultheria shallon is a taller species, reaching 1.2-1.8m (4-6ft) high, and the same across. It spreads by means of suckers to form a dense thicket of upright stems bearing mid to dark green, oval, leathery leaves. Sprays of pale pink or white flowers appear

in late spring to early summer. They are followed by round purple-black berries.

Cultivation
Plant in early autumn or mid to late spring, in moist acid soil enriched with lime-free organic matter. Gaultherias grow best in partial shade; they are excellent as ground cover but will not tolerate drips from overhead trees.
 Cut *G. shallon* hard back in mid to late spring to control growth.
Propagation Take heel cuttings of lateral shoots in mid to late summer. *G. shallon* can also be increased by detaching and replanting rooted suckers in autumn.
Pests and diseases Trouble free.

Gaultheria shallon

Griselinia
griselinia

Griselinia littoralis 'Variegata'

☐ Height 3-7.5m (10-25ft)
☐ Spread 1.8-4.5m (6-15ft)
☐ Foliage shrub
☐ Any ordinary soil
☐ Sunny or shaded site

This handsome, slightly tender shrub is grown for its foliage – oval, leathery, shiny yellow-green leaves. The green flowers, which appear in mid to late spring, are insignificant.
 Griselinia littoralis can be grown successfully only in mild parts of the country or in particularly sheltered spots. It makes an excellent screening or hedging shrub for seaside gardens as it tolerates salt spray and gales.
 Griselinia littoralis 'Variegata' has white-variegated leaves.

Cultivation
Plant in autumn or mid spring in any soil in a sunny or shaded site. For hedging, space plants 45cm (1½ft) apart and remove the growing tips of the shoots after planting to encourage bushy growth from low down. In winter protect young plants from frost.
 Regular pruning is not necessary, but loose, straggly growth can be shortened in mid spring or late summer. Trim hedges annually in summer.
Propagation Take 7.5-10cm (3-4in) heel cuttings of side-shoots in late summer to early autumn and root in a cold frame.
Pests and diseases Trouble free.

GERMANDER – see *Teucrium*

Halimium

halimium

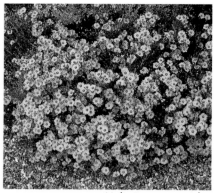

Halimium ocymoides

Halimium lasianthum

☐ Height 45-90cm (1½-3ft)
☐ Spread 60-120cm (2-4ft)
☐ Flowers late spring and early summer
☐ Any well-drained soil
☐ Full sun

Halimiums are related to the Mediterranean sun roses (*Cistus* and *Helianthemum* species), and as such grow especially well in mild seaside gardens. They are half-hardy and near-hardy compact shrubs, valued for their profusion of yellow flowers – these resemble single roses, and most have prominent blotches at the base of each of the five petals.

Popular species

Halimium commutatum is a half-hardy dwarf shrub, 60-90cm (2-3ft) high and wide. It has thin stems clothed with narrow leaves that are green on the upper surfaces and white beneath. Small clusters of 2.5cm (1in) wide, golden-yellow flowers are freely borne in early summer.

Halimium lasianthum (syn. *Cistus formosus* and *Helianthemum lasianthum*) is generally hardy in southern and western gardens. It grows 45-90cm (1½-3ft) high and up to 1.2m (4ft) wide, with thick, oblong, grey-green leaves. In late spring and early summer the foliage is almost

hidden by attractive golden-yellow flowers marked with purple-brown blotches. The variety 'Concolor' is pure yellow without blotches; on 'Sandling' the prominent markings are maroon coloured.

Halimium ocymoides (syn. *Helianthemum algarvense*) is the hardiest species. It grows 60-90cm (2-3ft) high, with a spread of 1.2m (4ft), and is of branching habit, bearing narrow oblong, grey-green leaves. The bright yellow flowers with chocolate-brown blotches are borne in clusters in early summer. The variety 'Susan' has broader leaves and is more compact and rounded in growth habit.

Halimium umbellatum grows about 60cm (2ft) high and across. It is a half-hardy species and resembles *H. commutatum* in growth habit, but bears white flowers in early summer.

Cultivation

Plant in early autumn or mid spring in any kind of soil, including poor ones, with sharp drainage. The shrubs require a site in full sun. Most species are not reliably hardy and should not be attempted in northern, cold and exposed gardens. Pruning is rarely necessary, but frost-dam-

aged tips should be cut back to healthy wood in spring.

Propagation Take 5-7.5cm (2-3in) long heel cuttings of lateral, non-flowering shoots in mid or late summer. Root them in a propagator unit at a temperature of 16°C (61°F), and pot the rooted cuttings up singly in a proprietary compost. Overwinter in a frost-free greenhouse. Pot them on the following spring and plunge outdoors until transplanting the young shrubs to their permanent sites in early autumn.

Pests and diseases Generally trouble free.

Halimium umbellatum

Hebe

shrubby veronica, hebe

Hebe 'Pink Wand'

- ☐ Height 15cm-1.8m (6in-6ft)
- ☐ Spread 45cm-1.8m (1½-6ft)
- ☐ Flowers late spring to mid autumn
- ☐ Ordinary well-drained soil
- ☐ Sunny site

The shrubs in this large New Zealand genus are grown for their attractive evergreen foliage and for their flowers – sometimes borne from late spring until early autumn. Some species are known as whipcord hebes, from their scale-like, overlapping leaves. Many species are half-hardy which restricts their range to mild coastal gardens in the south and west, and to sheltered inland spots. Being resistant to salt-spray and industrial pollution, they are excellent shrubs for seaside and sheltered town gardens.

Popular species and hybrids

Hebe albicans forms a dense rounded shrub reaching 60cm (2ft) high and across. The lance-shaped leaves are grey-green, and dense spikes of white flowers appear in early to mid summer. The species is generally hardy in most regions.
Hebe armstrongii is a moderately hardy shrub 90cm (3ft) high and 60-90cm (2-3ft) across. It is of rounded habit, with golden-green whipcord foliage. The small sparse clusters of white flowers appear between early and late summer. *Hebe ochracea* is similar (and often confused with it), although it has coppery leaves and flowers more freely.
Hebe 'Autumn Glory' is a moderately hardy hybrid with a height and spread of 60-90cm (2-3ft). Conical spikes of violet-blue flowers appear in late summer and

Hebe 'Autumn Glory'

continue into autumn. The oval dark green leaves are carried on purple stems.
Hebe 'Bowles' Hybrid' reaches 60cm (2ft) high and 45-60cm (1½-2ft) across. Its spikes of mauve flowers are borne from late spring until autumn. A moderately hardy hybrid, it has lance-shaped mid green leaves.
Hebe brachysiphon (syn. *H. traversii*) is a hardy shrub of bushy habit, 1.8m (6ft) high and 1.2-1.8m (4-6ft) across. The 5cm (2in) long sprays of white flowers appear in early and mid summer.
Hebe 'Carl Teschner' has a dense spreading habit, 30cm (1ft) high and 60-75cm (2-2½ft) across. It is a moderately hardy shrub and suitable for ground cover. Small spikes of violet-blue flowers appear in early and mid summer among grey-green leaves.
Hebe x *franciscana* 'Blue Gem' is a compact, near hardy hybrid with a height and spread of 1.2m (4ft). The bright blue flowers appear intermittently throughout the summer. It has rich green, rounded leaves. The smaller 'Variegata' has cream-edged leaves and mauve-blue flowers.
Hebe 'La Seduisante' is a half-

Hebe 'Simon Delaux'

hardy hybrid. Its spikes of magenta-purple flowers, borne from summer until autumn, make it worth considering for sheltered gardens. It reaches 1.5m (5ft) high and across and has dark green leathery and glossy leaves.
Hebe 'Marjorie' is a hardy shrub with a bushy spreading habit 90cm (3ft) high and 1.2m (4ft) across. It has fleshy leaves and light blue and white flowers borne from mid summer to early autumn.
Hebe 'Midsummer Beauty' grows into a rounded shrub 1.2m (4ft)

Hebe 'Marjorie'

Hedera

ivy

Hebe 'Midsummer Beauty'

Hedera colchica 'Dentata Variegata'

□ Height 60cm-30m (2-100ft)
□ Foliage climber
□ Any soil
□ Sunny or shaded site

high and across, with foliage that is purple-red on the undersides. An abundance of lavender-purple flower spikes are produced throughout summer. It is moderately hardy.

Hebe 'Pagei' is a hardy, dwarf dome-shaped hybrid only 15-23cm (6-9in) high but with a spread of 60-90cm (2-3ft). It has grey-green leaves and white flower spikes which appear in late spring and early summer. A good ground-cover or specimen plant for rock gardens.

Hebe 'Pink Wand' is a hardy, dense rounded shrub reaching 1.8m (6ft) high and across. In summer it produces long spikes of clear pink flowers among the green willow-like leaves.

Hebe 'Simon Delaux' is a half-hardy hybrid, suitable only for mild seaside gardens. It reaches 1.5m (5ft) high and 1.2-1.5m (4-5ft) across and has long, glossy, dark green leaves. The rich red flower spikes are produced from mid summer until autumn.

Cultivation

Plant in early to mid autumn or mid to late spring in any well-drained soil and in a warm sunny site.

Dead-head all hebes as soon as flowering is over. Leggy shrubs can be pruned hard back in mid spring.

Propagation Take tip cuttings of non-flowering shoots in summer and root in a cold frame.

Pests and diseases Downy mildew, leaf spot and honey fungus can be a problem.

Ivies are among the easiest and hardiest climbers to grow, tolerating any soil and any situation – from extreme heat to hard winters, heavy shade and town and industrial pollution. Though they produce both flowers and fruits, it is their evergreen foliage which makes them so popular. This comes in a range of shapes and colours – different shades of green, often with cream, gold or silver variegations and often with pink tints in winter.

Ivies produce two types of growth. In the juvenile stage the stems climb, clinging by means of aerial roots to any available support; they bear deeply lobed leaves. Adult growth is produced when the climbing stems reach the top of their supports; it ceases to climb and becomes bushy, beginning to produce greenish flowers followed by black fruits. Ivies propagated from the adult form retain the bushy characteristics and will grow into shrubs, often known as tree ivies.

As well as climbing, ivies also trail, forming dense ground cover beneath trees and seeding themselves in cracks between paving and in walls. They survive neglect and submit to hard pruning – tree ivies being favourite subjects for topiary designs.

Popular species

Hedera canariensis, Canary ivy, is slightly less hardy than the common ivy (*Hedera helix*). It thrives in most gardens in Britain, though the growth may die back in severe winters. Growing rapidly to reach a height of 4.5-6m (15-20ft), it is a good species for training up trellis as it has a more upright habit than *H. helix*. The leathery, lobed leaves are bright green in summer turning bronze-green in winter. 'Azorica' is a vigorous variety with slightly lobed, light green leaves; 'Gloire de Marengo' (syn. 'Variegata') is less hardy than the species; it is a vigorous climber or trailer, with large lobed leaves, dark green in the centre merging through silver-grey to white margins, most pronounced on young foliage; 'Margino Maculata' resembles 'Gloire de Marengo' but the red-stalked leaves are mottled with creamy-white; it is prone to frost damage though it usually recovers.

Hedera colchica, Persian ivy, is recognized by its large leathery leaves which are heart-shaped or oval. It is a rapid climber, capable of reaching a height of 6-9m (20-30ft). The young growth is covered with yellow down. In the species the leaves are dark green, but several varieties have been developed offering more interesting foliage: 'Arborescens' (adult shrubby form with large ovate leaves); 'Dentata' (extremely vigorous, the largest-leaved ivy variety and sometimes called elephant ears, with rich green foliage drooping from purplish stalks); 'Dentata Variegata' (bright green shading to grey, conspicuous and irregular creamy-yellow leaf mar-

Hedera helix 'Buttercup'

Hedera helix 'Goldheart'

gins); and 'Paddy's Pride' (syn. 'Sulphur Heart', leaves boldly splashed with yellow merging into shades of green; occasional leaves wholly yellow).

Hedera helix, common ivy, is one of the hardiest ivies and the most useful of all climbing plants – good for covering ground where little else will grow, as well as walls. Its glossy dark green, three- to five-lobed leaves are often marked with silver veins.

The species is capable of reaching 15-30m (50-100ft) high, but varieties developed from it are less vigorous. Favourites include 'Arborescens' (a bushy form); 'Atropurpurea' (almost entire leaves, dark purple-green especially in winter, good on exposed cold walls); 'Bird's Foot' (syn. 'Caenwoodiana' and 'Pedata', slow grower, narrowly lobed, dark grey-green leaves conspicuously veined with white); 'Buttercup' (outstanding golden form, five-lobed, rich yellow leaves turning lime-green in shade and with age); 'Cavendishii' (triangular grey-mottled green leaves with broad creamy-white margins); 'Chicago' (small leaves blotched bronze-purple); 'Congesta' (upright, non-climbing form, arrow-shaped, dark green veined leaves; good for rock gardens); 'Glacier' (silver-grey leaves edged white); 'Gold-

heart' (green leaves with yellow centres); 'Green Ripple' (green leaves with frilled edges); 'Hibernica' (syn. *H. helix hibernica*, large, five-lobed dark green leaves, good for ground cover); 'Ivalace' (large dark green crimped leaves, coppery-green in winter); 'Little Diamond' (dwarf shrubby form, excellent as ground cover in rock gardens, grey-green, white-edged leaves); 'Marginata Elegantissima' (syn. 'Tricolor', small greyish-green leaves edged white and usually flushed pink in winter); 'Parsley Crested' (strong grower, cascading stems with glossy pale green leaves twisted

and crimped at the edges, pinkish-red and crimson in winter); and 'Sagittifolia' (dark purple-green arrow-head-shaped leaves).

Hedera pastuchowii is an ultra-hardy ivy from the Caucasus. It is a vigorous grower with large leathery, heart-shaped leaves that are black-green in colour with paler veins and red midribs on the undersides. The species grows well on shady walls.

Hedera rhombea, Japanese ivy, resembles the common ivy (*H. helix*), but the dark green leaves are triangular and borne on long wiry stalks. In spite of its slender appearance, the species is fully hardy.

Cultivation
Plant at any time between early autumn and early spring. Any soil and any site is suitable, from full sun to deep shade. Ivies grow more slowly in a sunny site, and

Hedera helix 'Ivalace'

Hedera helix 'Buttercup'

Hedera helix 'Hibernica'

Hedera colchica 'Paddy's Pride'

Hedera canariensis 'Gloire de Marengo'

full sun often scorches variegated forms. However, these still need good light to maintain their leaf colours and should preferably be grown on west-facing walls. All ivies are highly tolerant of air pollution and exposure.

Ivy grown on walls or fences can be cut back close to its support during late winter to early spring. In the summer prune again to remove any unwanted growth. Prevent growth from becoming too matted and heavy by thinning out occasionally. Cut hard back before climbing stems reach guttering and roof tiles.

Propagation Take 7.5-10cm (3-4in) cuttings from the tips of shoots in mid to late summer. For shrubby tree ivies, take cuttings from mature growth; for climbing, trailing and ground-cover ivies, take cuttings from juvenile growth. Root the cuttings in a cold frame; pot them up and grow on outdoors until large enough to be planted in permanent sites.

Pests and diseases Scale insects can infest the leaves, making them sooty, and leaf spot can occur.

Helianthemum

rock rose, sun rose

Helianthemum nummularium 'Wisley Pink'

- ☐ Height 5-15cm (2-6in)
- ☐ Spread 30-60cm (1-2ft)
- ☐ Flowers early to mid summer
- ☐ Any well-drained soil
- ☐ Sunny situation

Few plants can equal rock roses as quick covering for sunny areas – after a year's growth a single specimen may have spread to 60cm (2ft). These hardy, low-growing shrubs provide 5-15cm (2-6in) high carpets of evergreen foliage, massed in summer with brightly coloured flowers – white, cream, yellow, orange, scarlet, bronze, crimson and pink. Foliage colour varies from deep glossy green to soft silver-grey.

Rock roses are suitable for banks, terrace walls, raised beds and rock gardens, though they should be sited carefully so they don't swamp less vigorous plants.

Popular species

Helianthemum alpestre, syn. *H. oelandicum*, comes from the mountains of central and southern Europe. It grows 7.5-10cm (3-4in) high and has a spread of

Helianthemum nummularium 'Amy Baring'

Helianthemum nummularium 'Raspbery Ripple'

Helianthemum 'Rose of Leeswood'

30cm (1ft). The bright yellow saucer-shaped flowers appear in abundance in early and mid summer. *H. alpestre* var. *roseum* is more prostrate, with a height of 5-7.5cm (2-3in) and a spread of 60cm (2ft). It has smaller, hairy grey-green leaves and silver-pink flowers.

Helianthemum nummularium, common rock rose or sun rose, is the parent of many garden varieties. Most reach 10-15cm (4-6in) high and spread to 60cm (2ft); they flower in early and mid summer. Popular varieties include 'Afflick' (orange with buff centres and green leaves); 'Amy Baring' (buttercup-yellow flowers and green leaves); 'Ben Dearg' (deep copper-orange and green leaves); 'Ben Hope' (deep pink with orange centres and green leaves); 'Ben Nevis' (deep yellow with bronzered centres, green leaves); 'Fire Dragon' (orange-scarlet and grey-green leaves); 'Jubilee' (double primrose-yellow); 'Mrs C.W. Earle' (brick-red with yellow flush, and dark green leaves); 'Praecox' (lemon-yellow and grey leaves); 'Raspberry Ripple' (red and white flowers, green leaves); 'Rose of Leeswood' (double rose-pink flowers and green leaves); 'The Bride' (white with yellow centres and grey leaves), 'Wisley Pink' (soft pink and grey leaves); 'Wisley Primrose' (yellow and grey leaves); and 'Wisley White' (pure white, grey leaves).

Cultivation
Plant between early autumn and early spring in any type of well-drained soil in a sunny position.

To keep *H. nummularium* varieties under control and maintain a neat shape, cut them hard back with shears after flowering.

Propagation Take 5-7.5cm (2-3in) long heel cuttings of non-flowering lateral shoots in summer. Root the cuttings in a cold frame. Pot up the rooted cuttings singly and overwinter in a cold frame. Pinch out the growing tips. Plant them out the following mid spring.

Pests and diseases Powdery mildew and leaf spot may occur.

Helianthemum nummularium 'Wisley White'

Helichrysum

everlastings

Helichrysum rosmarinifolium

□ Height 20cm-2.7m (8in-9ft)
□ Spread 30cm-1.5m (1-5ft)
□ Foliage shrub
□ Ordinary sharply drained soil
□ Sunny site

Shrubby everlastings are grown for their attractive grey-green or white woolly foliage which, in mild areas, remains evergreen.

Helichrysum angustifolium

Popular species

Helichrysum angustifolium, the curry plant, is a half-hardy species reaching 20-38cm (8-15in) high and 30-60cm (1-2ft) across. It has silver-grey, narrow, needle-like leaves and small mustard-yellow flower clusters in summer.

Helichrysum ledifolium, the kerosene bush, is generally hardy and reaches a height of 90cm (3ft) and a spread of 1.5m (5ft). The undersides of the narrow leathery leaves are coated with an inflammable yellow gum. Small white flowers appear in summer.

Helichrysum petiolatum is a half-hardy to moderately hardy species with semi-trailing stems bearing round grey felted leaves. Reaching 60cm (2ft) high and across, it is usually treated as a bedding plant for hanging baskets. The flowers are cream coloured.

Helichrysum rosmarinifolium is an upright near-hardy shrub, 1.8-2.7m (6-9ft) high and 60cm-1.5m (2-5ft) across. The young stems are woolly white with narrow leaves that are dark green above and white beneath. White flowers appear in early to mid summer.

Helichrysum splendidum is near hardy, 38cm (15in) high and 90cm (3ft) across. If cut back in spring it forms a mound of silver-grey downy foliage. Tiny yellow flowers appear in summer.

Cultivation

Plant in late summer and early autumn or in spring in any well-drained soil. The site should be sunny and sheltered. Trim the shrubs to shape in spring.

Propagation Take 7.5cm (3in) long heel cuttings of lateral shoots in mid to late summer.

Pests and diseases Downy mildew can affect the foliage.

Helichrysum petiolatum

Hypericum
St. John's wort

Hypericum calycinum

☐ Height 8-45cm (3-18in)
☐ Spread 30-60cm (1-2ft) and more
☐ Flowers mid summer to autumn
☐ Any well-drained soil
☐ Sunny site

The true evergreen species of St. John's wort are dwarf or prostrate shrubs suitable for ground cover on sunny banks and for growing in rock gardens. They are generally winter-hardy though they may be short-lived in very exposed gardens. The deciduous species, which make up the larger group, are often semi or fully evergreen in mild areas.

Valued for their year-round leaf carpets, hypericums are easily grown in any good soil. They are especially prized for their attractive golden or yellow flowers borne for many weeks through-

out summer and early autumn. The cup-shaped flowers open out flat to display a prominent centre of golden stamens.

Popular species
Hypericum balearicum is hardy in southern and western areas. It grows as a 60cm (2ft) high erect shrub, with a spread of 60cm (2ft). It bears tiny leaves and small, heavily fragrant yellow flowers from early summer to early autumn.

Hypericum calycinum, rose of Sharon or Aaron's beard, is a vigorous shrub, only 30-45cm (1-1½ft) high but spreading indefinitely by underground runners to form an attractive carpet of ovate leaves; these are bright green above, bluish-green on the undersides. The large, golden-yellow

flowers are borne singly or in pairs in great profusion from early summer onwards. The species is excellent for large-scale ground cover and thrives in the shade of trees.

Hypericum coris is suitable for a rock garden. It grows 15cm (6in) high and 30cm (12in) wide, with tufts of grey-green, heather-like leaves along the wiry stems. The golden-yellow flower clusters are borne in high summer at the tips of the stems. The species thrives on poor and limy soils.

Hypericum empetrifolium is another rock-garden species. It is almost prostrate, only 7.5cm (3in) high, but spreads to 30cm (12in). The slender stems bear small golden flowers in summer. It needs well-drained soil and a warm and sheltered site.

Ilex
holly

Ilex crenata 'Golden Gem'

- ☐ Height 60cm-7.5m (2-25ft)
- ☐ Spread 60cm-4.5m (2-15ft)
- ☐ Berrying foliage shrub
- ☐ Ordinary garden soil
- ☐ Sunny or shaded site

Holly is one of the few evergreens native to Britain and is represented in the garden by a host of varieties. Its glossy, dark green or variegated leaves provide interest throughout the year, while the colourful berries of the female hollies form a valuable source of winter colour. (For a female to produce berries, a male holly should be nearby.)

Hollies vary enormously in size. They are generally slow-growing – some attaining tree proportions (see page 35) while others remain compact or dwarf shrubs. They are adaptable to most soils and situations, withstanding pollution and exposure to wind. Shrubby hollies make admirable specimen shrubs and many are also excellent for hedging; with regular pruning, they can be kept at reasonable heights.

Popular species
Ilex x *altaclarensis* is the name given to a group of large-leaved hybrids 3-4.5m (10-15ft) tall. They make good windbreaks and hedges and thrive in town and seaside gardens. Popular varieties include: 'Camelliifolia' (female, of pyramidal shape, with spineless leaves and large red berries); 'Golden King' (female with almost spineless, golden variegated leaves and large red berries); 'Hodginsii' (male with purple

Hypericum coris

Cultivation
Evergreen hypericums do best in sheltered gardens. In cold regions they may lose their leaves in winter and the stems die back, but they usually sprout again from the base.

Plant in mid spring, setting out small, pot-grown specimens. Hypericums thrive in any soil that is quick-draining, and many prefer poor soil. They will tolerate light shade, notably *H. calycinum*, but flower most profusely in full sun.

Pruning is rarely necessary for these dwarf shrubs though frost-damaged shoots should be cut back to healthy wood in mid spring. If necessary, keep the invasive *H. calycinum* within bounds by cutting it back almost to ground level in spring every few years.
Propagation Increase the shrubs by 5cm (2in) softwood cuttings taken in late spring or early summer. Ideally root them in a moist propagator unit; otherwise in a closed cold frame. When rooted, pot the cuttings up singly in 7.5cm (3in) pots of a proprietary compost and overwinter them in a frost-free greenhouse. Set the young

plants in their permanent sites in spring of the following year.

H. calycinum can also be increased by division of the roots between mid autumn and mid spring; replant the divisions at once.
Pests and diseases Small orange or yellow spots on the leaves are caused by rust; orange and brown spore clusters appear later.

Hypericum empetrifolium

Ilex aquifolium

Ilex x altaclarensis 'Lawsoniana'

stems and large green spiny leaves); 'Lawsoniana' (female with spineless leaves splashed yellow, orange-red berries); and 'Silver Sentinel' (syn. 'Belgica Aurea', female with deep green leaves mottled grey and edged cream-white, orange-red berries).

Ilex aquifolium, common English holly, has given rise to a large number of varieties. The berries are red unless otherwise stated. Popular shrub-like varieties include: 'Ferox Argentea', hedgehog holly (male with leaves spined on upper surface as well as on the cream-white margins); 'Flavescens' (female, outstanding golden holly, leaves suffused bright yellow, best in full sun); 'Golden Milkboy/Milkgirl' (male and female with spiny, gold-splashed leaves); 'Golden Queen' (male, spiny dark green leaves shaded grey and light green, broad yellow edges); 'Handsworth New Silver' (female, grey-green leaves, cream-white margins); 'Ovata' (male, slow-growing, ovate, scalloped-edged leaves); 'Pendula' (female with weeping branches, dark green spiny

leaves); and 'Silver Queen' (male with white-edged leaves).

Ilex cornuta is a dense, slow-growing species, up to 2.4m (8ft) high and 1.8-2.4m (6-8ft) across, with rectangular, glossy dark green, very spiny leaves. Self-fertile, it bears bright red berries. The variety 'Burfordii', with spineless leaves, is particularly free-fruiting.

Ilex crenata, Japanese holly, grows slowly to 2.4m (8ft) high. A good hedging shrub, it has tiny, finely toothed, dark green leaves; female plants bear small black berries. The variety 'Convexa' grows no more than 30-60cm (1-2ft) and responds well to pruning; it has shiny leaves and a profusion of berries. 'Golden Gem', 30-60cm (1-2ft) high, is flat-topped with golden-yellow foliage; 'Helleri', female, with tiny glossy leaves, forms a hummock 60cm (2ft) high.

Ilex latifolia, from Japan, is 3-4.5m (10-15ft) high and bears exceptionally large leaves, glossy dark green with toothed margins. It is outstanding for its abundance of bright orange berries.

Ilex aquifolium 'Ferox Argentea'

Ilex x altaclarensis 'Silver Sentinel'

Ilex pernyi is a pyramidal-shaped holly with glossy green leaves which are almost triangular and spined. It has bright red berries. The hybrid 'Jermyn's Dwarf' is in part derived from this species; it forms a mound of arching stems with glossy dark green leaves and red berries.

Cultivation
Set out container-grown young plants in mid to late spring or early to mid autumn in sun or shade; variegated forms should be given a sunny position. Hollies will grow in any soil but thrive in moist loam. Water during dry weather until the plants are established. Set hedging plants 60cm (2ft) apart.

Trim specimen trees to shape in mid to late summer. Prune holly hedges in mid spring or in late summer. On variegated hollies, remove any green-leaved shoots that appear.

Propagation Layer long shoots in mid autumn and separate from the parent plant two years later. Alternatively take 5-7.5cm (2-3in) long heel cuttings in late summer and root in a cold frame. Cuttings are often slow to root.

Pests and diseases Birds feed on the berries, and holly leaf miners cause blotches on the foliage. Leaf spot and honey fungus can also affect holly.

IVY – see *Hedera*
JAPANESE CEDAR – see *Cryptomeria*
JASMINE NIGHTSHADE – see *Solanum*

Ilex cornuta

Jasminum polyanthum

Jasminum

jasmine

Jasminum humile 'Revolutum'

☐ Height 1.5-7.5m (5-25ft)
☐ Flowers spring and summer
☐ Any well-drained soil
☐ Warm sheltered position

The evergreen jasmines, grown for the heady scent of their flowers, are only moderately hardy. Most will survive the winters in southern Britain if grown against sunny sheltered walls; elsewhere they are better as greenhouse or conservatory shrubs and climbers.

Popular species

Jasminum humile 'Revolutum' is a moderately hardy, semi-evergreen shrub, about 1.8m (6ft) high and wide. It bears leathery dark green leaves, and clusters of yellow flowers in early summer.
Jasminum mesnyi, syn. *J. primulinum*, primrose jasmine, grows only in mild areas. Its semi-double yellow flowers are produced throughout spring. This climbing species can reach 4.5m (15ft) high.
Jasminum polyanthum needs a warm and sheltered wall even in frost-free gardens. It is vigorous and can reach 7.5m (25ft). The white flowers are borne from late spring to late summer.
Jasminum x stephanense is the hardiest species. It is a vigorous climber, 3-4.5m (10-15ft) high and suitable for covering archways and pergolas. Clusters of fragrant pale pink flowers appear in early summer.

Cultivation
Plant in mid or late spring in any well-drained but moist soil. All need a sheltered site in full sun, and winter protection. Prune after flowering, cutting out straggly stems and old weak shoots.
Propagation Long shoots can be layered in autumn. Alternatively take heel cuttings in late summer and root in a propagator unit.
Pests and diseases Frost damage may encourage grey mould.

JERUSALEM SAGE – see *Phlomis*

Juniperus

juniper

Juniperus communis 'Compressa'

☐ Height 5cm-1.8m (2in-6ft)
☐ Spread 15cm-1.8m (6in-6ft)
☐ Coniferous shrub
☐ Ordinary well-drained soil
☐ Sunny or lightly shaded position

Though many junipers grow to tree-like proportions (see pages 37-38), a large number of slow-growing, dwarf varieties have been developed. They are ideally suited to smaller gardens as they rarely reach more than 1.2-1.5m (4-5ft) in height.
Coming in a wide range of habits – columnar, prostrate, semi-prostrate and rounded – they are excellent for growing in rock gardens or as specimen shrubs in island beds; they associate well with heathers.
Junipers have two types of foliage: juvenile leaves on young growth are small, pointed and awl-shaped, while on older growth the leaves are scale-like and densely packed. Some dwarf varieties never produce adult foliage. The small cones resemble berries and are black or blue.

Popular varieties
Juniperus chinensis has given rise to numerous varieties which generally have a columnar habit.
'Kaizuka Variegata' grows up to 1.8m (6ft) high. Its mainly adult, green foliage is splashed with cream.
'Obelisk' grows 1.5m (5ft) or more high. It is of erect habit, with densely packed adult foliage that is bluish-green.

121

Juniperus x *media* 'Pfitzeriana Aurea'

'Pyramidalis' is a pyramid-shaped, slow-growing conifer reaching 1.5m (5ft) high and 60cm (2ft) across with juvenile blue-grey foliage.

Juniperus communis, the common juniper, is the parent of numerous dwarf varieties.

'Compressa' is a neat conical shrub 45cm (1½ft) high and 15cm (6in) wide, ideal for a rock garden. The leaves are dark green.

'Depressa Aurea' is a prostrate juniper 30cm (1ft) high, but with a spread of 1.2-1.5m (4-5ft). The summer foliage is golden-yellow and the winter foliage is bronze.

'Hornibrookii' is a mat-forming variety 15cm (6in) high, but with a spread of 90cm (3ft); excellent for ground cover. It has silvery-green leaves.

'Repanda', a low carpet-forming conifer 25cm (10in) high and 1.8m (6ft) across, has dark green foliage, sometimes bronze-coloured in winter.

'Sentinel' is very narrow and columnar with dense erect branches. It grows 1.8m (6ft) high and 30cm (1ft) across. Its bears deep blue-green foliage on purple shoots.

Juniperus horizontalis, creeping juniper, is useful for ground cover in full sun. The wholly adult foliage is blue-green, and the main stems root where they touch the soil. Several fine varieties have been bred from the species.

'Blue Chip' reaches 30cm (1ft) high and 1.2-1.5m (4-5ft) across, and has feathery silver-blue foliage.

'Emerald Spreader' is a prostrate ground-hugging variety 5-10cm (2-4in) high, but spreading to 1.5m (5ft) across. The foliage is bright green.

'Glauca' is a carpeting juniper which forms low mounds of rich blue-green foliage. It is 10cm (4in) high and 1.2m (4ft) across.

'Hughes', a prostrate but vigorous variety, reaches 30cm (1ft) high and 1.5-1.8m (5-6ft) across. It has grey-green foliage.

'Wiltonii', syn. 'Blue Rug', 10cm (4in) high, spreads its long branches to a silver-blue carpet.

Juniperus x *media*, a hybrid group of junipers sometimes listed as forms of *J. chinensis*, includes several popular varieties of conical or spreading habit.

Juniperus chinensis 'Pyramidalis'

'Gold Coast' is a dense, flat-topped, semi-prostrate juniper 60-90cm (2-3ft) high and 90-120cm (3-4ft) across. The green leaves are tipped with golden-yellow.

'Mint Julep', a semi-prostrate conifer with arching branches covered in rich green foliage, reaches 75cm (2½ft) high and 1.2m (4ft) across.

Juniperus communis 'Depressa Aurea'

Juniperus squamata 'Meyeri'

'Old Gold' is compact and semi-prostrate. Reaching 90cm-1.2m (3-4ft) high and 1.2-1.5m (4-5ft) across, it has bronze-gold leaves throughout the year.

'Pfitzeriana' grows to a height of 90cm (3ft) and a spread of 1.8m (6ft). The branches, bearing grey-green juvenile foliage, curve at the tips. A flat-topped variety with gold-tipped foliage, 'Pfitzeriana Aurea', is also available.

'Plumosa Aurea' is semi-prostrate with branches which droop at the tips. It reaches 75cm (2½ft) high and 90cm (3ft) across and has yellow-bronze feathery foliage.

'Sulphur Spray' is slow-growing but eventually reaches a height of 1.8m (6ft) and a spread of 1.2-1.5m (4-5ft). The leaves have a pale sulphur-yellow colour.

Juniperus sabina, the savin juniper, is usually represented by the variety 'Tamariscifolia'. This is a dense spreading shrub with feathery, blue-green foliage. It grows 45cm (1½ft) high, spreading eventually to 3m (10ft) or more; it is excellent for ground cover.

Juniperus squamata is the parent of several outstanding blue-grey leaved varieties.

'Blue Carpet' is prostrate and grows 30cm (1ft) high and 1.5m (5ft) across.

'Blue Star' grows into a dense, bun-shaped conifer 30-38cm (12-15in) high and 45cm (1½ft) across.

'Meyeri' the deepest blue of all junipers, is an irregularly shaped variety 1.2-1.5m (4-5ft) high and 1.5m (5ft) across, with ascending branches.

Juniperus virginiana is the parent of two popular dwarf junipers.

'Globosa' is a dense neatly-rounded conifer, 90cm (3ft) high and across, with bright green adult foliage.

'Grey Owl', a vigorous variety, eventually grows 1.5m (5ft) high and across, with silver-grey leaves.

Cultivation

Plant in mid spring in ordinary well-drained garden soil in full sun or light shade. The forms with golden, silver or blue foliage colour best in sunny sites. Keep young plants well watered in dry periods in summer; once established, they are drought-tolerant.

No pruning is required.

Propagation Heel cuttings taken in early autumn are difficult to root. It is safer to buy in new stock.

Pests and diseases Scale insects and caterpillars can attack the foliage; rust may be a problem in spring.

Juniperus virginiana 'Globosa'

123

Kalmia
kalmia

Kalmia latifolia

- Height 90cm-3m (3-10ft)
- Spread 90cm-2.4m (3-8ft)
- Flowers early summer
- Moist, acid soil
- Partially shaded position

Kalmias – all hardy shrubs – grow best in semi-woodland conditions where the soil is moist and acidic and there is light shade. They are often planted with azaleas and rhododendrons.

The clusters of cup-shaped flowers appear in early summer at the end of the previous season's growth. Out of flower, the shrubs resemble rhododendrons, though the glossy leaves are slightly narrower.

Popular species
Kalmia angustifolia, sheep laurel, bears clusters of rose-red flowers in early summer. The lance-shaped leaves are glossy and mid green. It has a height and spread of 90cm-1.2m (3-4ft). 'Rubra' is a variety with deep red flowers and deep green foliage.
Kalmia latifolia, calico bush or mountain laurel, has bright pink flowers with conspicuous stamens in early summer. Each flower is crimped like calico – an effect which gives the plant its common name. Reaching 1.8-3m (6-10ft) high and 2.4m (8ft) across, it has lance-shaped leathery mid green leaves.

Cultivation
Plant in early to mid autumn or mid to late spring in good, moist, lime-free soil. The site should be partially shaded.

No pruning is required, though faded flower clusters should be removed. Overlong and crowded shoots can be cut hard back after flowering.
Propagation Layer shoots of the current season's growth in late summer to early autumn. By the following autumn, the layers should have rooted sufficiently to be severed from the parent plant.
Pests and diseases Trouble free.

Kalmia angustifolia 'Rubra'

Laurus
bay laurel

Laurus nobilis

- Height 3-4.5m (10-15ft)
- Spread 3-4.5m (10-15ft)
- Foliage shrub
- Ordinary garden soil
- Sheltered sunny site

This hardy aromatic shrub is the laurel of the ancient Romans and Greeks, who crowned the victors at games and festivals with laurel wreaths.

Bay laurel (*Laurus nobilis*) is grown for its foliage of lance-shaped, glossy dark green leaves which have culinary as well as decorative uses. Insignificant yellow-green flower clusters in mid spring are followed by purple-black berries on female plants.

Though bay laurel can attain tree size, it usually grows no more than 3-4.5m (10-15ft) high. It is frequently tub-grown and pruned to a neat pyramid shape or standard.

Cultivation
Plant in early to mid spring in any type of soil in a sunny sheltered position. The shrubs are tolerant of town pollution and maritime exposure. Container-grown shrubs should be protected from frost during the winter.

Trim trained bay laurel to shape during the summer. Remove any sucker shoots which appear from stems of trained standards.
Propagation In late summer to early autumn take 10cm (4in) heel cuttings of half-ripe lateral shoots and root in a cold frame.
Pests and diseases Scale insects may infest the stems and the undersides of the leaves, making the plants sticky and sooty.

Lavandula

lavender

Lavandula stoechas

Lavandula angustifolia 'Munstead'

☐ Height 30cm-1.2m (1-4ft)
☐ Spread 30cm-1.2m (1-4ft)
☐ Flowers late spring to early autumn
☐ Any well-drained soil
☐ Sunny site

Lavender has been grown and loved for so long that there can be few gardeners who do not know this little hardy shrub. Flowers and leaves are both aromatic, and the unique lavender scent is exuded as much in winter by the silver-grey foliage as in summer by the dense flower spikes. The flowers range in colour from deepest purple to white.

Lavenders make excellent low-growing informal hedges, and are also useful as edging plants. They tend to grow leggy with age unless regularly pruned.

The flowers can be dried for use in pot-pourris. Pick the blooms when they are showing colour, but before they are fully out. Hang in bunches to dry, in a cool airy place.

Popular species

Lavandula angustifolia (syn. *L. spica*), English lavender, has pale grey-blue flowers borne in 6cm (2½in) spikes between mid summer and early autumn. It forms a shrub 90cm-1.2m (3-4ft) high, and has narrow, silver-grey leaves. Popular varieties developed from it include: 'Alba' (pinkish white flowers); 'Grappenhall' (lavender-blue flowers); 'Hidcote' (compact, 60-80cm/2-2¾ft high with dense violet-purple flowers); 'Hidcote Pink' (similar, but only 60cm/2ft high, with pale pink flowers); 'Loddon Pink' (compact, to 75cm/2½ft high, pale pink flowers); 'Munstead' (compact, 30-60cm/1-2ft high, with clear blue flowers and green leaves); 'Nana Alba' (30cm/1ft high, with white flowers); and 'Twickel Purple' (60-90cm/2-3ft high, with long purple-blue flower spikes). 'Vera', the Dutch lavender, is sometimes listed as *L. vera*, but resembles *L. angustifolia*. It is

a robust shrub, up to 1.2m (4ft) high and wide, with grey foliage and blue-purple flowers.

Lavandula stoechas, French lavender, bears shorter spikes of dark purple tubular flowers from late spring to early summer. Each flower spike is topped by a tuft of purple bracts. This species grows up to 60cm (2ft) high and across and has grey-green leaves.

Cultivation

Plant between early autumn and early spring in any well-drained soil in a sunny situation. For hedges, set young plants 23-30cm (9-12in) apart.

Remove dead flower stems and lightly trim the plants in late summer. Straggly plants can be cut hard back in early to mid spring to encourage new growth from the base. Clip hedges to shape in early to mid spring.

L. stoechas is not fully hardy and may need winter protection in cold areas.

Propagation Take 7.5-10cm (3-4in) cuttings of non-flowering shoots in late summer and root in a cold frame. Transplant to the flowering position in spring.

Alternatively take 15cm (6in) long cuttings in early autumn and plant in the flowering position.

Pests and diseases Shoots injured by frost may die back; grey mould may occur on dead shoots.

LAVENDER – see *Lavandula*

Lavandula angustifolia 'Hidcote'

Leptospermum

tea tree

Leptospermum scoparium

Leptospermum scoparium 'Nichollsii'

☐ Height 15cm-3m (6in-10ft)
☐ Spread 90cm-1.8m (3-6ft)
☐ Flowers late spring to early summer
☐ Well-drained lime-free soil
☐ Sunny sheltered position

Originating from Australia and New Zealand, leptospermums are hardy only in sheltered southern gardens. They thrive in mild coastal areas and do particularly well against south-facing walls.

Between late spring and early summer they bear a profusion of small, saucer-shaped, white or pink flowers which are good for cutting as well as garden decoration. Some are prostrate, others have an upright growth habit and branch freely. They bear narrowly oblong and pointed, dark green leaves.

Tea trees are unrelated to the commercial tea plant; they take their common name from the beverage brewed from the leaves by early Australian settlers as a precaution against scurvy.

Popular species
Leptospermum humifusum is a prostrate mat-forming species, 15cm (6in) high, but with a spread of 90cm (3ft). It is the hardiest species and will survive all but the coldest winters. In early summer the white flowers almost obscure the foliage.

Leptospermum scoparium, when planted against a wall, reaches 1.8-3m (6-10ft) high and 1.2-1.8m

(4-6ft) across. It has star-shaped white flowers. Varieties developed from the species include 'Chapmanii' (rose-red flowers and bronze leaves); 'Kiwi' (dwarf, 30cm/1ft high, with crimson flowers); 'Nanum' (dwarf, 30cm/1ft high, with rose-pink flowers); 'Nichollsii' (carmine-red flowers); and 'Red Damask' (double, deep rose-pink flowers).

Cultivation
Plant container-grown leptospermums in mid to late spring in good, well-drained lime-free soil in a sunny sheltered position. In mild coastal areas plants can be grown without protection, but inland they need a site against a south-facing wall.

Remove straggly branches in mid spring. Otherwise no pruning is required.

Propagation In early to mid summer take 5cm (2in) cuttings of half-ripe, non-flowering shoots and root in a propagating unit at a temperature of 16°C (61°F). Set the rooted cuttings in pots of a proprietary lime-free potting compost and overwinter under glass. Grow on for a further year before planting out in the flowering site in late spring.

Pests and diseases Trouble free.

Leucothoë

leucothoë

Leucothoë fontanesiana

☐ Height 1.2m (4ft)
☐ Spread 2.4m (8ft)
☐ Flowers late spring
☐ Moist acid soil
☐ Lightly shaded site

Thriving on acid soils, this hardy elegant shrub is valuable for the contrasting shapes and textures it can bring to gardens dominated by rhododendrons and heathers. From autumn onwards its thick and leathery, lance-shaped leaves develop bronze and purple tints. In late spring the shrub is equally spectacular, with drooping spikes of small white, urn-shaped flowers.

Leucothoë fontanesiana is useful for ground cover, developing a wide-spreading thicket of gracefully arching stems. A mature specimen can grow 1.2m (4ft) high, with a spread of twice that.

Popular varieties
Three outstanding varieties have been bred from *Leucothoë fontanesiana*.

'Nana' is a compact, low-growing version of the species.

'Rainbow' has leaves variegated with cream, yellow and pink. The young shoots, too, are pink.

'Rollissonii' is similar to the species but with narrow green leaves.

Cultivation
Plant in autumn or spring in moist acid soil and in a lightly shaded site. In early spring, prune old and overgrown shoots back to ground level.

Propagation Increase by removing and replanting rooted suckers in autumn or spring.

Pests and diseases Trouble free.

Ligustrum
privet

Ligustrum ovalifolium and golden 'Aureum'

Ligustrum lucidum 'Tricolor'

☐ Height 1.5-5.5m (6-18ft)
☐ Spread 1.2-5.5m (4-18ft)
☐ Flowers mid to late summer
☐ Ordinary garden soil
☐ Sunny or shaded position

The evergreen privets are used extensively for hedging and screening, in spite of their fast growth rate. They are hardy shrubs, tolerant of pollution and shade and amenable to severe pruning and topiary work.

As well as their ubiquitous use in hedges, privets make fine specimen shrubs. If allowed to grow naturally they produce clusters of pungent cream-white flowers in summer, followed by small blue-black long-lasting berries.

Popular species

Ligustrum japonicum, Japanese privet, reaches 1.8-2.4m (6-8ft) high and 1.2-1.8m (4-6ft) across. It has a dense, compact habit and glossy dark green, camellia-like leaves. Panicles of white flowers appear in late summer. 'Macrophyllum' is an outstanding variety, with glossy, broad camellia-like foliage.

Ligustrum lucidum is an elegantly symmetrical shrub, 3-5.5m (10-18ft) high and up to 3m (10ft) across. It needs shelter from cold north and east winds. The large ovate leaves are glossy dark green; handsome white flower panicles are produced in late summer and early autumn. The variety 'Tricolor' has narrower leaves marked with grey-green and margined white or cream-yellow, pink tinged when young.

Ligustrum ovalifolium, oval-leaved privet, is evergreen in all but the severest winters. It is the common privet, with glossy, oval, mid green leaves. Unpruned shrubs bear panicles of pungent cream-white flowers in mid summer. Varieties include 'Argenteum' with cream-edged leaves; and the popular golden privet ('Aureum'), which has broadly edged yellow leaves.

Ligustrum 'Vicaryi' grows as a densely branched shrub up to 3m (10ft) high and wide. The broadly oval leaves are golden-yellow, turning bronze-purple in winter. Unpruned, it bears dense white flower clusters in mid summer.

Cultivation

Plant privets between autumn and spring in any kind of soil, in sun or shade. They survive poor soils, drought and neglect; but for a long-lived hedge, prepare the soil thoroughly, improving drainage if necessary and digging in plenty of organic matter.

For hedging, set 30-90cm (1-3ft) high plants about 30-45cm (1-1½ft) apart; cut them back by at least half in mid spring to encourage bushy growth from the base. The following spring, prune all new shoots by half again and repeat in early autumn. Continue this hard pruning annually, in late summer/early autumn, until the hedge has reached the desired height.

Established hedges and topiary will need trimming to shape at least twice a year – in late spring and in early autumn. Free-growing shrubs need little pruning, except for cutting long shoots back to side-shoots in spring.

Propagation Take 30cm (1ft) hardwood cuttings of *L. ovalifolium* in mid autumn and insert them in a sheltered outdoor nursery bed. A year later plant out the rooted cuttings in their permanent position.

For *L. japonicum* and *L. lucidum*, take 10-15cm (4-6in) hardwood cuttings in early to mid autumn and root in a cold frame. The following spring transfer to an outdoor sheltered nursery bed. Plant out in autumn.

Pests and diseases Leaf miners and thrips may affect the leaves.

LILY-OF-THE-VALLEY BUSH
– see *Pieris*
LING – see *Calluna*

Ligustrum japonicum 'Macrophyllum'

Ligustrum 'Vicaryi'

Ligustrum 'Vicaryi', hedge

Lonicera

honeysuckle

Lonicera japonica

Lonicera hildebrandiana

The evergreen honeysuckles described here are, with one exception, all climbers.

Popular species

Lonicera giraldii is hardy in all but the coldest areas. It is a vigorous grower, useful for a low wall, where it can trail its slender hairy stems. These are clothed with narrowly oblong leaves thickly covered with velvety hairs. The purple-red flowers, with yellow stamens, are borne in clusters in summer; they are followed by purple-black berries.

Lonicera henryi is a fully hardy, vigorous but non-invasive species reaching a height of 9m (30ft). The slender downy stems are set with dark green, heart-shaped leaves. Yellow and purple-red flowers are borne in pairs during summer; the berries are black.

Lonicera hildebrandiana, giant honeysuckle, is semi-hardy and suitable only for the mildest areas. Under favourable conditions it will reach a height of 25m (80ft); elsewhere it is a magnificent greenhouse or conservatory climber. The broadly oval leaves are up to 15cm (6in) long, glossy dark green and a handsome foil for the richly fragrant flowers borne in clusters throughout summer; they are creamy-white on opening, maturing to deep yellow flushed with orange. The large berries are near black.

Lonicera japonica, Japanese honeysuckle, is a vigorous climber which grows into a tangled mass of slender stems 7.5-9m (25-30ft) high. Its fragrant, white to pale yellow flowers are borne from early summer to mid autumn. The pale green, ovate leaves are downy on both sides. 'Aureoreticulata',

☐ Height 1.5-24m (5-80ft)
☐ Spread 1.5-1.8m (5-6ft)
☐ Flowers summer and autumn
☐ Ordinary well-drained soil enriched with humus
☐ Sunny or partially shaded site

The large *Lonicera* genus contains shrubby and climbing plants, evergreen or deciduous, frost-hardy or tender. They display great diversity in their growth habits and their suitability for garden decoration, and not all species are noteworthy for their blooms.

The typical honeysuckle flowers are tubular, borne in pairs, clusters or whorls. They are often, but not always, sweetly fragrant and are usually followed by clusters of berries.

Climbing honeysuckles have woody twining stems which need sturdy supports, such as strong trellis fixed to walls and fences. They are also ideal for tumbling over arbours and pergolas and for hiding unsightly sheds and other eyesores.

Without support, honeysuckles will flop along the ground; some types, notably *L. japonica* and the less vigorous *L. henryi*, can successfully be grown as ground cover to prevent soil erosion on large sunny banks.

Lonicera japonica 'Aureoreticulata'

Lonicera sempervirens

which has bright green leaves netted and veined with yellow, is a popular garden variety. It is susceptible to frost and may lose its leaves in winter, but the plant itself is rarely killed. 'Halliana' is an outstanding form with deeply fragrant flowers that change from white to yellow with age.

Lonicera nitida, fully hardy with a height and spread of 1.5-1.8m (5-6ft), makes an excellent dense hedging shrub. Its oval, glossy dark green leaves are tiny and respond well to clipping. Insignificant yellow-green flowers, which open in mid to late spring, are followed by globular, semi-translu-

cent violet berries if the shrub is left unpruned. 'Baggesen's Gold' is a popular variety, with round, golden-yellow leaves which turn yellow-green in autumn. 'Ernest Wilson' is widely used for hedging; it is of spreading and arching habit and rarely flowers or fruits. *Lonicera sempervirens*, trumpet honeysuckle, is a semi-evergreen climber reaching 3-6m (10-20ft) high. It has ovate mid green leaves, but the distinguishing feature is the bright orange-scarlet blooms which are borne in whorls during summer. They are followed by dark red berries. This species is not fully hardy and is

best grown against a warm and sheltered wall.

Cultivation
Plant evergreen honeysuckles in mid to late spring, in any ordinary well-drained soil enriched with organic matter. Hardy species will grow in sun or partial shade, but half-hardy and tender types should be grown against sunny and sheltered walls, with a protective straw mulch over the roots in winter. Mulch all climbers with well-rotted manure or leaf-mould annually in spring.

For hedging with *L. nitida*, set the young plants 23-30cm (9-12in)

Lonicera nitida 'Baggesen's Gold'

apart; cut the plants back by half at the time of planting. Cut off the tips of young shoots two or three times during the summer to encourage bushy growth. Each year cut all new growths back by half until the hedge reaches the desired height. Thereafter, shear the hedge to shape annually in late spring and again in early autumn.

Prune climbing honeysuckles after flowering, thinning out older shoots and removing entirely a proportion from the base of the plants to encourage new shoots.

Propagation Increase climbing species and varieties by 10cm (4in) long stem sections taken in mid to late summer; root them in a cold frame. The following spring pot the rooted cuttings individually and plunge them outdoors. Move them under frost-free cover for the winter and plant out in the permanent flowering positions in mid spring.

Increase *L. nitida* and its varieties by 23-30cm (9-12in) hardwood cuttings taken in autumn and rooted in an outdoor sheltered spot. They should be ready for transplanting after a year.

Pest and diseases Aphids may attack young climbing shoots. Leaf spot shows as small green or large round brown spots. If growing conditions are unsuitable, the leaves may turn yellow or brown, and die-back can occur. Powdery mildew shows as a white powdery deposit on the leaves.

LOQUAT – see *Eriobotrya*

Lupinus
tree lupin

Lupinus arboreus

☐ Height 60cm-1.2m (2-4ft)
☐ Spread 60cm-1.2m (2-4ft)
☐ Flowers early to late summer
☐ Well-drained, lime-free soil
☐ Sunny site

Despite its common name the tree lupin is little more than a sub-shrub. Nonetheless it is an extremely attractive and useful plant. It grows rapidly – even from seed it flowers in the second year – making it excellent for providing almost instant effect in new gardens. After three years it makes a shrub 1.2m (4ft) high and measuring at least as much across. On sandy banks the plants seed themselves freely though they are comparatively short-lived. They are good for preventing soil erosion and thrive in coastal gardens.

Lupinus arboreus is a typical lupin. Like its annual and perennial relatives it bears large, deeply divided leaves and spikes, 15cm (6in) long, of pea-like flowers from early to late summer. The flowers are mainly yellow, though occasionally mauve or white types appear. Whatever the colour, they have a delicate fragrance.

Being more or less evergreen, the fingered, pale green foliage provides year-round interest.

Popular varieties
Two popular varieties are generally available.

'Golden Spire' has yellow flowers which are a deeper shade than those in the true species.

'Snow Queen' has pure white flower spikes.

Cultivation
Plant between mid autumn and early spring in any well-drained, lime-free soil. Though they will grow on heavy soil, they are longer-lived on light soils. Tree lupins are particularly suitable for growing in seaside gardens; on rich soils they produce excessive foliage rather than flowers.

Dead-head unless seeds are wanted for propagation; prune any wayward shoots back to shape after flowering.

Propagation Increase by seed sown in autumn or spring.

Pests and diseases Powdery mildew sometimes shows as a white powdery coating on the leaves. Honey fungus may rapidly kill the plants.

Mahonia

mahonia

Mahonia aquifolium, fruits

Mahonia aquifolium

□ Height 75cm-3m (2½-10ft)
□ Spread 1.5-3.5m (5-12ft)
□ Flowers early winter to mid spring
□ Any well-drained soil
□ Lightly shaded site

The hardy mahonias have four great attributes: sweetly scented winter flowers, attractive foliage, grape-like berries and an architectural habit which makes them suitable for growing as specimen plants. The flowers and foliage can be cut for decoration.

The yellow, bell-shaped or globular flowers appear between early winter and late spring, held in upright or pendent clusters. The often spiny foliage is glossy green.

Popular species

Mahonia aquifolium, Oregon grape, is a 90cm-1.5m (3-5ft) high suckering shrub with a spread of 1.5-1.8m (5-6ft). Its fragrant, rich yellow flowers are borne in dense clusters and are followed by tight clusters of berries. Varieties include 'Atropurpurea' (purple-red leaves in winter) and 'Moseri' (pink-tinted young leaves).

Mahonia japonica is a 2.4-3m (8-

10ft) high shrub with a spread of 2.4-3.5m (8-12ft). Its glossy green, holly-like leaflets sometimes become flushed with red as they age. Lemon-yellow flowers, with a lily-of-the-valley scent, are borne in drooping spikes from mid winter to early spring.

Mahonia x *media* 'Charity' bears fragrant, deep yellow flowers in upright spikes between late autumn and late winter. It is 2.4-3m (8-10ft) high and 1.8-2.4m (6-8ft) wide, with leathery dark green

leaves. 'Winter Sun' bears upright, densely packed flower spikes.

Mahonia repens is a suckering shrub up to 75cm (2½ft) high, spreading to form ground-covering colonies. It has spineless, matt green leaves, and rounded yellow flower clusters in late spring followed by black berries. The variety 'Rotundifolia' bears sea-green foliage and rich yellow flowers.

Cultivation

Plant in early to mid spring or early to mid autumn in any well-drained soil. A partially shaded site is best. Regular pruning is unnecessary, though mahonias grown as ground cover can be cut hard back in spring.

Propagation Take tip or leaf cuttings in autumn and root in a propagator.

Pests and diseases Leaf spot, powdery mildew and rust may affect mahonias.

Mahonia x *media* 'Charity'

Mahonia x *media* 'Winter Sun'

Mahonia japonica (winter)   *Mahonia japonica* (mature foliage)   *Mahonia repens* 'Rotundifolia'

Mahonia repens

Melianthus
honey flower

Melianthus major

- ☐ Height 2.4m (8ft)
- ☐ Spread 3m (10ft)
- ☐ Foliage shrub
- ☐ Any well-drained soil
- ☐ Sunny sheltered site

The honey flower (*Melianthus major*) is grown for its striking foliage – large grey-green leaves which are deeply divided, serrated along the edges, and have a pungent aroma. In spring, the young leaves are pale green and give the impression of being luminous. The deep maroon flower spikes are rarely produced in Britain.

The honey flower is only semi-hardy. It is suitable only for the mildest areas; the top growth is easily killed by frost though it often recovers from the base. As a foliage plant, it provides a stunning source of fresh grey-green foliage. It grows 2.4m (8ft) high and 3m (10ft) across.

Cultivation
Plant in mid spring, in well-drained soil in a sheltered sunny spot.

Pruning is not necessary.

Propagation Buy new stock, or try tip cuttings taken in summer and rooted in a propagator unit.

Pests and diseases Trouble free.

MEXICAN ORANGE BLOSSOM – see *Choisya*
MOUNTAIN LAUREL – see *Kalmia*
MOUNTAIN SPURGE – see *Pachysandra*

Myrtus
myrtle

Myrtus communis

- ☐ Height 90cm-3m (3-10ft)
- ☐ Spread 60cm-3m (2-10ft)
- ☐ Flowers in summer
- ☐ Ordinary well-drained soil
- ☐ Sunny sheltered position

Myrtle is an attractive, easily-grown shrub thriving in mild seaside gardens. The lance-shaped oval leaves are dark green and lustrous and give off a pleasant aromatic scent when bruised. In summer rounded buds open into white fragrant flowers with prominent stamens; they are often followed by purple-black berries.

Common myrtle (*Myrtus communis*) is half-hardy and suitable only for mild frost-free areas. It is best grown in the shelter of a sunny wall, where it seldom grows more than 3m (10ft) high before being cut back by frost. *Myrtus communis tarentina* ('Jenny Reitenbach') is a hardier more compact shrub, 90cm (3ft) high and 60cm (2ft) across with smaller, narrower leaves.

Cultivation
Plant in late spring in any well-drained soil against a sunny sheltered wall.

Remove straggly and frosted shoots from the base in spring.

Propagation Take 5-7.5cm (2-3in) heel cuttings of non-flowering side-shoots in summer and root in a propagator unit.

Pests and diseases Trouble free.

Nandina
Chinese sacred bamboo

Nandina domestica

- ☐ Height 1.2-1.8m (4-6ft)
- ☐ Spread 60-90cm (2-3ft)
- ☐ Flowers in mid summer
- ☐ Rich, moist but well-drained soil
- ☐ Sunny sheltered position

This semi-hardy shrub, with its erect stems, resembles bamboo in habit, but the leaves, which are pale to mid green, are tinted red and purple in spring and autumn. Clusters of white flowers appear in summer and may be followed by scarlet fruits which ripen in late summer and persist on the plant throughout the winter.

Chinese sacred bamboo (*Nandina domestica*) is suitable only for sunny sheltered gardens in the milder parts of Britain. In severe winters the tips of the shrub may be killed by frost, but the shrub usually recovers.

A dwarf variety with purplish leaves, 'Nana Purpurea', is also available.

Cultivation
Plant in spring in rich, moist but well-drained soil in a sunny and sheltered position. Thin out dead wood and weak shoots after flowering.

Propagation In early autumn, take 7.5-10cm (3-4in) heel cuttings of side-shoots and root in a cold frame. Transfer to a nursery bed the following late spring and grow on for two or three years before planting out in mid spring.

Pests and diseases Trouble free.

Olearia
daisy bush

Olearia x haastii

Olearia macrodonta

☐ Height 1.2-4.5m (4-15ft)
☐ Spread 1.2-4.5m (4-15ft)
☐ Flowers late spring to late summer
☐ Any well-drained soil
☐ Sunny sheltered position

Daisy bushes, native to Australasia, are popular hedging shrubs for seaside gardens. Although not all species in this large genus are fully hardy, they are easily grown shrubs, revelling in full sun and tolerant of salt sea spray and coastal wind. In inland gardens, they need a sheltered site.

Most olearias bear large clusters of daisy-like white flowers, at any time from late spring to late summer. The foliage, which in some species resembles spineless holly leaves, has white-felted undersides.

Popular species
Olearia avicenniifolia is generally hardy and a very good hedging shrub in mild coastal areas. It grows up to 4.5m (15ft) high and wide, bearing grey-green pointed leaves. The large clusters of sweetly scented flowers are borne in late summer.
Olearia x haastii is a hardy species tolerating pollution and is frequently grown in town gardens. Reaching 1.8-2.4m (6-8ft) high and 2.4-3m (8-10ft) across, it produces a mass of fragrant flowers from mid to late summer. The leaves are broadly oval and glossy mid green on the upper surfaces.
Olearia macrodonta is a 1.8-2.4m (6-8ft) high hardy shrub with sage-green, holly-like leaves. Tiny scented flowers are borne in large clusters in early to mid summer. 'Major' has larger leaves and flower clusters while 'Minor' is a dwarf form, smaller than the species in all its parts.
Olearia moschata is a slow-growing, usually hardy shrub of round habit, up to 2.4m (8ft) in height and 3m (10ft) across. It bears small grey-green, glossy leaves and, in high summer, clusters of white and yellow flowers. Foliage and flowers emit a musky scent.
Olearia x scilloniensis, a smaller species with a height and spread of 1.2-1.5m (4-5ft), flowers between late spring and early summer and is almost smothered with a profusion of brilliant white blooms. The narrow leaves are bright green.

Olearia semidentata, more correctly known as *O*. 'Henry Travers', is one of the loveliest of the olearias, but also the least hardy. In mild favoured seaside gardens, it can reach a height and spread of 2.4m (8ft). The lance-shaped leaves are grey-green. The flowers are solitary, pale purple in colour with deeper purple centres; they are borne in mid summer.

Cultivation
Plant in mid autumn or in early to mid spring; *O. semidentata* should be planted in late spring. The shrubs do well on any well-drained soil and thrive on chalk. The site should be sunny and sheltered, though in mild seaside areas the shrubs tolerate greater exposure. In mid spring cut any dead shoots back to healthy wood.
Propagation Take 10cm (4in) half-ripe cuttings of lateral shoots in late summer and root in a propagating frame. Pot the rooted cuttings up singly and overwinter under glass. Pot on and plant out a year later, in mid to late spring.
Pests and diseases Trouble free.

OREGON GRAPE – see *Mahonia*

Osmanthus

osmanthus

Osmanthus delavayi

Osmanthus delavayi

☐ Height 1.8-4.5m (6-15ft)
☐ Spread 1.8-4.5m (6-15ft)
☐ Flowers spring, autumn and winter
☐ Well-drained soil
☐ Sunny or partially shaded site

Osmanthus combines the best attributes of any garden-worthy shrub: handsome foliage and attractive fragrant flowers. The shrubs, which often resemble hollies (*Ilex*), do well in any kind of soil, and while a few species are too tender for the British climate, those described here are generally hardy.

These graceful shrubs, of slow growth and neat habit, can be grown as specimen shrubs or included in shrub and mixed borders. Some are also useful for hedging and screening.

Popular species

Osmanthus x *burkwoodii*, syn. x *Osmarea burkwoodii*, has a height and spread of 1.8-3m (6-10ft), and oval, glossy dark green leaves. The fragrant white flower clusters appear during mid and late spring.

Osmanthus decorus grows to a height and spread of 1.8-3m (6-10ft). It is a robust, dome-shaped shrub, with large leathery leaves, lance-shaped and glossy rich green, as much as 12.5 cm (5in) long on young plants. Clusters of white scented flowers are freely borne in spring, sometimes followed by purple-black berries.

Osmanthus delavayi reaches 1.8-2.4m (6-8ft) and has glossy dark green leaves which are oval in shape and toothed. A profusion of white, sweetly scented flowers are borne in mid spring. The variety 'Latifolius' is taller-growing with broader, more rounded leaves.

Osmanthus x *fortunei* is a vigorous shrub, 3m (10ft) or more in height and spread, with large holly-like leaves, spiny-toothed and shiny dark green with prominent veins. The fragrant white flower clusters are produced in autumn.

Osmanthus heterophyllus, syn. *O. aquifolium*, is a slow-growing species but eventually reaches a height and spread of 1.8-3m (6-10ft). It is often mistaken for a holly, from its dark, glossy green leaves; these vary considerably on the same plant, some being prickly,

Osmanthus heterophyllus 'Variegatus'

Pachysandra

mountain spurge

Pachysandra terminalis 'Variegata'

☐ Height 25-30cm (10-12in)
☐ Spread 60-90cm (2-3ft)
☐ Foliage shrub
☐ Fertile moist soil
☐ Shaded site

Mountain spurge is an excellent and hardy ground-cover shrub for shady or partially shaded sites, as it has a low spreading habit and evergreen foliage. Flowers do appear in mid spring but they are tiny and have no petals – only white, purple-tinted stamens.

Popular species
Pachysandra procumbens reaches 30cm (1ft) high and 90cm (3ft) across and has glossy semi-ever-green leaves. Dense flower spikes are borne in spring.
Pachysandra terminalis has smaller, narrower leaves than *P. procumbens* and is a lower-grow-ing species reaching 25cm (10in) high but spreading to 60cm (2ft). 'Variegata' has white-variegated leaves.

Cultivation
Plant during mild spells between mid autumn and early spring in any moist fertile soil. The plants thrive in a shady site, even deep shade. Pruning is not necessary.
Propagation Lift, divide and replant in early spring.
Pests and diseases Trouble free.

Osmanthus x burkwoodii

others only spine-tipped. Dense clusters of scented white flowers are borne in early and mid autumn. The species and its vari-eties are good for dense hedging. Several varieties include 'Aureo-marginatus' (deep yellow leaf margins); 'Gulftide' (lobed or twisted, strongly spiny foliage); 'Myrtifolius' (compact habit, small spineless leaves); 'Sasaba' (Japanese variety, leaves deeply divided into spiny lobes); and 'Variegatus' (leaves edged cream-white).
Osmanthus yunnanensis, syn. *O. forrestii*, is a vigorous shrub or small tree, 4.5m (15ft) high and wide. The handsome, dark olive-green, lance-shaped leaves are up to 15cm (6in) long, sometimes wavy and toothed, sometimes flat and entire, on the same plant. It is hardy if given shelter from cold

winds. Clusters of fragrant, cream-white flowers are borne in late winter and early spring.

Cultivation
Plant between mid autumn and early spring in ordinary well-drained garden soil in a sunny or partially shaded site sheltered from cold north or east winds.
Pruning is rarely necessary, but established hedges should be trimmed to shape in mid to late spring.
Propagation Take 10cm (4in) heel cuttings of half-ripe shoots in summer. Root in a propaga-ting frame at a temperature of 18°C (64°F).
Pests and diseases Trouble free.

Pachystegia
pachystegia

Pachystegia insignis

- ☐ Height 75-90cm (2½-3ft)
- ☐ Spread 1.8m (6ft)
- ☐ Flowers late summer
- ☐ Any well-drained soil
- ☐ Sunny sheltered site

Related to the daisy bushes (*Olearia*) and sometimes known as Marlborough rock daisy, the small *Pachystegia insignis* (syn. *Olearia insignis*) is a near-hardy dwarf but wide-spreading shrub, rarely more than 90cm (3ft) high. Pachystegia is particularly suitable for seaside gardens, being tolerant of salt spray, and its tough foliage withstands coastal gales. The leaves are oval, up to 15cm (6in) long, and dark green with white woolly undersides. In late summer, the shrub is studded with large white, daisy-like flowers with yellow centres; they are borne on stiff and erect, hairy stems.

The variety *P. insignis* var. *minor* is smaller and less woolly; it is suitable for a sunny rock garden.

Cultivation
Plant in mid autumn or mid spring in any well-drained soil and in a sunny and sheltered site. The shrub does well on chalky soils and thrives in mild maritime positions. Pruning is rarely necessary; any frost-damaged shoots should be cut back to healthy wood in mid spring.

Propagation Take 10cm (4in) half-ripe cuttings of non-flowering side-shoots in late summer and root in a cold frame.

Pests and diseases Trouble free.

PARTRIDGE BERRY – see *Gaultheria*

Passiflora
passion flower

Passiflora caerulea 'Constance Elliott'

- ☐ Height 6-9m (20-30ft)
- ☐ Flowers summer to early autumn
- ☐ Ordinary well-drained soil
- ☐ Sheltered sunny site

Passion flowers originate in South America, where they are grown commercially for their edible fruits. Most species are too tender to be grown outdoors in Britain, though a few will survive average winters in southern counties if given sun and shelter. They are sometimes damaged by frosts but usually shoot again from the base.

The passion flower takes its name, according to legend, from the shape of its dramatic blooms, usually borne singly on long stalks. Each bloom consists of a long tube which opens out into five petals and five sepals surrounding a centre, or corona, of thread-like filaments above which rise five prominent anthers and three stigmas. The corona is said to represent the crown of thorns, and the five petals and five sepals the Apostles, with Peter and Judas absent; the whole flower structure is likened to Christ's passion.

Climbing evergreen or semi-evergreen shrubs, passion flowers put on a magnificent display throughout summer and early autumn when fully established. The edible fruits are rarely produced in open gardens.

Popular species
Passiflora caerulea is one of the hardier species and, where suited, is a vigorous even rampant climber up to 9m (30ft) high. It bears light to mid green, five- or seven-lobed leaves and slightly fragrant flowers, up to 10cm (4in) across, white with a blue-purple corona. After long hot summers, orange-red ovoid fruits are sometimes produced. The variety 'Constance Elliott' is outstanding, with ivory-white flowers; it is hardier than the species.

Passiflora umbellicata is the hardiest species. It grows fast, up

Passiflora caerulea 'Constance Elliott'

Pernettya
pernettya

Pernettya mucronata 'Signal'

Passiflora caerulea

to 6m (20ft) high and bears dark green, tri-lobed leaves. The flowers, from mid summer to early autumn, are 7.5-10cm (3-4in) wide and purple-violet in colour. Round yellow fruits may sometimes occur.

Cultivation
Plant in late spring in any well-drained soil. Choose a sheltered site in full sun or light shade. Train the climbers up trellis or wire mesh attached to a wall; although they are self-clinging by tendrils, they should be tied in until they become self-supporting. For the first few winters after planting, protect the roots with straw, cloches or polythene sheeting. Climbers that have come through the winter unscathed can be pruned in early spring, overgrown shoots being thinned out at ground level or cut back to the main stems.
Propagation Take 7.5-10cm (3-4in) long stem sections in summer and root in a propagator.
Pests and diseases Trouble free.

☐ Height 60-90cm (2-3ft)
☐ Spread 60-90cm (2-3ft)
☐ Flowers late spring to early summer
☐ Moist, lime-free soil
☐ Sunny or shaded site

This Chilean shrub displays its beauty at two different times of year. First, in late spring and early summer, the wiry stems are whitened with tiny heather-like flowers. Then, through the autumn and winter, the shrubs are laden with bright marble-sized, glowing berries.

As a hardy low-growing shrub, *Pernettya mucronata* and its varieties make excellent ground-cover plants in gardens with acid soil.

Popular varieties
A male variety must be grown among the fruiting female varieties for colourful fruits to be produced. **'Alba'** has white fruits lightly tinged with pink.
'Bell's Seedling', a self-pollinating variety with dark carmine-red berries.
'Lilacina', reddish-lilac berries.
'Sea Shell' has delicately coloured shell-pink berries.
'Signal' has deep red berries.

Cultivation
Plant pernettyas between early autumn and early spring in moist

Pernettya mucronata 'Bell's Seedling'

lime-free soil. They will grow in a shaded site, though the shrubs will be more compact and will produce more berries in full sun.

Old plants tend to become leggy and can be cut hard back into the old wood in late winter or early spring to encourage new growth.
Propagation Take 5cm (2in) long cuttings in early to mid autumn and root in a cold frame.
Pests and diseases Trouble free.

PERIWINKLE – see *Vinca*

Phlomis
Jerusalem sage

Phlomis fruticosa

☐ Height 90cm-1.2m (3-4ft)
☐ Spread 60cm (2ft)
☐ Flowers early and mid summer
☐ Any well-drained soil
☐ Sunny position

Jerusalem sage (*Phlomis fruticosa*) is a low-growing Mediterranean shrub, hardy in all but the coldest areas. It is valued for its textured foliage – woolly grey-green, wedge-shaped leaves – and for its whorls of hooded, bright golden flowers which appear in early to mid summer.

Reaching 90cm-1.2m (3-4ft) high, it is ideally grown in association with other sun-loving shrubs and perennials to impart a Mediterranean feel to the garden. It also makes fine ground cover for large sunny banks.

In cold winters the shrub may die back, but new growth usually appears in spring.

Cultivation
Plant between mid autumn and mid spring in any well-drained fertile soil in a sunny sheltered site.

Pruning is unnecessary, but frost-damaged and untidy shoots can be trimmed back in spring.
Propagation Take heel cuttings in late summer to early autumn and root in a cold frame. Plant out in nursery rows in mid spring for a further year before transplanting to the permanent positions in mid spring.
Pests and diseases Trouble free.

Photinia
photinia

Photinia 'Red Robin'

☐ Height 1.5-3m (5-10ft)
☐ Spread 1.5-3m (5-10ft)
☐ Foliage shrub
☐ Any well-drained soil
☐ Sunny sheltered site

If you do not have the acid conditions needed for growing *Pieris*, *Photinia* x *fraseri* is an excellent substitute. In spring this near-hardy shrub becomes a mass of rich coppery-red as the young leaves unfurl. As summer arrives the leathery leaves mature to dark green.

Popular varieties
Two varieties of *Photinia* x *fraseri* are commonly grown.
'Red Robin' is the smaller variety, reaching 1.8m (6ft) high and 1.5m (5ft) across; it bears sharply toothed leaves and brilliant red young foliage.
'Robusta' is a vigorous shrub, 3m (10ft) high and the hardiest type.

Cultivation
Plant in any well-drained but moist soil between mid autumn and early spring. The site should be sheltered and sunny.

Prune in early summer to keep the shrubs tidy.
Propagation Take semi-ripe cuttings in summer and root in a propagating case. Alternatively, layer in spring and sever from the parent plant one year later.
Pests and diseases Trouble free.

Phyllodoce
phyllodoce

Phyllodoce x *intermedia*

☐ Height 15-25cm (6-10in)
☐ Spread 30-1.2m (1-4ft)
☐ Flowers mid spring to early summer
☐ Moist lime-free soil
☐ Cool shaded site

The species in this genus of hardy, heather-like sub-shrubs thrive in cool, moist and acid soil. They are essentially moorland shrubs and useful as ground cover for shady sites.

The narrow heath-like leaves are pale to dark green and arranged in whorls along the stems. Flowering is between mid and late spring, though some blooms may appear in autumn.

Popular species
Phyllodoce aleutica has green-yellow pitcher-shaped flowers. The plants reach 15-30cm (6-12in) high but spread 30cm (1ft) or more across.
Phyllodoce x *intermedia* grows 15-25cm (6-10in) high and up to 1.2m (4ft) across; it bears mauve-purple flowers.

Cultivation
Plant in spring or autumn in moist acid soil in a cool shaded site. Regular pruning is not necessary.
Propagation Take heel cuttings from young lateral growth between mid summer and autumn and root in a cold frame.
Pests and diseases Die-back can affect the plants and honey fungus may kill them.

Pieris

pieris, lily-of-the-valley bush

Pieris formosa 'Wakehurst'

Pieris formosa 'Forest Flame'

Pieris japonica 'Blush'

☐ Height 1.2-3.5m (4-12ft)
☐ Spread 1.2-4.5m (4-15ft)
☐ Flowers mid to late spring
☐ Moist lime-free soil
☐ Sheltered site in partial shade

These hardy handsome shrubs are favourites in gardens with acid soil, and are grown for their attractive foliage and lily-of-the-valley-like flowers. As soon as the spring flowers fade, new brightly coloured leaves unfurl to put on another eye-catching display. In winter, the narrow oval leaves provide a handsome mass of glossy, dark green foliage.

Popular species

Pieris floribunda, syn. *Andromeda floribunda*, is useful for small gardens as it grows only 1.2-1.8m (4-6ft) high and across. It has narrow, dark green, leathery foliage throughout the year, and dense erect spikes of white flowers in mid to late spring.

Pieris formosa is usually represented by varieties of the 'Forrestii' group. All grow 1.8-3.5m (6-12ft) high and have a spread of 3-4.5m (10-15ft). They have bril-

liant red young foliage and sprays of white flowers. Favourites include: 'Charles Michael' (bronze young leaves, large flower sprays); 'Forest Flame' (red young leaves fading to pink, then cream and finally green); and 'Wakehurst' (vivid red young leaves).

Pieris japonica, syn. *Andromeda japonica*, and its varieties bear an abundance of drooping waxy white flowers in spring. They also have attractive young leaves which are copper-red at first and then turn light green. The shrubs have a height and spread of 1.8-3m (6-10ft). Popular varieties include: 'Blush' (rose-coloured buds opening to pale pink flowers); 'Christmas Cheer' (early, deep pink buds opening to rose-coloured flowers); 'Purity' (compact; pure white flowers); and 'Variegata' (white flowers, narrow cream-edged leaves tinted pink).

Cultivation

Plant in autumn or spring in moist lime-free loam in a sheltered, partially shaded site.

In mid spring top-dress the shrubs with leaf-mould or coir; do

not allow the soil to dry out during the summer months.

After flowering, remove faded flower heads and lightly cut back any straggly shoots.

Propagation In late summer take 7.5-10cm (3-4in) cuttings of half-ripe shoots and root in a cold frame. In spring transfer to pots of lime-free compost and grow on for two or three years before planting out.

Pests and diseases Trouble free.

PINE – see *Pinus*

Pieris japonica 'Purity'

Pinus

pine

□ Height 20cm-2m (8in-7ft)
□ Spread 25cm-1.5m (10in-5ft)
□ Coniferous shrubs
□ Well-drained soil
□ Open sunny position

Pinus is a large genus of hardy coniferous trees and shrubs, native to most forested areas in the Northern Hemisphere. They range from tall-growing forest trees and shelter-belts in exposed coastal positions to ornamental garden trees (see pages 43-45) and compact shrubby conifers suitable for rock gardens and specimen planting.

Pines are distinguished by their needle-like leaves which range in colour from blue to green to golden-yellow, depending on variety. The woody cones are broad and squat or long and tapering.

The shrubby and compact pines described here thrive in full sun; they dislike town and industrial pollution.

Popular species and varieties

Pinus densiflora 'Umbraculifera' grows slowly into a domed shrub

Pinus leucodermis 'Compact Gem'

Pinus pumila 'Globe'

90cm (3ft) high and across with an umbrella-like head of branches. It bears a profusion of tiny cones.

Pinus leucodermis, the lime and drought-tolerant Bosnian pine, has several shrubby varieties: 'Compact Gem' is a rounded variety eventually to 2m (7ft) high and 1.5m (5ft) across. Its foliage is dark green. 'Schmidtii' (syn. 'Pygmy') is a dense globular or pyramid-shaped dwarf pine, 25cm (10in) high and across, with bright green leaves.

Pinus mugo, mountain pine, is parent to a number of ultra-hardy, dense and shrubby varieties, all of which are tolerant of lime-rich soils. 'Gnom' grows into a dense, globular, dark green mound 50cm (20in) high and 75cm (2½ft) across. 'Humpy' is an extremely compact round conifer 38cm (15in) high and 50cm (20in) across. Its winter buds are red-brown. 'Mops' is a dense, globular variety reaching 38cm (15in) high and 50cm (20in) across. 'Ophir' is grown for its spectacular foliage – dark green, gold-tipped needles which

become entirely gold in winter; it is a compact rounded pine 45cm (1½ft) high and 60cm (2ft) across. *Pinus nigra* 'Hornibrookiana', reaching 45cm (1½ft) high and 90cm (3ft) across, has a broad spreading habit. The needles are a rich dark green colour. It is extremely slow-growing and thrives on chalky soils.

Pinus parviflora and its varieties are distinguished by their conical habit and light blue-green needles. Popular shrubby types include 'Adcock's Dwarf', a compact pine with a height of 1.5m (5ft) and a spread of 75cm (2½ft); the grey-green foliage is borne in bunches at the tips of the shoots. *Pinus pumila*, the dwarf Siberian pine, is the parent of two popular varieties. They are ultra-hardy and often included in heather and large rock gardens. 'Dwarf Blue'

Pinus mugo 'Mops'

Pinus sylvestris 'Aurea'

bears bluish needles banded with white. It reaches 60cm (2ft) high and spreads to 1.2m (4ft). 'Globe' is rounded, 75cm (2½ft) high and wide, and has blue-grey foliage.

Pinus strobus 'Nana' is a small bushy pine 75cm (2½ft) high and 90cm (3ft) across with dense blue-green leaves.

Pinus sylvestris, the familiar Scots pine, has given rise to several popular dwarf varieties. They include: 'Aurea' (a slow-growing pine, 1.8m/6ft high and 90cm/3ft across, but eventually developing into a small tree; it has striking golden winter foliage); 'Beuvronensis' (a broad domed or flat-topped shrub 75cm (2½ft) high and 90cm (3ft) across with grey-green foliage); 'Doone Valley' (an irregularly conical-shaped, compact pine reaching 1.2m (4ft) high and 90cm (3ft) across with grey-green leaves); and 'Windsor' (slow-growing dwarf pine, bun-shaped and with grey-green foliage).

Cultivation

Plant in late autumn or early spring in well-drained soil, acid, neutral or alkaline. While some species succeed on poor soils none can tolerate shallow ground. The site should be open and in full light.

Pruning is not recommended.

Propagation Named varieties can only be increased by grafting techniques best left to professionals.

Pests and diseases Canker and die-back can affect injured or weak trees. Honey fungus may kill pines and rust can occur.

Pittosporum

pittosporum

Pittosporum tenuifolium 'Purpureum'

□ Height 3-4.5m (10-15ft)
□ Spread 1.5-2.1m (5-7ft)
□ Foliage shrub
□ Well-drained fertile soil
□ Sunny sheltered site

These shrubs from Australia and New Zealand are half-hardy in Britain. They are suitable only for mild locations but thrive in frost-free coastal areas and stand up well to sea spray.

Pittosporums are chiefly grown for their attractive foliage which comes in a range of variegations and colours and is popular with flower arrangers. The dense, small-leaved shrubs respond well to clipping, and make excellent hedges. Insignificant bell-shaped flowers appear in spring.

Popular species

Pittosporum crassifolium has oval leathery leaves that are dark green above and brown or off-white and felted below. Reaching 3-4.5m (10-15ft) high and 1.8m (6ft) across, it bears maroon flowers in mid to late spring. In mild coastal areas it makes an excellent dense hedge. 'Variegata' has grey-green leaves edged white.

Pittosporum tenuifolium can reach 4.5m (15ft) high, with a spread of 1.5-2.1m (5-7ft). It is popular for hedging and for cut greenery. The pale green oval leaves have attractively waved edges carried on almost black stems. Chocolate-purple flowers with a strong vanilla-like fragrance appear in late spring. Popular varieties include: 'Garnettii' (green leaves edged white, often tinged pink); 'Irene Paterson' (cream young leaves becoming

Pittosporum tenuifolium 'Warnham Gold'

Prunus
laurel

Pittosporum tenuifolium 'Garnettii'

green mottled with white – and pink in winter); 'Purpureum' (reddish-purple leaves); 'Silver Queen' (grey-green leaves edged white); and 'Warnham Gold' (young green leaves mature to golden-yellow).

Cultivation
Plant container-grown plants in mid to late spring in well-drained fertile soil in a position sheltered from north and east winds. For hedging, set plants 45cm (1½ft) apart. Tip the leading shoots twice in the first growing season. When a hedge has reached the desired size, clip to shape every year in mid spring and mid summer.

Pittosporums grown as specimen shrubs should have straggly shoots trimmed to shape in spring.
Propagation In mid summer take 7.5-10cm (3-4in) heel cuttings of half-ripe lateral shoots and root in a propagating unit. Pot up the rooted cuttings and overwinter in a frost-free greenhouse. Plant out the following late spring.
Pests and diseases Trouble free.

PORTUGAL LAUREL – see *Prunus*
POTATO VINE – see *Solanum*
PRIVET – see *Ligustrum*

Prunus laurocerasus 'Otto Luyken'

- ☐ Height 1.2-6m (4-20ft)
- ☐ Spread 1.8-9m (6-30ft)
- ☐ Foliage and flowering shrub
- ☐ Deep well-drained soil
- ☐ Sun or shade

The evergreen laurels are easily grown hardy shrubs, invaluable for screening and tall hedging, and tolerant of shade and overhead drips from trees. Although chiefly grown for their attractive glossy foliage, laurels also make fine specimen shrubs bearing clusters of cream-white flowers in spring.

Popular species
Prunus laurocerasus, cherry laurel, is a vigorous shrub reaching 4.5-6m (15-20ft) high and 6-9m (20-30ft) across. The leathery leaves are shiny mid green above and pale green beneath. Arching spikes of white flowers appear in mid spring followed by small black fruits. Popular varieties include: 'Magnoliifolia' (6m/20ft high and wide, with particularly large leaves); 'Marbled White' (syn. 'Variegata', slow-growing, grey-green leaves heavily marbled

with white); and 'Otto Luyken' (narrow-leaved, 1.2m/4ft high and 1.8m/6ft across).
Prunus lusitanica, Portugal laurel, is the hardiest species. It grows 4.5-6m (15-20ft) high and wide and bears dark green, glistening foliage. Sprays of cream-white scented flowers are borne in early summer, followed by small red fruits. 'Variegata' is slow-growing with white edged leaves.

Cultivation
Plant in autumn in any well-drained soil and in shade or sun. Unlike *P. laurocerasus*, the hardier *P. lusitanica* thrives on shallow chalky soils. For hedging, set young plants 60-90cm (2-3ft) apart; after planting, cut them back by one-third to promote bushy growth.

Prune large unsightly laurels hard back into old wood in spring. Trim hedges in spring or summer.
Propagation Take 7.5-10cm (3-4in) long heel cuttings in late summer or early autumn and root in a cold frame.
Pests and diseases Leaf spot and powdery mildew may occur.

Prunus lusitanica 'Variegata'   *Prunus laurocerasus*, fruit   *Prunus laurocerasus* 'Marbled White'

Prunus lusitanica, flowers

Pyracantha

firethorn

Pyracantha 'Orange Glow'

- ☐ Height 2.4-4.5m (8-15ft)
- ☐ Spread 1.8-4.5m (6-15ft)
- ☐ Flowers early to mid summer
- ☐ Any fertile, well-drained soil
- ☐ Sunny or partially shaded site

Many shrubs grown for their berries are struck down in their moment of glory. Either the birds devour the fruit or they are damaged by frost. *Pyracantha* – or firethorns as these hardy shrubs are commonly called – are less subject to such ravages. Their masses of orange, red or yellow berries decorate the thorny branches in heavy swags from autumn through winter.

The leaves are attractive too, being glossy and a particularly fresh bright green on the young shoots. In mid summer, white hawthorn-like flowers cluster thickly on the stems.

Firethorns are usually grown as wall shrubs or hedging plants, but when they are pruned to shape they will not bear many berries. Alternatively they can be treated as specimen shrubs and left unpruned to grow into large broad shrubs. They are tolerant of exposure and pollution.

Popular species and hybrids

Pyracantha angustifolia bears rounded clusters of cream flowers in early to mid summer, followed by bright orange-yellow berries which usually persist all winter. It reaches 3m (10ft) high and 1.8-2.4m (6-8ft) across and has narrow leaves which are dark and glossy above but grey and hairy beneath. *Pyracantha atalantioides* is an

Pyracantha rogersiana

upright fast-growing shrub, height and spread 3-4.5m (10-15ft), with large, glossy deep green leaves. Flat clusters of white flowers appear in early summer, followed by crimson berries in autumn. 'Aurea' (syn. 'Flava') is a yellow-berried variety.

Pyracantha coccinea reaches 3-4.5m (10-15ft) high and across and has narrow, pointed mid green leaves. Its wide clusters of white flowers appear in early summer and are followed by dense clusters of rich red berries.

Pyracantha 'Fiery Cascade' grows to a height and spread of 3m (10ft). It is of upright habit, small-leaved and with a profusion of small, orange-red berries.

Pyracantha 'Golden Charmer' is a vigorous shrub, up to 4.5m (15ft) high and across, with arching branches bearing bright green, finely toothed leaves. The orange-yellow berries are exceptionally large and borne in great profusion.

Pyracantha 'Mohave' grows up to 3m (10ft) high and across. It is outstanding for its mass of bright red berries, but is unfortunately prone to scab.

Pyracantha 'Navaho' is smaller than most firethorns, rarely more than 1.5m (5ft) high, but wide-spreading. The berries appear late in the season; they are small but borne in heavy clusters, orange or orange-red in colour.

Pyracantha 'Orange Glow' is dense and vigorous, 3m (10ft) or more high and wide. In autumn, its branches are weighed down with bright orange, persistent berries.

Pyracantha rogersiana, syn. *P. crenulata rogersiana*, reaches 2.4-3m (8-10ft) high and 3.5-4.5m (12-15ft) across. It has small mid green leaves and an abundance of white flower clusters followed by bright orange-red berries. The variety 'Flava' bears yellow berries.

Pyracantha 'Soleil d'Or' grows up to 3m (10ft) high and wide. It is of upright habit, with reddish stems and glossy dark green foliage. Large clusters of golden berries persist through autumn and winter.

Cultivation

Plant container-grown specimens between mid autumn and early spring in fertile well-drained garden soil, including chalky soil.

Pyracantha 'Mohave'

Rhamnus
buckthorn

Pyracantha rogersiana 'Flava'

Firethorns thrive in either full sun or partial shade.

Set hedging plants 38-60cm (15-24in) apart and cut the current season's growth back by half. Pinch out the growing tips of young shoots when they reach 15-20cm (6-8in), and repeat in late summer to induce bushy growth from low down. Clip established hedges to shape between late spring and mid summer.

Provide trellis or wire support for wall-grown pyracanthas; they do well on north and east-facing walls. Tie in vigorous growth each year between mid summer and early autumn. Prune out unwanted shoots between late spring and mid summer.

Pruning is not necessary on free-standing shrubs.

Propagation Take 7.5-10cm (3-4in) cuttings of the current year's shoots in mid to late summer and root in a propagator unit.

Pests and diseases Scale insects and aphids may infest stems; fireblight and scab are the most common problems.

Rhamnus alaternus 'Argenteovariegata'

☐ Height 0.3-3m (1-10ft)
☐ Spread 2.4m (8ft)
☐ Foliage shrub
☐ Any well-drained soil
☐ Sunny site

This large genus of trees and shrubs include a few evergreen types grown primarily for their attractive foliage and fruits. They are easy to cultivate in well-drained soils and tolerate salt sprays and industrial pollution, making them a popular choice for sunny coastal or town gardens.

Popular species
Rhamnus alaternus, a moderately hardy shrub, grows rapidly to reach a height of 3m (10ft) and a spread of 2.4m (8ft). The stiff branches are covered with small lance-shaped, shiny green leaves. Clusters of yellow-green flowers in mid spring are followed by red berries that ripen to black. In mild gardens, fruiting is often prolific. The variety 'Argenteovariegata' has leaves irregularly edged with cream.

Rhamnus procumbens is a mound-forming creeping species suitable for a rock garden. It bears tiny, glossy green leaves and black berries.

Cultivation
Plant in autumn or spring in any well-drained soil in a sunny or lightly shaded position.

Regular pruning is not necessary though dead or frost-damaged shoots should be removed in early spring.

Propagation Increase by layering in spring. Separate from the parent plant one to two years later. *R. procumbens* roots where it touches the ground.

Pests and diseases Trouble free.

Rhododendron

rhododendron

Rhododendron 'Furnivall's Daughter'

☐ Height 30cm-15m (1-50ft)
☐ Spread 30cm-12m (1-40ft)
☐ Flowers mid winter to early summer
☐ Moist, rich acid soil
☐ Lightly shaded site

For many people the word rhododendron conjures up one enduring image – the large purple-flowered shrub that dominates the early summer scene wherever acid soil exists. But purple is only one shade of the huge kaleidoscope portrayed by the rhododendron genus. The thousands of species, hybrids and varieties vary enormously, in size, colour, performance and hardiness. They include deciduous and evergreen types, true rhododendrons, azaleas and azaleodendrons – hybrids between azaleas and rhododendrons.

There is a vast range of flower colours (white, cream, yellow, orange, pink, scarlet, crimson, purple, violet and lavender) and of flower shapes, textures and scents. Flowering is by no means limited to late spring and early summer. *R. lutescens*, for instance, blooms in mid winter.

The beauty of rhododendrons is not restricted to their flowers. The leaves of many species are another asset, with sizes varying widely. They may be little larger than those of heathers or as huge as those of *R. sinogrande*, which can grow nearly 75cm (2½ft) long.

The rhododendrons described here are hardy evergreen shrubs; by nature they are woodland plants, and though they will grow in a sunny position they give off their best in dappled shade.

Popular species

Rhododendron aberconwayi bears loose clusters of saucer-shaped flowers which are whitish-pink spotted with maroon. They open in late spring against a backdrop of brittle, leathery leaves. It grows into a 2m (7ft) high shrub with a spread of 1.5m (5ft).

Rhododendron arboreum has compact clusters of deep red, pink or white bell-shaped blooms in late winter and early spring. The dark green shiny leaves have silver or brown-felted undersides. It grows 6-12m (20-40ft) high and across and, being moderately hardy, is suitable for mild gardens only.

Rhododendron yakusimanum

Rhododendron augustinii bears clusters of trumpet-shaped flowers in mid and late spring. They range in colour from mauve to dark blue, and the throats are spotted with green. The pointed dark green leaves are scaly beneath. Reaching 1.8-3m (6-10ft) high and 1.5-1.8m (5-6ft) across, the shrub is fairly fast-growing with an upright habit.

Rhododendron lutescens

Rhododendron campylogynum, an ultra-hardy dwarf species reaching only 45cm (1½ft) high and wide, bears bell-shaped flowers in varying shades of purple. They appear in late spring and early summer. The small dark green leaves turn bronze in winter.

Rhododendron ciliatum has clusters of red flower buds which open into pink bell-shaped blooms in mid spring. Given a site sheltered from spring frost, the flowers appear in abundance. The dull green leaves are bristly. This species is of spreading habit, growing 1.2-1.5m (4-5ft) high and 1.8-2.4m (6-8ft) across.

Rhododendron cinnabarinum is distinguished by its large clusters of waxy, tubular orange-red blooms. They open in late spring and early summer against grey-green leaves. It reaches 1.8-3m (6-10ft) high and 1.2-1.8m (4-6ft) across.

Rhododendron decorum has fragrant funnel-shaped flowers, pale pink or white with green centres, opening in mid to late spring. The smooth leaves are grey-green above and smoky blue beneath. The shrub grows 1.8-3m (6-10ft) high and wide.

Rhododendron haematodes is a low-growing shrub of dense habit (90cm-1.2m/3-4ft high and 1.8m/6ft across). Its clusters of brilliant red funnel-shaped flowers appear in late spring among the leathery mid-green leaves whose undersides are covered in orange-brown felt.

Rhododendron hippophaeoides is one of the hardiest of the early-flowering species and will grow in the coldest gardens. The early to mid spring blooms – in shades of mauve and pink – are funnel-

Rhododendron rubiginosum

Rhododendron racemosum

153

Rhododendron yunnanense

shaped. The shrub throws up suckers and grows 1.2-1.5m (4-5ft) high and wide. The leaves are grey-green and scaly.

Rhododendron lutescens is a variable 3m (10ft) high species with a spread of 1.5-2m (5-7ft), best grown in woodland shelter. An abundance of wide funnel-shaped yellow flowers are carried singly or in pairs from mid winter to mid spring. The lance-shaped leaves are glossy bronze to dull green.

Rhododendron macabeanum reaches tree-like proportions – 7.5m (25ft) high with a spread of 3-4.5m (10-15ft). It has yellow bell-shaped flowers marked purple at the base of the petals, borne in compact clusters in mid spring. The dark green leaves, up to 30cm (1ft) long, are silvery-white and hairy on the undersides.

Rhododendron moupinense has tubular white or pink flowers speckled with red in late winter and early spring. It is a dwarf shrub, 60cm-1.5m (2-5ft) high and 90cm-1.2m (3-4ft) across. The leaves are mid green and glossy.

Rhododendron neriiflorum bears large clusters of rich scarlet-red flowers in early to mid spring. It has a height and spread of 1.2-2.4m (4-8ft). The undersides of the leaves are grey-white.

Rhododendron pseudochrysanthum, a slow-growing, compact species reaching 2.4m (8ft) high and 1.8m (6ft) across, has bell-shaped pink flowers. The young leaves and shoots are grey-white and covered with fine hairs.

Rhododendron racemosum is a free-flowering species reaching 30cm-1.8m (1-6ft) high and 90cm-1.5m (3-5ft) across. It has funnel-shaped flowers in shades of pink between early and late spring, and grey-green leaves.

Rhododendron rubiginosum is one of the few rhododendrons to tolerate limy soils. Its funnel-shaped lilac-pink blooms appear between early and mid spring among dull green leaves that are scaly and rust-coloured beneath. It grows to a height of 1.8-3m (6-10ft) and a spread of 1.2-2.4m (4-8ft).

Rhododendron scintillans, a dwarf species 60-90cm (2-3ft) high and 60cm-1.2m (2-4ft) across, bears funnel-shaped violet-blue flowers in mid spring. The leathery leaves are mid green above and grey on the undersides.

Rhododendron sinogrande is of tree-like proportions, reaching 9-15m (30-50ft) high and 4.5-6m (15-20ft) across. The magnificent leaves, glossy dark green above and silvery beneath, are up to 75cm

(2½ft) long and 30cm (1ft) wide. The cream to canary-yellow bell-shaped flowers appear in enormous clusters in mid spring. This species is only suitable for woodland conditions in mild southern gardens.

Rhododendron sutchuenense, with a height and spread of up to 3.5m (12ft), has rose-lilac bell-shaped blooms speckled with purple. They appear in early spring. The leaves are grey-green.

Rhododendron thomsonii bears clusters of blood-red flowers with a waxy texture in mid to late spring. It reaches 2.4m (8ft) high, with a spread of 1.8m (6ft) and is clothed with shiny dark green leaves.

Rhododendron yakusimanum has pink buds which open into white bell-shaped flowers in late spring and early summer. A dwarf species reaching only 60cm (2ft) high and 60-90cm (2-3ft) across, it has dark green leathery leaves which are felted and fawn-coloured beneath.

Rhododendron yunnanense bears an abundance of white or pale pink flowers in late spring and early summer. This compact shrub reaches 3-3.5m (10-12ft) high and across and may be semi-deciduous after a cold winter. The brittle, dark green leaves are hairy on top.

Rhododendron 'Purple Splendour'

Rhododendron pseudochrysanthum

Rhododendron 'Bluebird'

Rhododendron 'Praecox'

Rhododendron sutchuenense

Popular hybrids

A large number of hybrid rhododendrons have been developed. Most are free-flowering in late spring and early summer. The blooms are generally funnel-shaped and borne in large clusters while the leaves are glossy and dark green. The hybrids are generally hardier than the species, tolerating cold and exposure; they are ideal for large-scale planting, and taller types are much used for screening.

'**Anna Rose Whitney**' is a vigorous shrub up to 3m (10ft) high and 2.4m (8ft) or more across. It bears dense clusters of deep rose-pink flowers spotted with brown.

'**Betty Wormald**' has crimson-red buds opening to rose-pink wavy-edged blooms with inner red-black speckles. Maximum height is 3-4.5m (10-15ft) and spread is 2.4-3.5m (8-12ft).

'**Bluebird**' is a small neat shrub with rich violet-blue blooms in mid spring. It reaches 90cm-1.5m (3-5ft) high and 90cm-1.2m (3-4ft) across.

'**Blue Diamond**' bears tight clusters of small rich violet-blue flowers. A slow-growing shrub, it grows 90cm (3ft) high and across.

'**Blue Peter**' has an abundance of cobalt-violet, frilled blooms. It reaches 1.5-3m (5-10ft) high and 1.2-2.4m (4-8ft) across.

'**Blue Tit**' bears lavender-blue flowers in mid spring. It is a compact shrub 90cm (3ft) or more high and the same across.

'**Chikor**' has pale yellow flowers and at only 30-60cm (1-2ft) high and across is ideal for a rock garden.

'**Chink**' is an early spring-flowering hybrid with pale yellow-green blooms. It is 90cm-1.5m (3-5ft) high and 90cm-1.2m (3-4ft) across.

'**Corona**' has coral-pink blooms and grows slowly to 1.5-3m (5-10ft) high and 1.2-2.4m (4-8ft) across.

'**Crest**' (syn. 'Hawk Crest') bears primrose-yellow flowers above exceptionally large leaves. It has a height of 1.5-3m (5-10ft) and a spread of 1.2-2.4m (4-8ft).

'**Elizabeth**' is a spreading shrub with large scarlet-red trumpet-shaped flowers. It grows 90cm-1.5m (3-5ft) high and 90cm-1.2m (3-4ft) across.

'**Exbury Naomi**' has lilac-pink flowers tinged with yellow; it grows 4.5-6m (15-20ft) high and 3.5-5m (12-17ft) across.

'**Fastuosum Flore Pleno**' bears double mauve flowers and is exceptionally hardy, reaching 4.5-6m (15-20ft) high and a little less across.

'**Furnivall's Daughter**' has light pink flowers blotched with crimson. A vigorous hybrid, it grows 3-4.5m (10-15ft) high and about 2.4-3.5m (8-12ft) across.

'**Gomer Waterer**' bears white flowers flushed with pale mauve and reaches 3-4.5m (10-15ft) high and 2.4-3.5m (8-12ft) across.

'**Grumpy**' has cream flowers flushed with pink and spotted with orange-yellow. It is dwarf, only 60-90cm (2-3ft) high and wide.

'**Lady Clementine Mitford**', with peach-pink flowers in early and mid summer, reaches 3-4.5m (10-15ft) high and 2.4-3.5m (8-12ft) across.

'**Loderi King George**' has soft pink buds which open to pure white flowers. It is 4.5-6m (15-20ft) high and 3.5-5m (12-17ft) across.

'**Mrs Charles E. Pearson**' has pink-mauve flowers spotted brown. Average height is 3-4.5m (10-15ft) and spread is 2.4-3.5m (8-12ft) across.

'**Pink Pearl**' bears rose-pink flowers which fade to white. It is one of the taller and most popular hybrids, reaching 4.5-6m (15-20ft) high and 3.5-5m (12-17ft) across.

'**Praecox**', an early-flowering variety with rose-purple blooms, is 90cm-1.5m (3-5ft) high and has a spread of 90cm-1.2m (3-4ft).

Rhododendron 'Anna Rose Whitney'

Rhododendron sinogrande

Rhododendron 'Elizabeth'

'Purple Splendour' has royal purple flowers with black markings. It grows 1.5-3m (5-10ft) high and has a spread of 1.2-2.4m (4-8ft).

'Sapphire', a dwarf hybrid, bears pale lavender-blue flowers in mid spring. It grows 60cm (2ft) high and 1.2m (4ft) across.

Cultivation
Rhododendrons will not grow in alkaline or chalky soil. The ideal is a well-drained but moist acid loam – light soils can be enriched, and heavy soils can be lightened with peat substitute or leaf-mould. The site should be lightly shaded and sheltered from cold drying winds.

Plant in autumn or spring, choosing a site where spring-flowering types are protected from early-morning sun.

Every spring feed the plants with a specially formulated rhododendron fertilizer. Pruning is unnecessary, but shrubs should be dead-headed after flowering.

Propagation Layer large-leaved species rhododendrons at any time of year. Sever after two years. Increase small-leaved species and hardy hybrids by semi-ripe cuttings in summer.

Pest and diseases Rhododendron bugs, weevils and caterpillars are the pests to watch out for. Honey fungus may kill the shrubs and rust and silver leaf can cause problems.

Rhododendron 'Chink'

Rhododendron (azalea)

azalea

Rhododendron 'Hatsugiri' (Kurume)

☐ Height 15cm-3m (6in-10ft)
☐ Spread 30cm-3m (1-10ft)
☐ Flowers mid spring to early summer
☐ Moist rich, acid soil
☐ Sheltered partially shaded site

The evergreen azaleas are among the most stunning of spring-flowering shrubs. They are also of moderate size and more suitable for small gardens than the related large-leaved rhododendrons. Dwarf types are ideal for rock gardens and raised beds. Botanically, azaleas belong in the vast *Rhododendron* genus, but they are popularly regarded as a separate group although they share the same growing needs of acid soil and light shade.

Azaleas, like other rhododendrons, thrive in woodland conditions; because of their modest size they are best planted as edgings to clearings, at the front of lightly shaded shrub borders or along streamside banks.

Azaleas are either deciduous or evergreen, the latter sometimes known as Japanese azaleas because the hybrid types were first bred there. The hardy evergreen azaleas described here are generally low-growing and of a spreading habit. Their funnel-shaped or flat flowers are borne in small clusters at the tips of the shoots. Colours are predominantly pink, red and mauve, though they also include white and varying shades of cream, yellow and orange. The small green leaves sometimes colour in autumn.

Popular species and varieties

Rhododendron indicum (syn. *Azalea indica*) is a small dense shrub, 90cm-1.8m (3-6ft) high and 90cm-1.2m (3-4ft) across. The lance-shaped, glossy dark green leaves, and the shoots, are bristly; the foliage often turns crimson and purple in autumn. Wide funnel-shaped flowers, pink or bright red, are borne singly or in pairs in early summer.

The species is variable in performance, but several more reliable varieties are available and include 'Balsaminiflorum' (dwarf, with double salmon-pink flowers); 'Coccineum' (large scarlet-red flowers in mid summer); 'Hakata Shiro' (large ivory-white flowers in late spring, moderately hardy); 'Salmonea' (low-growing, large salmon-red flowers); and 'Zangetsu' (white-throated, pale crimson flowers).

Rhododendron kaempferi has orange, salmon-pink or brick-red blooms with darker speckles in late spring. Reaching 1.5m (5ft) high and across, it is almost deciduous as only a few of the small dark green leaves persist through the winter. Outstanding varieties include 'Highlight' (bright salmon-orange flowers); and 'Mikado' (syn. 'Daimio', late-flowering, apricot-salmon flowers). The species is very hardy and free-flowering and one of the parents of Kurume and other hybrid azaleas.

Rhododendron 'Betty' (Kaempferi)

Rhododendron kiusianum, syn. *R. obtusum japonicum*, is sometimes semi-evergreen or even deciduous. It grows to a height of 90cm (3ft), with a spread of 1.5m (5ft). The small oval leaves are dark glossy green. Clusters of funnel-shaped flowers are borne in late spring and early summer; they are usually purple though sometimes in shades of pink or crimson. The Kurume azaleas were bred in part from this species.

Rhododendron nakaharae is a near-prostrate, creeping species, only 15cm (6in) high, but 30cm (1ft) or more across. The densely hairy shoots are clothed with small, dark green leaves, pale green on the undersides. Clusters of two or three funnel- or bell-shaped flowers are borne in mid summer; they are bright red in colour.

Rhododendron obtusum, from Japan, is sometimes known as Kirishima azalea. It is a small shrub, rarely more than 90cm (3ft) high and as much or more across. The hairy branches are set with small glossy green leaves and almost hidden by an abundance of flower clusters in late spring; they are scarlet-crimson. The variety 'Amoenum' bears brilliant magenta or rose-purple hose-in-hose flowers.

Rhododendron simsii is a half-hardy species and suitable only for greenhouse cultivation. The 'Indian azaleas', sold as pot plants at Christmas, are derived from this species and *R. indicum*. They flower indoors during winter in a range of colours and can be moved outdoors to a shaded spot for the summer months.

Azalea hybrids

A vast number of evergreen azalea hybrids has been raised in Europe, the United States and

Rhododendron 'Kirin' (Kurume)

Rhododendron 'Ivette' (Kaempferi)

Rhododendron 'Palestrina' (Vuykiana)

Japan. They are arranged in groups according to main parentage and flower size. Those described here are hardy, with an average height of 60-120cm (2-4ft) and a spread of 90-180cm (3-6ft).

Glen Dale hybrids are free-flowering shrubs and though hardy not recommended for cold districts. The individual flowers are up to 10cm (4in) wide. Popular types include 'Buccaneer' (vivid orange-red); 'Chanticleer' (brilliant purple); 'Gaity' (purple-pink); 'Niagara' (white, frilly-edged and yellow-blotched); and 'Violetta' (purple-pink).

Kaempferi hybrids are very hardy and free-flowering, with blooms up to 5cm (2in) wide. Some types have one flower set within another (hose-in-hose). Mainly raised in Holland, they include 'Betty' (bright salmon-pink); 'Blue Danube' (violet-blue); 'Christina' (red, hose-in-hose); 'Ivette' (brilliant carmine-pink); 'John Cairns' (dark orange-red); 'Naomi' (salmon-pink, late); 'Orange Beauty' (salmon-orange); and Royal Pink (purple).

Kurume hybrids originated in Japan in the 19th century. The largest of the hybrid groups, the shrubs are hardy in sheltered sites, low-growing and floriferous, the small flowers rarely more than 2.5cm (1in) across. Popular varieties include 'Addy Wery' (deep orange-scarlet); 'Azuma Kagami' (bright cyclamen-pink, hose-in-hose); 'Beni Giri' (crimson); 'Hatsugiri' (vivid crimson-purple); 'Hino Crimson' (crimson-scarlet); 'Hinode Giri' (bright crimson); 'Hinomayo' (clear pink); 'Iroha Yama' (white edged lavender); 'Kirin' (silver-pink, hose-in-hose); 'Rosebud' (rose-pink, hose-in-hose); and 'Surprise' (pale orange-red).

Vuykiana hybrids, from Holland, are fully hardy, with large flowers up to 7.5cm (3in) wide. They include 'Beethoven' (orchid-purple, fringed); 'Florida' (dark

Rhododendron 'Hinode Giri' (Kurume)

red, hose-in-hose); 'Königin Wilhelmina' (dwarf, vermilion-red); 'Palestrina' (white, faint green stripes); 'Purple Triumph' (deep purple); and 'Vuyk's Rosyred' (deep rose-red, dark markings).

Cultivation
Azaleas have the same cultural needs as other rhododendrons – moist acid soil rich in organic matter. They need shelter from cold winds, and while they will tolerate full sun if the roots can be kept moist, azaleas do better in light shade, especially as the flowers tend to fade in hot sun.

Plant in autumn or early spring; mulch annually with a peat substitute or leaf-mould to keep the shallow-growing roots cool and moist; a yearly application in spring of an acid-based fertilizer is beneficial for established shrubs. Pruning is unnecessary, but faded flowers should be dead-headed; snap them off by hand, taking care not to damage the new small buds at the base.

Propagation Take 5-7.5cm (2-3in) cuttings from non-flowering side-shoots in summer and root in a cold frame.

Pests and diseases Azaleas are affected by the same disorders as rhododendrons (see page 158).

Rhodothamnus
rhodothamnus

Rhodothamnus chamaecistus

☐ Height 25cm (10in)
☐ Spread 30cm (12in)
☐ Flowers mid and late spring
☐ Moist rich soil
☐ Cool and shady site

A member of the heather family, the little *Rhodothamnus chamaecistus* is a dwarf shrublet of neat habit, suitable for the rock garden. It rarely grows more than 25cm (10in) high, with the bright green leaves arranged in whorls along wiry stems. From mid spring onwards, the foliage is almost hidden by pale rose-pink, saucer-shaped flowers.

Like other members of the heath family, this hardy shrub will not grow on shallow chalky soils, but unlike them it is tolerant of alkaline conditions as it grows wild on the limestone mountains of the Austrian Alps.

Cultivation
Plant in spring or autumn in any moist soil rich in organic content. The site should be cool, with shade over the root area; the plant will grow in dense shade, but then produces fewer flowers. Pruning is unnecessary.
Propagation Take heel cuttings from young side-shoots in summer or early autumn and root in a cold frame.
Pests and diseases Die-back can affect the plants, and honey fungus may kill them.

Ribes
ribes

Ribes laurifolium

☐ Height 0.9-1.5m (3-5ft)
☐ Spread 1.2-1.8m (4-6ft)
☐ Flowers early spring, summer
☐ Any well-drained soil
☐ Sun or light shade

The *Ribes* genus includes the culinary gooseberries and currants as well as deciduous spring-flowering shrubs. Ornamental evergreen species are less common, in spite of being easily grown, fully hardy shrubs. They lack the vicious spines of gooseberries and the pungent aroma of flowering currants and are worthy of a place in the shrub border or large rock garden.

Popular species
Ribes gayanum grows up to 1.5m (5ft) in height, with a spread of 1.8m (6ft). It is a suckering shrub, the young shoots covered with soft hairs. The three-lobed, toothed leaves are velvety soft and grey-green in colour. In early summer, the shrub bears dense upright clusters of yellow bell flowers with a scent of honey.
Ribes laurifolium is a sparsely branched shrub, rarely more than 90cm (3ft) high and wide. The ovate, leathery and coarsely toothed leaves are dark green above, pale green and lustrous on the undersides. The species is valued for its early flowering, beginning in late winter and continuing into spring, with male and female flowers on separate plants. The male flowers are more conspicuous, borne in long drooping, greenish-yellow sprays.

Cultivation
Plant in autumn or spring in any good, well-drained soil, in sun or light shade. Pruning is unnecessary, but old stems on overgrown shrubs can be cut out at ground level after flowering.
Propagation Take 7.5-10cm (3-4in) long heel cuttings in early autumn and root in a cold frame.
Pests and diseases Leaf spot, showing as small brown spots, occasionally occurs.

ROCK ROSE – see *Cistus, Helianthemum*
ROSE OF SHARON – see *Hypericum*

Ribes laurifolium

Rosmarinus
rosemary

Rosmarinus officinalis

☐ Height 90cm-1.2m (3-4ft)
☐ Spread 90cm-1.2m (3-4ft)
☐ Flowers late spring
☐ Well-drained to dry soil
☐ Sunny site

Rosemary (*Rosmarinus officinalis*), one of the classic Mediterranean herbs, has its place in the ornamental border as well as the herb garden. As an evergreen, its narrow white-felted leaves – which release their aromatic oils freely – are a source of year-round interest. They are used fresh or dried for flavouring. Another attraction is the blue-grey flowers which open in late spring.

Although coming from hot limestone hillsides, rosemary will nevertheless prosper in colder, wetter climates, provided it is given a sheltered and sunny position. However, in severe winters the foliage turns brown and whole branches may be killed.

Popular varieties
Several varieties have been developed from *Rosmarinus officinalis*. Those with a tall upright habit can be used for informal hedging, while prostrate forms make excellent ground cover.
'Miss Jessop's Upright' is a strong-growing upright variety with deep blue-green leaves and pale mauve flowers.
'Prostratus' is a mat-forming variety with fresh green leaves and lavender-blue flowers; it is half-hardy only.
'Roseus', up to 90cm (3ft) high, bears lilac-pink flowers.
'Severn Sea', a compact dwarf form 60cm (2ft) high and 90cm (3ft) across, bears an abundance of brilliant blue flowers.

Cultivation
Plant in spring in ordinary well-drained soil in a sunny position. Cut out any dead shoots in early spring and shorten long straggly shoots by up to half. Lightly trim hedging plants after flowering.

Protect half-hardy varieties with a straw mulch over the roots in winter.
Propagation Take 10cm (4in) cuttings of half-ripe shoots in mid to late summer and root in a cold frame. Pot on and overwinter under glass, before planting out in late spring.
Pests and diseases Trouble free.

RUE – see *Ruta*

Ruscus
butcher's broom

Ruscus aculeatus

☐ Height 60-90cm (2-3ft)
☐ Spread 60-90cm (2-3ft)
☐ Berrying shrub
☐ Ordinary soil
☐ Sun or shade

Butcher's broom (*Ruscus aculeatus*) is one of those plants that hovers vaguely between being a shrub and a perennial. Its 60-90cm (2-3ft) high evergreen shoots do not die down in winter, but neither do they have any apparent leaves. In bud, the tiny cream flowers are little bigger than pinheads, and when they open in early to mid spring they are barely visible. Male and female flowers are borne on separate plants.

Small though the flowers may be, on female plants they are followed by marble-sized berries of pillar-box red if plants of both sexes are grown. This display is stunning and long-lasting especially in a shady spot similar to the woodland and hedge habitats where the shrub may occasionally be seen growing wild.

Cultivation
Plant in mid spring in ordinary well-drained soil in sun or shade. The plants do equally well on heavy clay and on shallow chalk, in full sun or dense dry shade. Grow in groups of three to five containing both sexes.

Remove any dead wood in early to mid spring.
Propagation Lift, divide and replant large clumps in spring.
Pests and diseases Trouble free.

Ruta
rue

Ruta graveolens 'Jackman's Blue'

☐ Height 60-90cm (2-3ft)
☐ Spread 45cm (1½ft)
☐ Foliage shrub
☐ Ordinary well-drained soil
☐ Sunny site

Ruta graveolens, a hardy evergreen sub-shrub, was once widely used as a medicinal and disinfectant herb, but is now chiefly grown for its decorative value. It grows 60-90cm (2-3ft) high and 45cm (1½ft) across and is distinguished by the filigree-like, bitterly aromatic, blue-green foliage that clothes the plant.

Above the leaves, clusters of flowers are borne in early to mid summer or later. They are sulphur-yellow with cupped, fringed petals. Most gardeners remove the flowers as they appear.

'Jackman's Blue', a compact form which seldom flowers and has almost metallic blue leaves, is a striking variety.

Cultivation
Plant between early autumn and early spring in ordinary well-drained soil in a sunny position. Trim the plants back to old wood in mid spring.
Propagation Take cuttings of lateral shoots 7.5-10cm (3-4in) long in mid summer.
Pests and diseases Trouble free.

SAGE – see *Salvia*
ST. DABEOC'S HEATH – see *Daboecia*

Santolina
cotton lavender

Santolina neapolitana 'Sulphurea'

☐ Height 45-75cm (1½-2½ft)
☐ Spread 45cm-1.2m (1½-4ft)
☐ Flowers mid summer
☐ Ordinary well-drained soil
☐ Sunny site

These hardy dwarf shrubs with silver-grey feathery leaves grow into attractive low mounds suitable for the front of a shrub border. Here their strong aromatic scent will be released by bruising. They can also be grown in rock gardens or as low informal hedges.

Popular species
Santolina chamaecyparissus, syn. *S. incana*, is a dense mound-forming plant reaching 45-60cm (1½-2ft) high and across, with silver-grey feathery leaves. The flowers are bright lemon-yellow.
Santolina neapolitana grows into a dome 60-75cm (2-2½ft) high of long feathery grey leaves. It bears bright yellow blooms; 'Sulphurea' has lemon-yellow blooms.
Santolina virens, syn. *S. viridis*, bears vivid green thread-like leaves. Reaching 60cm (2ft) high and 90cm-1.2m (3-4ft) across, it has bright yellow flowers. 'Primrose Gem' has pale yellow blooms.

Cultivation
Plant in autumn or spring in well-drained soil in a sunny site. Remove dead flower stems. Cut back untidy specimens into old wood in mid spring or after flowering. Plants grown as hedges should not be allowed to flower.
Propagation Take cuttings of half-ripe side-shoots, 5-7.5cm (2-3in) long in mid summer.
Pests and diseases Trouble free.

Santolina chamaecyparissus

Sarcococca

Christmas box

Sarcococca hookeriana

- ☐ Height 60cm-1.2m (2-4ft)
- ☐ Spread 60cm-1.2m (2-4ft)
- ☐ Flowers late winter to early spring
- ☐ Any good soil
- ☐ Sunny or shaded site

Sarcococcas are grown for their handsome foliage and for their tiny but fragrant white winter flowers. Their dwarf suckering habit makes them excellent ground cover for shady and sunny sites. Glossy black berries appear in spring.

Popular species
Sarcococca confusa is a dense dome-shaped shrub, 90cm (3ft) high and 1.2m (4ft) across. It has dark green leathery leaves and very fragrant flowers.
Sarcococca hookeriana is of upright suckering habit. It grows 1.2m (4ft) high and 60cm (2ft) across and carries narrow light green leaves.
Sarcococca humilis is a dwarf species, 60cm (2ft) high and 90cm (3ft) across. The leaves are glossy dark green.

Cultivation
Plant in autumn or spring in any good soil. Sarcococca thrives on chalky soil, in shade or sun. Pruning is not necessary.
Propagation Remove and replant rooted suckers.
Pests and diseases Trouble free.

Senecio

senecio

Senecio 'Sunshine'

- ☐ Height 60cm-1.8m (2-6ft)
- ☐ Spread 60cm-1.8m (2-6ft)
- ☐ Flowers early to mid summer
- ☐ Any well-drained soil
- ☐ Sunny site

Senecio is a large genus of more than 1500 species. It includes not only shrubby species, but also tender climbers and hardy perennials (now more correctly listed as *Ligularia*) and half-hardy annuals among which cinerarias are popular as pot and bedding plants.

The evergreen shrubby species originate in New Zealand, but they have been much cross-bred to produce several hybrid clones, and most of the plants in general cultivation are of hybrid parentage. Evergrey rather than evergreen, senecios are generally hardy though they do not tolerate long frosty periods. They thrive in full sun and are extremely wind-resistant; they are often grown as informal hedges in seaside gardens.

Senecios are valuable in mixed and herbaceous borders where their foliage introduces pockets of calm. Long-stalked, loose clusters of daisy-like flowers are borne in summer; many gardeners find that the blooms detract from the beauty of the foliage and snip off the flower stems.

Popular species and hybrids
Senecio compactus is a dense, compact shrub about 1m (3½ft) in height and with a spread of 1.8m (6ft). It resembles S. 'Sunshine', but is less wide-spreading. The oval wavy-edged leaves are dark green above, covered with a white felt on the undersides; the young shoots and flower stalks, too, are white. Bright yellow flower clusters are borne throughout summer. The shrub may suffer frost damage in severe winters.
Senecio greyi is a rarely grown species. Most plants offered as S. *greyi* or S. *laxifolius* are hybrids between this species, S. *compactus*

Senecio greyi hybrid, in flower

Senecio greyi hybrid

and *S. laxifolius*. Hybrids are generally hardier than the species; they are spreading shrubs up to 1.2m (4ft) high and often spreading to 2.4m (8ft). The oval leaves and the shoots are covered with a soft white felt. Yellow flower heads are borne in summer.

Senecio laxifolius is rare in cultivation, having been superseded by named hybrids. It is a spreading, generally hardy shrub, 90cm (3ft) high and twice that across, with thin oval, grey-white leaves that age to dark green. Large, loose clusters of golden-yellow flowers appear in summer.

Senecio monroi grows as a hardy, dense and domed shrub, 1.2-1.8m (4-6ft) high, with a spread of 60-120cm (2-4ft). The oblong leaves differ from other senecios in having prominent wavy edges; they are thickly covered with fine white hairs on the undersides, and are mid to deep green above. This species is one of the best in flower, with large and bright yellow clusters in mid summer.

Senecio reinoldii is a robust, fully hardy shrub tolerant of strong seaside gales. It grows 90cm (3ft) or more high and wide and bears rounded, thick and leathery, glossy dark green leaves. The yellow flower heads in mid summer are insignificant.

Senecio 'Sunshine' grows to a broad mound, 60-90cm (2-3ft) high and twice as much or more across. It is the best known and the most popular of the shrubby senecios, frequently offered as *S. greyi* or *S. laxifolius*, but it properly belongs to the hybrid group known as 'Dunedin Hybrids'. The oval to elliptic leaves, often with fine wavy margins, are silvery-white on both sides when young, the upper surfaces ageing to grey-green. Large bright yellow flower clusters are borne from early to late summer, sometimes into autumn.

Cultivation

Plant between mid autumn and mid spring in any well-drained soil. The site should be in full sun.

All species and varieties do particularly well in coastal gardens; while they are highly tolerant of exposure to strong winds, they rarely survive prolonged spells of hard frost.

For hedges, space young shrubs 45cm (1½ft) apart; during the first growing season, pinch out the growing tips of leading shoots several times, to induce bushy growth from low down.

Remove faded flower stems and cut out any straggly shoots which spoil the rounded shape of the shrubs. Hedges should not be clipped but cut faded flower stems back to healthy leafy shoots in autumn.

Propagation In late summer to early autumn, take 7.5-10cm (3-4in) cuttings of half-ripened lateral shoots and root in a cold frame over winter.

Transfer the rooted cuttings to an outdoor nursery bed in mid spring and let them grow on until they are moved to their permanent positions in autumn.

Pests and diseases Trouble free.

Skimmia

skimmia

Skimmia japonica, berries

- ☐ Height 60cm-1.5m (2-5ft)
- ☐ Spread 90cm-1.8m (3-6ft)
- ☐ Flowers mid to late spring
- ☐ Ordinary well-drained soil
- ☐ Lightly shaded or sunny site

Skimmia japonica, male flowers

Skimmias are easily grown, bright-berried shrubs, thriving in light shade – as ground cover beneath trees – or in a sunny site provided they are shaded from strong midday sun. They also do well in seaside gardens and tolerate town and industrial pollution. Although these accommodating shrubs are hardy, the emerging young leaves can suffer damage from late spring frost in exposed and cold gardens.

Small cream-white, sometimes fragrant flowers are borne in rounded clusters in spring. Most skimmias are unisexual, bearing female and male flowers on separate plants. For the females to produce their splendid autumn display of brilliant berries, it is essential that a male form is grown close by.

Popular species

Skimmia japonica is a spreading shrub, usually 90cm (3ft) high but occasionally to 1.5m (5ft), and 1.5-1.8m (5-6ft) across. Its oval lance-shaped leaves are pale green and leathery. Male shrubs have the largest and most fragrant flowers, but the female shrubs produce the round bright red berries. Popular varieties include: 'Foremanii' syn. 'Veitchii' (female with large flowers and brilliant red fruit clusters); 'Fragrans' (male, broadly dome-shaped, large clusters of scented white flowers); 'Fructo-albo' (low-growing, compact female, small leaves, white berries); 'Nymans' (female, particularly large and profuse scarlet berries); and 'Rubella' (male, large clusters of deep red winter buds open in early spring to white flowers; leaves often edged crimson in cold winters).

Skimmia laureola, a male species, is also listed as *S. × confusa.* It grows 90cm (3ft) high and about 1.5m (5ft) across, with aromatic, oblong and pointed leaves clustered together at the tips of the shoots. It is the best species for flowering, bearing large scented clusters of cream-white flowers in spring. Most plants are male, but 'Isabella', a female, produces bright red berries.

Skimmia reevesiana is now regarded by most authorities as a subspecies of *S. japonica.* It is a compact, spreading shrub, 60-90cm (2-3ft) high and 90-120cm (3-4ft) across. It bears narrow lance-shaped, mid to dark green leaves often with paler margins. The white flowers, in late spring, are bisexual and followed by oval crimson berries that persist through the winter.

Cultivation

Plant in early to mid autumn or early to mid spring in ordinary well-drained soil. Set the shrubs in a lightly shaded site or in sun. In cold northern gardens, protect young plants with a winter mulch over the roots.

Pruning is generally unnecessary, except for cutting back any frost-damaged shoots. Berrying stems can be cut for indoor decoration in winter.

Propagation Take 7.5cm (3in) heel cuttings of half-ripe side-shoots and root in a cold frame. The following spring, transfer the rooted cuttings to an outdoor nursery bed and grow them on for two or three years before planting them out in their permanent positions, in autumn or spring.

Pests and diseases Few pests trouble skimmias; other disorders are generally due to adverse growing conditions: whitening of the leaves is caused by frost – in spring cut damaged shoots back to healthy wood. Yellowing of the leaves and die-back of the shoots can be due to lime-induced chlorosis – an application of fritted trace elements is beneficial.

Skimmia japonica 'Rubella'

Solanum

potato vine

Solanum jasminoides 'Album'

☐ Height 3-6m (10-20ft)
☐ Flowers early summer to mid autumn
☐ Any well-drained soil
☐ Sunny sheltered site

When these splendid climbers are in full bloom it is hard to believe that they belong to the same genus as the potato. From early summer to autumn the dark green foliage is hung with great clusters of slightly fragrant, purple or white, starry flowers with prominent stamens. The plants are suitable for sheltered gardens only.

Popular species

Solanum crispum has dark green leaves and reaches 4.5-6m (15-20ft) high. 'Glasnevin', the most popular variety, has purple-blue, star-shaped flowers.
Solanum jasminoides, jasmine nightshade, is a slender species with twining stems reaching 3-4.5m (10-15ft) high. It has glossy pale green leaves and pale blue flowers. 'Album' has white flowers with yellow anthers.

Cultivation

Plant in late spring in any well-drained soil against a sheltered south- or west-facing wall. Tie the stems to wires or trellis.

In spring thin out weak growth and cut back any stems damaged by frost. To control *S. crispum*, cut the previous season's shoots back to 15cm (6in) in spring.
Propagation In summer take 7.5-10cm (3-4in) cuttings of side-shoots; root in a propagator unit.
Pests and diseases Aphids may infest stems and shoots and make the plants sticky and sooty.

Solanum crispum 'Glasnevin'

Sophora

sophora

Sophora tetraptera

☐ Height 3.5m (12ft)
☐ Spread 1.8m (6ft)
☐ Flowers mid to late spring
☐ Fertile well-drained soil
☐ Sunny sheltered position

Sophora tetraptera, a near-hardy shrub growing some 3.6m (12ft) high and half that across, is the national flower of New Zealand. It bears elegant foliage, the long, narrow leaves made up of a dozen or so pairs of leaflets. Most of the old leaves fall in mid spring as bunches of golden waxy pea flowers open.

After flowering, the current year's leaves unfold from furry new shoots, and seed pods develop, hanging like strings of four-winged beads.

Cultivation

Plant in early to mid spring in fertile well-drained soil in a sunny position against a south- or west-facing wall sheltered from cold winds. Pruning is not necessary.
Propagation Seed is the usual means of increase.
Pests and diseases Trouble free.

SPOTTED LAUREL see –
Aucuba
SPURGE LAUREL – see *Daphne*

Stranvaesia

stranvaesia

Stranvaesia davidiana

- ☐ Height 3.5-5.5m (12-18ft)
- ☐ Spread 3.5-5.5m (12-18ft)
- ☐ Flowers in early summer
- ☐ Fertile well-drained soil
- ☐ Sunny or partially shaded site

Looking like a distinguished cotoneaster, *Stranvaesia davidiana* was one of the many fine discoveries by the plant collector Ernest Wilson. He introduced it to Britain from western China in 1901.

This hardy shrub's attraction is the display of brilliant scarlet berries which hang in clusters along the branches from autumn to spring – birds generally leave the berries alone. The wide-spreading branches carry wavy-edged, leathery dark green leaves, some of which turn vivid red in autumn. Clusters of white hawthorne-like flowers are borne in early summer.

Cultivation

Plant in mid autumn or spring in any fertile well-drained soil in sun or partial shade.

Propagation Take 7.5-10cm (3-4in) heel cuttings of half-ripe side-shoots and root in a propagator unit.

Pests and diseases Fireblight may affect the shrubs.

STRAWBERRY TREE – see *Arbutus*
SUN ROSE – see *Helianthemum*
SWEET BAY – see *Laurus*

Taxus

yew

Taxus baccata 'Fastigiata'

- ☐ Height 45cm-3.5m (1½-12ft)
- ☐ Spread 30cm-1.8m (1-6ft)
- ☐ Coniferous shrub
- ☐ Any well-drained soil
- ☐ Sunny or shaded site

Yews are extremely long-lived and eventually develop into magnificent specimen trees, too tall for garden planting (see page 49). But these fine conifers are also slow-growing; they respond well to clipping and topiary work and can easily be kept at a manageable size.

Most garden-worthy yews have been developed from *Taxus baccata* and include varieties of shrubby or dwarf habit, with attractive dark green or golden foliage. They rarely produce berries.

Popular varieties

'Aurea', golden yew, is a compact conifer reaching 2.4m (8ft) high and 1.8m (6ft) across. The foliage is a luminous golden-yellow.

'Cavendishii' grows less than 90cm (3ft) high, but the branches, which droop at the tips, spread to at least twice the height. The foliage is dark green.

'Elegantissima' is a dense, bushy upright yew with golden foliage; it grows 2.4m (8ft) high and 1.5m (5ft) across. It is one of the most popular golden yews for a sunny site; in shade it is pale green.

'Fastigiata', Irish yew, grows into an upright columnar conifer 3.5m (12ft) high and 60cm (2ft) across. The leaves are dark green.

Teucrium
germander

Taxus baccata 'Semperaurea'

Teucrium chamaedrys

'Semperaurea', an irregularly shaped variety with a height and spread of 1.8m (6ft), has gold or yellow foliage.

'Standishii' is a particularly slow-growing variety. Reaching 90cm-1.2m (3-4ft) high and 30cm (1ft) across, it is of upright columnar habit with attractive golden-yellow foliage.

'Summergold', a low-growing conifer reaching 45cm (1½ft) high and 90cm (3ft) across, has golden leaves which are particularly bright in summer.

Cultivation
Yews thrive in any type of soil and any site except a wet, boggy one. Plant between mid autumn and mid spring.

Pruning is unnecessary, but the shrubs can be clipped to shape at any time of year.

Propagation Take 7.5-10cm (3-4in) heel cuttings of lateral shoots in early to mid autumn. Root in a cold frame. Transplant to a nursery bed and grow on for two or three years. Plant out in permanent positions in spring.

Pests and diseases Colonies of scale insects, particularly yew scale, may infest the stems.

TEA TREE – see *Leptospermum*

- ☐ Height 20cm-1.5m (8in-5ft)
- ☐ Spread 30cm-1.2m (1-4ft)
- ☐ Flowers early summer to early autumn
- ☐ Any well-drained soil
- ☐ Sunny, sheltered site

Germanders vary from creeping shrublets to medium-sized evergreen shrubs and are valued for their year-round, small-leaved foliage and for their flower spikes which are produced abundantly throughout summer. Low-growing types are suitable for rock gardens and for ground covers, the taller germanders for shrub borders and walls.

Popular species
Teucrium chamaedrys (wall germander) is a fully hardy sub-shrub, only about 20cm (8in) high but spreading its downy branches to 30cm (12in) or more from a creeping rootstock. The small aromatic, toothed leaves are ovate, bright green above and grey beneath. Purple-pink flower spikes are borne from mid summer until autumn. Wall germander is suitable for a rock garden or as ground cover; in the wild it inhabits old walls and ruins.

Teucrium fruticans (shrubby germander) is much taller, 1.5m (5ft) or more high and almost as much across. It is not completely hardy but makes a handsome specimen shrub in milder areas, especially by the sea. The grey-green leaves are pleasantly aromatic when bruised. Pale lavender flowers appear from early summer until early autumn. 'Azureum' is an attractive deep blue variety, but more tender than the species.

Cultivation
Plant *T. chamaedrys* from early autumn to mid spring, *T. fruticans* in late spring. Both thrive in any well-drained soil, *T. chamaedrys* often doing best on poor soil. They need a site in full sun; in all but the mildest gardens, *T. fruticans* should be grown against a sheltered south- or west-facing wall. Pruning is rarely necessary, but on *T. fruticans* cut any frost-damaged shoots back to healthy wood in spring; the shrub can be trimmed to shape after flowering.

Propagation Increase *T. chamaedrys* from 5-7.5cm (2-3in) cuttings of basal shoots in late spring and root in a cold frame. *T. fruticans* is propagated from 7.5-10cm (4-10in) heel cuttings of side-shoots taken in mid or late summer and rooted in a propagator unit.

Pests and diseases Trouble free.

Thuja
thuja

Thuja occidentalis 'Danica'

Thuja occidentalis 'Rheingold'

☐ Height 30cm-3.5m (1-12ft)
☐ Spread 30cm-1.5m (1-5ft)
☐ Coniferous shrub
☐ Any moist soil
☐ Sheltered sunny position

Thuja, a genus of hardy coniferous trees (see also pages 49-50), contains a few slow-growing dwarf species and varieties. They make handsome specimen shrubs for small gardens, and some are dwarf enough for rockeries. The foliage is aromatic and usually borne in flat sprays; it is in various shades of green and golden-yellow, often changing colour in autumn and winter.

Popular varieties

Thuja occidentalis, the white cedar, is parent to several slow-growing, shrubby varieties.
'Caespitosa' is slow-growing, eventually forming a low hummock 40cm (16in) high and wide, with grey-green foliage. Good rock-garden variety.
'Danica' is rounded and reaches 50cm (20in) high and 38cm (15in) across. The leaves are dark green.
'Golden Globe' grows 90cm (3ft) high and wide; it is of rounded habit, with golden foliage.
'Hetz Midget' is extremely slow-growing, to 30cm (12in) high and wide; the foliage is dark green.
'Lutea Nana' forms a conical shrub 1.8m (6ft) high and 1.5m (5ft) across. The foliage is yellow-green

in summer, deep golden in winter.
'Rheingold', conical-shaped, 1m (3ft) high and 75cm (2½ft) across, has copper-gold leaves. It is much planted in association with winter-flowering heathers.
'Smaragd', a 1.8m (6ft) high conical conifer with a spread of 90cm (3ft), has emerald-green leaves.
'Sunkist', a pyramidal-shaped variety with golden foliage, slowly reaches 1.8m (6ft) high.
'Wansdyke Silver' grows slowly to 1.5m (5ft) high; it is conical in habit, with foliage conspicuously variegated cream-white.
Thuja orientalis bears foliage in frond-like vertical sprays. It is less aromatic than that of *T. occidentalis*, and the growth habit is

Thuja plicata 'Stoneham Gold'

more erect. Several dwarf varieties are available.
'Aurea Nana' is a rounded shrub, 60-75cm (2-2½ft) high with golden green leaves.
'Conspicua' is of dense, compact habit, 1.8m (6ft) high and 90cm (3ft) or more wide. The golden-yellow foliage colour is retained in winter.
'Rosedalis' grows slowly to a rounded shrub, 60cm (2ft) high and 45cm (1½ft) across. The soft juvenile foliage is canary-yellow in spring, sea-green in summer and plum-purple in winter.
Thuja plicata is conspicuous for the pineapple scent of its foliage; several slow-growing varieties occur.
'Cuprea' is broadly pyramid-shaped, to 90cm (3ft) high and wide, with yellow-tipped dark green foliage.
'Rogersii' is small and rounded, 30-45cm (1-1½ft) high and across with golden-bronze leaves.
'Stoneham Gold' has a squat conical habit, 60-90cm (2-3ft) high and 60cm (2ft) across. The green foliage is gold-tipped.

Cultivation
Though easily grown in ordinary soil, thujas thrive in deep, moist conditions. The site should be sheltered and in full sun. Plant between late autumn and early spring. Pruning is unnecessary.
Propagation Take 5-10cm (2-4in) tip cuttings in autumn and root in a cold frame.
Pests and diseases Trouble free.

Trachelospermum

star jasmine

Trachelospermum jasminoides

- ☐ Height 3-4.5m (10-15ft)
- ☐ Flowers mid to late summer
- ☐ Fertile, well-drained soil
- ☐ Sheltered sunny wall

Star jasmine is a self-clinging climber grown for its fragrant flowers and oval, glossy dark green leaves. It is not fully hardy but usually succeeds on a sheltered south- or west-facing wall in mild localities. The blooms appear in mid to late summer.

Popular species
Trachelospermum asiaticum can grow 4.5m (15ft) high. It is of dense habit, the branching and hairy stems covered with a curtain of foliage. It is the hardier species, with creamy-white to yellow flowers.
Trachelospermum jasminoides reaches 3-3.5m (10-12ft) high. It is slow-growing but outstanding in foliage and in the fragrance of its white flowers.

Cultivation
Plant in mid to late spring against a sheltered sunny wall. These climbers thrive in well-drained soil enriched with organic matter. Thin out over-vigorous shoots in early to mid spring.
Propagation Layer stems in autumn and sever a year later.
Pests and diseases Aphids may infest young shoots.

TREE HEATH – see *Erica*
TREE LUPIN – see *Lupinus*

Tsuga

hemlock

Tsuga canadensis 'Pendula'

- ☐ Height 30-90cm (1-3ft)
- ☐ Spread 75cm-1.5m (2½-5ft)
- ☐ Coniferous shrub
- ☐ Moist, well-drained soil
- ☐ Partially shaded site

Most hemlocks are tall graceful trees (see page 51), but a few dwarf varieties have been developed from *Tsuga canadensis*. They are suitable for small gardens where their attractive weeping branches and graceful outline make them excellent as specimen shrubs or as focal points in large rock gardens.

Popular varieties
'Bennett' is a slow-growing, spreading shrub 30cm (1ft) high and 75cm (2½ft) across. The dense foliage is mid green.
'Jeddeloh' forms a low hummock, 30cm (1ft) high and 60cm (2ft) across, of pale green foliage.
'Pendula' grows into a dense mound of weeping branches clothed with rich green foliage. It grows 90cm (3ft) high and 1.5m (5ft) across.

Cultivation
Plant between mid autumn and mid spring in any deep, well-drained but moisture-retentive soil. The site should be partially shaded and sheltered from east winds. Pruning is not necessary.
Propagation Take 2.5-7.5cm (1-3in) long heel cuttings in early autumn and root in a cold frame.
Pests and diseases Trouble free.

Ulex

gorse

Ulex europaeus

- ☐ Height 1.5-1.8m (5-6ft)
- ☐ Spread 1.5-1.8m (5-6ft)
- ☐ Flowers spring and summer
- ☐ Any well-drained soil
- ☐ Sunny site

There is an old saying that 'kissing is out of season when gorse is out of bloom'. Although the main display of these hardy native shrubs is in late spring and early summer, they continue to produce their fragrant golden flowers intermittently until early winter. Gorse (*Ulex europaeus*) grows as a dark green spiny shrub, 1.5-1.8m (5-6ft) high and across. It thrives on poor soil and is useful for covering dry banks or growing in exposed seaside gardens.

Cultivation
Plant out container-grown specimens between mid autumn and early spring in any well-drained soil in full sun. Keep the soil ball intact to avoid root disturbance. Cut back tall leggy plants to within 15cm (6in) of the ground in early spring to encourage new growth from the base.
Propagation Take 7.5cm (3in) cuttings of the current year's sideshoots in late summer and root in a cold frame.
Pests and diseases Trouble free.

VERONICA – see *Hebe*

Viburnum
viburnum

Viburnum davidii

Viburnum tinus

- ☐ Height 60cm-4.5m (2-15ft)
- ☐ Spread 1.2-4.5m (4-15ft)
- ☐ Flowers early winter to early summer
- ☐ Good moist soil
- ☐ Sunny or partially shaded site

The evergreen viburnums are invaluable in the shrub border for their attractive, year-round foliage and for their flat clusters of often fragrant flowers followed by decorative berries. For the finest display of berries, plant viburnums in groups of three to ensure cross-pollination.

These hardy, easily grown shrubs thrive in woodland conditions; in the garden they need cool, moist but well-drained soil.

Popular species
Viburnum x burkwoodii grows 2.4m (8ft) high and 2.7-3.5m (9-12ft) across. The waxy, sweetly scented white flowers (pink in bud) are borne in flat wide heads between early and late spring. The leaves are glossy dark green, brown-felted on the undersides.
Viburnum davidii has a low spreading habit reaching 60-90cm (2-3ft) high and 1.2-1.5m (4-5ft) across. The glossy dark green leaves are prominently veined. Small clusters of white flowers appear in early summer, but the shrub is chiefly grown for its decorative turquoise-blue berry clusters that persist well into winter.
Viburnum henryi is of erect habit, the stiff branches set with narrow leathery leaves that are glossy green. The shrub grows about 1.8m (6ft) high and wide and bears drooping clusters of fragrant white flowers in early summer. The berries are bright red, ripening to black.
Viburnum rhytidophyllum is a fast-growing handsome species with horizontal branches; it grows 3-4.5m (10-15ft) high and 3-3.5m (10-12ft) across. Flat wide heads of white flowers open in late spring and early summer, followed by red berries which eventually turn black. The large leaves are lance-shaped and corrugated. The species thrives on chalky soils.
Viburnum tinus grows into a large, domed shrub 2-3m (7-10ft) high and 2m (7ft) across. It is one of the most popular winter-flowering shrubs, closely set with lance-shaped mid to deep green leaves. The white, pink-budded flowers are carried in flat heads at the end of shoots intermittently from early winter to late spring. The berries are black. 'Eve Price' has pinkish flowers, and 'Variegatum' has foliage heavily variegated with cream-yellow.

Cultivation
All viburnums do best in good moist but well-drained soil and in light shade or sun. Give early-flowering shrubs a site sheltered from cold north and east winds, and where morning sun after a frost cannot damage the flowers. Plant in autumn or spring.

Thin out old overgrown shoots in late spring.
Propagation Take 7.5-10cm (3-4in) heel cuttings of side-shoots in summer or early autumn and root in a cold frame.
Pests and diseases Whiteflies infest the foliage. Grey mould, leaf spot and honey fungus can also occur.

Viburnum davidii, berries

Vinca
periwinkle

Vinca major

Vinca minor 'Gertrude Jekyll'

☐ Height 5-30cm (2-12in)
☐ Spread 90cm-1.2m (3-4ft)
☐ Flowers early spring to mid summer
☐ Any well-drained soil
☐ Partially shaded or sunny site

Hardy and invasive, periwinkles are popular low-growing ground-cover plants, trailing and creeping to form extensive carpets of ever-green foliage. They are useful beneath deciduous trees and shrubs and for covering steep banks, growing equally well in sun and light shade. Flowering is most profuse in sun while the shrubs make dense weed-proof cover in shade.

Periwinkle's five-petalled, blue, purple or white flowers are borne singly from the leaf axils from early spring through summer and intermittently until autumn.

Popular species and varieties
Vinca major, greater periwinkle, reaches 15-30cm (6-12in) high and 90cm-1.2m (3-4ft) across. It is a rampant species with erect shoots that later trail and root where the tips touch the ground. The small heart-shaped leaves are glossy and mid to dark green. Bright blue flowers appear from mid spring to early summer, often with a second flush of bloom in autumn.

Several varieties are available: 'Maculata' has foliage splashed with greenish-yellow; 'Oxyloba' bears narrow hairy leaves and deep violet-blue flowers; 'Reticulata' has young foliage strongly veined with yellow; and 'Variegata' (syn. 'Elegantissima') has leaves blotched and margined with cream-white; the flowers are lavender-blue.

Vinca minor, lesser periwinkle, reaches only 5-10cm (2-4in) high and 90cm-1.2m (3-4ft) across and has smaller oval, deep glossy green leaves on wiry stems, and smaller flowers than *V. major*. It makes a denser and neater ground cover. The flowers are 2.5cm (1in) across and bright blue in the species but several different varieties are available: 'Argenteo-variegata' (blue flowers, leaves variegated cream-white); 'Atro-purpureum' (deep plum-purple flowers); 'Azurea Flore Pleno' (double sky-blue flowers);

'Bowles' Variety' (small light blue flowers); 'Gertrude Jekyll' (small freely borne, glistening white flowers); and 'Multiplex' (double, plum-purple flowers).

Cultivation
Plant between early autumn and early spring in ordinary well-drained garden soil in a partially shaded or sunny position. The plants tolerate hard clipping and benefit from annual trimming in early spring, when old shoots can be pruned out.

Propagation The trailing stems of these plants root from every node that is in contact with the soil; if necessary, they can be dug up, divided and replanted between autumn and spring. Alternatively, take 15cm (6in) long stem sections in early autumn or spring and insert them obliquely where they are to grow; they root easily.

Pests and diseases Rust may attack the plants. A parasitic virus occasionally attacks *V. major*, causing the leaves to turn yellow and eventually killing the plants.

WINTER'S-BARK – see *Drimys*
WINTERGREEN – see
Gaultheria
WIRE-NETTING BUSH – see
Corokia
YEW – see *Taxus*

Yucca
yucca

Yucca filamentosa 'Variegata'

Yucca gloriosa 'Variegata'

☐ Height 60cm-1.8m (2-6ft)
☐ Spread 90cm-1.8m (3-6ft)
☐ Flowers mid summer to late autumn
☐ Any well-drained soil
☐ Sunny site

Yuccas are excellent shrubs for introducing an exotic air to a garden. Despite their tropical appearance, they are quite hardy, thriving in warm sunny places in town as well as seaside gardens. They can be included in mixed borders, but are even better as focal points and specimen plants where their architectural qualities can be fully appreciated.

The popular belief that yuccas only flower every seven years and die afterwards is erroneous. They are all long-lived shrubs, flowering from about five years old and carrying their huge spikes well above the foliage.

Popular species
Yucca filamentosa, Adam's needle, has stiff upright narrow blue-green leaves, the margins of which are covered with curly white hairs. It has a height of 60-75cm (2-2½ft) and a spread of 90cm-1.2m (3-4ft). The cream-white bell-shaped flowers are carried in plume-like spikes 90cm-1.8m (3-6ft) high in mid to late summer and appear on two- or three-year-old plants. 'Variegata'

has cream-edged or yellow-edged leaves.
Yucca flaccida, syn. *Y. puberula*, is very similar to *Y. filamentosa*, except that its deeper green leaves arch outwards and droop at the tips. Varieties include 'Ivory' (large spikes of cream flowers) and 'Golden Sword' (leaves centred cream).
Yucca gloriosa bears dense rosettes of stiff deep green leaves at the top of a slow-growing woody trunk. Its bell-shaped cream-white flowers, which are tinged red on the outside, appear in dense upright spikes, held 90cm-1.8m (3-6ft) above the foliage, between late summer and late autumn. It does not flower until it is at least five years old. 'Variegata' has leaves striped yellow.

Cultivation
Plant in mid spring or mid autumn in any well-drained soil – including poor, sandy ones – in full sun.

Pruning is not necessary.
Propagation Remove rooted suckers in early to mid spring and replant in permanent positions.
Pests and diseases Brown spots with grey centres on the leaves are due to leaf spot.

ACKNOWLEDGEMENTS

Photographer's Credits
A-Z Botanical Collection 34(tc), 46(tr), 50(b) 65(r) 74(tl), 97(tr), 106(b); Heather Angel 61(tc), 62(tl), 107(tl,b), 108, 112(b), 115(tr), 118(b), 133(tr), 142(l), 158(tl); Gillian Beckett 22, 110(tr,b), 113(b), 115(tl,b); Brian Carter 68(b); Eric Crichton 13(t), 24(t), 26(tr), 31(tl), 32(r), 37(r), 38(tl), 41(bl), 43(cr), 44(cl), 60, 61(bl), 64(l), 67(l), 70(tl), 78(bl), 79(tc), 80(tl), 81(tr,b), 85(tl,b), 86-88, 94, 95(b), 96(b), 98(b), 99, 106(tr), 119(b), 121-122, 123(tr), 125, 127(l,c), 128, 132, 133(tl,b), 136(l,c), 137(l), 138(tl), 139(l), 146(tl), 147(r), 149(r), 151(l), 152, 153(b), 154, 155(t), 156(l), 158(b), 163(r), 164(t), 165(l), 168, 170(l), 171(tl), 172(tl,tr), 173(tr); Philippe Ferret 11(b), 12(t), 13(b), 172(tc); Garden Picture Library (David Askham) 135(tl), (Rex Butcher) 117(b), (Brian Carter) 49(tl,tr), 66(t), 148(tr), (C Fairweather) 162(b), (John Glover) 2-3, 15(t), 28(tr), 33(t), 69(bc), 135(tc), 148(tc), 167(tc); (Neil Holmes) 31(cl), 62(tc); (Lamontagne) 130(tl), (JS Sira) front cover(tr), 82(r), 59(b), 82(r); (Brigitt Thomas) 15(br), (John Wright) 18(b); Bob Gibbons 28(b), 47(b), 148(tl); John Glover front cover (cr), 6-8, 14(l), 25(l), 42(tl), 45(b), 50(tr), 62(tr), 68(tr), 71(r), 72, 73(b), 76(r), 78(br), 79(tl), 84(r), 103(r), 120, 126, 129(bl), 136(r), 149(l); David Gould 79(tr), 93(c), 95(t), 96(t), 98(t); Jerry Harper 17(t), 18(tr); Photos Horticultural front cover (cl,br), 1, 10, 11(t), 12(b), 15(bl), 16, 23, 24(b), 28(tl), 29, 32(l), 35(t), 36, 37(l), 38(tr,b), 39(r), 41(t,br), 42(cl), 43(t), 44(t), 45(t), 46(tr), 47(tl), 48(tl,tr), 52, 54, 55(t), 56(b), 57(t), 58(b), 61(tr), 66(b), 68(tl), 69(br), 70(b), 71(l), 74(tc,b), 75, 82(l), 85(tr), 89(tr), 91(t), 92(l), 93(l), 101, 104, 105(r), 107(tr), 110(tl), 111, 112(tl), 114, 116, 117(tl), 118(tr), 119(t), 123(tl,b), 124(tr,b) 127(r), 129(t), 130(b), 134, 135(tr,b), 137(r), 138(b), 140(tr), 141(r), 142(c,r), 146(tr), 147(l), 148(b), 151(r), 169(l), 170(r), 173(b); Lamontagne 18(tl), 18-19(b),19, 21(b), 26(cr), 27(tl), 40(l), 42(tr), 44(br), 48(tc), 50(tl), 83(l), 167(b); S & O Mathews front cover (tc), 21(t), 27(tr), 35(cr), 113(b), 153(tl), 155(bl), 158(tr), 159, 160(b), 161(tl); Tania Midgley 14(r), 17(b), 20, 26(tl), 27(cr), 34(tl), 39(c), 49(tc), 56(t), 57(b), 63(l), 65(l), 74(r), 77(r), 78(t), 80(tr), 89(b) 90, 91(b), 97(tl), 100(tr), 102(t), 103(l), 138(tr), 153(tr), 155(br), 156(r), 160(t), 161(tr), 166(tl), 171(b); Natural Image (R Fletcher) 51(r), 55(t), 59(t), (P Wilson) 34(tr); Clive Nichols front cover (tl, c, bl, bc,), 4-5, 33(b), 69(t), 83(r), 92(r), 100(tl), 109(r), back cover; Harry Smith Collection 25(r), 30, 31(tr), 39(l), 40(r), 47(tr), 51(l), 58(t), 61(tl), 63(r), 64(r), 67(r), 69(bl), 70(tr), 73(t), 76(l), 77(l), 81(tl), 84(l,c), 89(tl), 93(r), 97(b), 100(b), 102(b), 105(b), 106(tl), 109(l), 112(tr), 117(tr), 118(tl), 124(tl),129(br), 130(tr), 131, 139(r), 140(tl,b), 141(l), 145, 146(b), 162(t), 163(l), 164(b), 165(r), 166(b), 167(tl), 169(r), 171(tr), 173(tl), 174, 175.

Illustrators
Elisabeth Dowle 14